David Chipperfield

David Chipperfield
Architectural Works
1990–2002

edited by Thomas Weaver

Princeton Architectural Press
New York

Published by
Princeton Architectural Press
37 East Seventh Street
New York, New York 10003
For a free catalog of books, call 1.800.722.6657.
Visit our web site at www.papress.com.

Published simultaneously in Spain by Ediciones Polígrafa

For Princeton Architectural Press
Project coordinator: Mark Lamster
Specials thanks to: Nettie Aljian, Nicola Bednarek, Janet Behning,
Megan Carey, Penny Chu, Russell Fernandez, Clare Jacobson,
Nancy Eklund Later, Linda Lee, Katharine Myers, Jane Sheinman,
Scott Tennent, Jennifer Thompson, Joe Weston, and Deb Wood
of Princeton Architectural Press—Kevin C. Lippert, publisher

Library of Congress Cataloging-in-Publication Data for this title
is available from the publisher.

ISBN: 1-56898-407-3
Dep. Legal: B. 2.783 - 2003 (Printed in Spain)

Contents

David Chipperfield
by Kenneth Frampton

To date David Chipperfield's architecture has depended to a rather unusual degree on the perimeter wall and on its planar potential as a generator of both volume and mass and even more importantly, on its capacity to transform one into the other and vice-versa. This prismatic oscillation is at once evident in two labyrinthic works that may be regarded as typical of his brief yet exceptionally fertile Japanese career, during which he seems to have stumbled upon his characteristic domestic syntax, in part deriving from the work of Tadao Ando. I have in mind the five-storey mixed-use building realized in Kyoto for Toyota Auto in 1991. The layered character of this work would seem to derive from the typically deep plots to be found in Japanese cities. We find the juxtaposition of symmetrical and asymmetrical volumetric sequences receding in depth from a narrow entry facade facing the street. In the Toyota complex, this would entail an overlay of a set of parallel interconnected patios, sequentially enfolding the exterior volume into the interior of the building. These patios rise up through the structure to create a compressed spatial spiral culminating in a pavilion-cum-belvedere overlooking the city. The sequence is reinforced by an equally fugal juxtaposition of different materials, setting up an interplay between fair-faced concrete walls (enclosing the main body of the structure) and steel balustrading and fenestration, together with the liberal use of timber and steel revetment. Thus, where steel siding is used to emphasize the form of the horizontal superstructure at the top of the block, wood appears in various incarnations throughout, as paneling, grillwork, flooring and exterior decking. In each instance, wood serves as a tactile counterform, not only to the grey opacity of the fair-faced

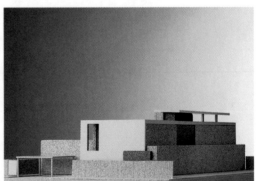

From left, drawing of Jazzie B House,
model of Aram House

concrete but also to the luminosity of glassblock and long stretches of plate glass fenestration that parallel a shallow reflecting pool lined with pebbles, evocative of the Japanese garden tradition. Apart from its tactility, this work also recalls, by virtue of its powerful, abstract, planar composition, the *art concret*, avant-gardist artists of the 1930s, figures such as Theo van Doesburg, Vordemberge Gildewart and Jean Gorin.

A similar compressed and layered *parti* informs a number of patio houses projected by Chipperfield at virtually the same time; works which, unfortunately, have remained for the most part, unrealized. The Jazzie B, Aram, Kao and Lockhart houses are all variations on a similar labyrinthic theme since they are each made up of layered, orthogonal volumes, contained by full-height bounding walls, combined with either a recessed garden court or an elevated belvedere terrace, depending on the circumstances. Where the modest Jazzie B house in Camden Town, North London, literally steps down as a continuum from a top-lit living hall, through a lower dining room into a garden court, the luxurious Lockhart house, designed for Umbria, Italy, ascends from the surrounding rural landscape via a narrow stair, to culminate in a generous terrace situated on top of the double-height art gallery. In each instance, the external court is enlivened by the presence of a swimming pool. Two subsequent works would seem to bring this formal paradigm to some kind of provisional summation; the so-called Olivetti project of 1994 and a monumental villa realized in Germany in 1996.

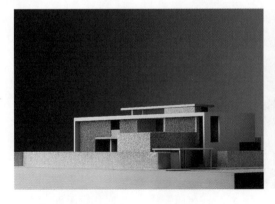 

From left, model of Aram House,
model of Lockhart Saatchi House

Moving away from the domestic format, the Olivetti project consisted of a small, quasi-hypothetical mixed-use office building, cruciform in plan, rising to three stories in height and surrounded on all four sides by a two-storey masonry wall, systematically pierced and interrupted according to a pin-wheeling pattern of openings. Apart from providing thermic and acoustical isolation, this wall also serves to modulate the light and the microclimate onto which the offices open. As in the Toyota building, the top floor of the offices, T-shaped in plan was envisaged as being clad in sheet steel. The counterpoint of symmetrical and asymmetrical volumes, providing for a reciprocal expansion and contraction of the interior space, recalls Mies van der Rohe's courthouse projects of the mid-1930s; the common bond being the neo-constructivist G-Group and De Stijl artists by which Mies had been influenced in the previous decade. Chipperfield's courthouse permutations would find their momentary fulfillment in Germany in 1996, where the brick syntax of Mies's Esters and Lange Houses, built in Krefeld in the late 1920s, comes to be adopted in pursuit of plastic ends that are, on balance, more cubistic than constructivist in character, particularly with regard to volumetric displacements in section and the homogeneity of the mass, both of which Mies would have handled in a very different way, given his lifelong insistence on the continuity of the ceiling plane and the horizontality of the internal space. By way of contrast, Chipperfield is preoccupied with the mutual configuration of both mass and volume as the following description makes sufficiently clear.

> The spatial composition is considered in three dimensions, enjoying the manipulation of various ceiling heights. This compression and expansion in the vertical is expressed on the exterior of the building, where once again, the game between physical 'restraint' and abstract freedom is played out. All external surfaces are clad in handmade brick. Soffits of balconies are constructed to allow the continuous surface treatment, ambiguously expressing the brickwork, both as a massive physical presence and at the same time manipulating it to respond to abstract and formal compositions.

Olivetti Bank Project

While an enclosed court and spiraling *promenade architecturale* are still in evidence, the planar character of the bounding wall so prominent in the Toyota and Olivetti schemes is now abandoned in favour of a cubistic configuration comprised of a single material, interrupted only by ample steel-framed glazing. Here the homogeneity of the handmade brickwork gives way at the window frame to the plastered continuity of the interior, momentarily interrupting the free flow of space in order to prepare the ground for the quieter, top-lit character of the interior.

The shift to a civic scale will cause the architect to break with this configured domesticity in order to embody works of a much more public character. We first encounter this in the River and Rowing Museum designed for Henley-on-Thames in 1989 and realized some seven years later. With this work, won in open competition, Chipperfield turned to the vernacular for its potential to serve both as an origin and as an interpretive key, thus providing a convincing *parti*, while simultaneously affording the society a contextual paradigm through which to comprehend and appropriate the work. Nonetheless, one immediately senses that the scale is hardly local, even though an existing moat and a line of poplars, paralleling the main face of the building, suggest the presence of something that has always existed. Part outsized Oxfordshire barn, part Japanese *minka*, this largely windowless structure is raised off the ground on a grid of cylindrical concrete columns so as to elevate its entry above the current high-water mark of the Thames in flood. Like the German villa, the Rowing Museum assumes its full plastic strength by virtue of being clad throughout in a single material – this time thick oak siding, held in place over relatively short intervals by double sets of stainless steel screws. Suspended on concrete columns, which are set back from the face, the opaque bulk of the museum is separated from its raised deck by continuous floor-to-ceiling glazing. There large sheets of plate glass encompass entrance, cafeteria, exhibition foyer, shop, ticket office, stair hall and restaurant. Each of these sub-spaces enjoys variously sweeping views over the flat flanking fields and the tree-lined banks of the river. At the same time the external platforms running along the northern face of the complex tend to reinforce the subtly Shintoesque feeling underlying the elevation of the building above the ground.

Of mixed concrete and steel frame structure, the pitched roofs of the sheds are finished in standing seam, sheet metal construction. Exceptions to this all-encompassing timber and steel enclosure, lit only by skylights in the apex of the roof, extend to a small amount of clerestory glazing on one gable end and to a concrete and glass bridge running between the first and second phases of the complex in 1997. The 'long house', white-walled interior of the original building is fittingly anthropological in its character, a mood that is consummated by rowing skiffs of every conceivable size and vintage being hung from its walls as well as by the complementary mythic celebration of the Upper Thames as though it was the outreach of some tribal watershed culminating in Henley.

The break into monumental form takes an even greater leap forward in two major complexes designed in the second half of the 1990s; first a Centre for Performing Arts in Bristol (1994) to be built on the old harbour waterfront and then a 'runner up' competition entry in 1999 for a Centre of World Cultures to be built in Göteborg, Sweden. Returning to the once fashionable 'egg in the box' formula (c.f. Leslie Martin's Royal Festival Hall, London and Mies's entry for the Mannheim Theater competition of 1953-5) Chipperfield predicated his performing arts center on two distinctly different physical propositions, on the one hand, an exterior cage of timber, largely comprised of vertical blades on the exterior face, on the other, "...an internal plastic mass, responding to the organic development of the auditorium mass. The interstitial space between the external wooden boxes and the internal mass is to be occupied by the public circulation and hospitality functions." This strategy enabled the architect to handle the relatively

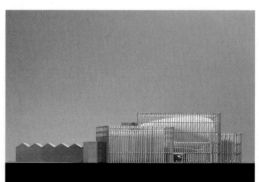

Models of Bristol Centre for Performing Arts, UK

large and difficult masses of the twin auditoria on a prominent but awkward site through the stepped modulation of a brightly illuminated timber enclosure, thereby avoiding the necessity of having to provide a singular mass-form. As Chipperfield puts it in his project description: "This material proposition generates a form of great civic presence without adopting either the novelty of architectural fantasy or the pomposity of monumental facades." A very similar strategy on an equally difficult undulating site will be tried out for encompassing the stepped volumes of the Centre of World Cultures; a project which would seem to have been taken further in a series of in-house study models.

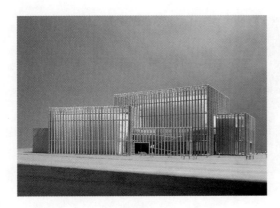

During the last decade Chipperfield has become a European rather than a British architect with commissions widely dispersed throughout the continent, either as projects or as ambitious civic works currently under construction ranging from a modernized reworking of Stüler's heavily bomb-damaged Neues Museum in Berlin, adjacent to Schinkel's canonical Altes Museum, to the San Michele cemetery expansion in Venice and a new law court complex for Salerno. Chipperfield's Italian commissions have much in common in that they have both been approached as 'cities in miniature', that is to say, as a city of the dead in the first instance and as a city of justice in the second. The somewhat common *parti pris* employed for both of these projects is perhaps to be found in Chipperfield's competition entry for the development of the historic center of Salerno. The deployment of bounding walls in relation to the grid of the city is virtually the conceptual matrix of this urban renewal, which was largely based on the restoration of existing structures and on the clarification of prevailing monuments, together with the reintegration of interstitial public space and the reorganization of vehicular and pedestrian access to the historic core. This new heart of the city built from basalt would have elaborated the topographic nature of site, in part by an extension of the existing ramp system.

This image of agglomerated horizontal masses bounded by walls is clearly the idea behind Chipperfield's cloister *parti* for the enlargement of the San Michele cemetery in Venice, where, instead of continuing the serried rows of graves of which the present cemetery is composed, Chipperfield proposes a series of 'free-standing' garden courts enclosed by columbaria. In other words, instead of being overwhelmed by the retrospective prospect of an infinite array of graves, as is the case in most cemeteries around the world today, what Chipperfield is currently building in Venice is a series of walled memorial gardens where survivors may mourn their departed ones in a state of intimacy and protection.

Neues Museum, Berlin

In a not dissimilar manner, the law courts in Salerno are predicated on breaking down the overwhelming scale of a bureaucratic program, since here the proliferation of courtrooms and their ancillary facilities (judge chambers, public foyers, prisoners' holding cells, etc.) is subdivided into a series of relatively small pavilionated structures fed by interstitial patios and linked by an outriding pergola that assures a sense of urban continuity at the larger scale.

The Neues Museum is a reparatory exercise in urban continuity at another level since it not only entails a large scale minimalist addition, fronting onto the Spree, but also a subtle reconstitution of the bombed-out fabric of the original museum through a series of tectonic interventions into the body of Stüler's ruined stair hall and its adjacent gallery spaces. This operation will be carried out in consultation with the preservation expert Julian Harrap in a procedure that the architect has characterized as 'soft preservation', in which the blue and gold papered ceilings will be left in their ruined, tattered state, while the continuity of the original decorative sequence will be provided by subtle forms of digitally modulated simulation. As the architect has put it: "Soft restoration keeps everything that is original and makes sure nothing synthetic creeps in. Don't take off the render on the face and redo the whole thing. Keep it, paint it, use the same color – but make sure it is now seen to be new. Not glaringly evident but then not faking it either."

Model of Salerno Old Town redevelopment, Italy

In addition to civic buildings, Germany has also been the occasion wherein the architect has had to respond to everyday needs as in the ten-storey Kaistrasse 'studio' tower built on the waterfront in Dusseldorf. Comprising an *in situ*, fair-face concrete jacket cast over a steel frame, this is a 'bottom, middle and top' structure in which the ground floor is a cafeteria facing into a public podium, the intermediate floors are double and single-height studio-cum-office spaces and the crowning floor is a grand, three-storey loft, with a mezzanine. The dualistic, frontalized, symmetrical character of the plans, together with the evident articulation of servant and served elements seems to return Chipperfield to the tectonic ethos of his Japanese work.

In his various theoretical statements, Chipperfield may be seen as following the German philosopher Hans Georg Gadamer in particular, with regard to the latter's concern for sustaining the creative interplay between tradition and innovation. As he puts it "The architect must stand apart, both in front of and behind the present reality. In front of, in order to give shape to possibilities . . . To be behind, to understand that the continuum of creative ideas ensures meaning. Significance in the contemporary world requires us to ensure the relevance of our work within a developing sociological reality and its meaning within an established tradition of forms and language . . . Progress is a continuum that benefits from resistance as well as encouragement. We should not live in a bright new shining future anymore than we should hide in a comfortable pastiche of the past . . ."

While readily acknowledging the manifest advantages of the information age, Chipperfield cautions against the cybernetic iteration of form and while recognizing the current fascination with high technology, he still insists on the relative 'low-tech', permanent character of architecture. As his laconic sketches suggest, like Alvaro Siza, his initial approach stems from an intuitive, hands-on appraisal of the site, while bearing in mind the weight of the brief, the load that is, that the concept has to carry. While his architecture tends to derive, as Joseph Rykwert has remarked, from sectional configuration, he remains categorically opposed to any attempt to reduce architecture to a literary or configurative operation, to the spectacular or representational drives of deconstruction and pastiche or to the idea that architecture is nothing more than art writ large. He insists instead on its irreducible materiality and on the capacity of architects to transcend this limitation through the poetics of fabrication. At the same time, he stresses its ethical responsibility to create an appropriate context for the conduct of everyday life. As he puts it, architecture " . . . can make our lives more comfortable, and can offer a vision of order in a world of chaos. It can make our world more 'material' and bring us in touch with the very elements it shelters us from . . . " While he is only too conscious of the abstract potential of any given gestalt, he remains equally preoccupied with the sensuous craft dimension of the discipline as this is invariably revealed through the tacticity of material and the luminosity of light.

While having, by definition, to accept the benefits and freedoms made available by the current triumph of capitalism, along with its material potential and necessary constraints, Chipperfield also feels that in order to survive, the métier has no choice but to distance itself from the destructive and cynical excesses that are also an integral part of the system; the Scylla and Charybdis, as it were, of the architect on the threshold of the twenty-first century. To this end, topographic continuity, imagistic character and the dynamic experience of the subject in space are intimately interconnected in his work. Along with the eurhythmic potential of abstract form they serve to guarantee the critical character of his architecture.

RN   Departing from the book at hand, I thought it quite interesting how it is structured. Although it covers thirty projects in what seems to be a random order, we soon realize that they follow in alphabetical sequence. Even if we could debate the naming of the projects, some interesting juxtapositions have arisen from this classification system. Was there any particular reason for this order?

DC   There is an uncomfortable question as to why you publish your work in the first place. What is it you are trying to show in each of those projects? One feels a sense of vanity in describing what you are trying to establish, but it is actually quite useful to be forced to try and put things together again. I suppose from a critical point of view, what you really can use the process of doing a monograph for is to check on ideas and their development.

    As for the juxtaposition of projects in a non-chronological order that you are referring to, it shows how ideas can be seen in a body of fifteen years work: not just as a linear progression but as a string of ideas. There are certain things that I suppose are genetically conditioned as opposed to conditionally defined. You start off with certain ideas and you always keep reworking those same ideas, come what may, notwithstanding the fact that it would be stupid to deny that the architect or the designer develops through experience. This sequence tends to emphasize the themes and ideas consistent through the work.

RN   The Gotoh museum in Japan is followed by the house in Corrubedo. It is surprising that they are almost ten years apart.

DC   I like to believe that the viewpoint is not that different from the early days. What one believes architecture is about and what one thinks are the limits of architecture or what makes good architecture has not changed. I still adhere to what I would call architectural presence. Something which is of a solid nature, which builds itself around an interpretation of a daily ritual of life. If there is a development in the work, it is to do with language and formal exploration. Compositional rules still seem quite consistent, I think that the work is grounded by the fact that both interior space and exterior volume have always been conceived as an integrated idea.

The proposal for a Centre for Performing Arts in the dockland area of Bristol attempted to assure a nearly industrial quality, standing up to the bold simple structures surrounding the Victorian docks. The language of 'posts and beams' investigates a developing interest in volumes that are both transparent but massive.

Bristol Centre for Performing Arts, UK

RN   You often talk about the experiential qualities of architecture and the rejection of
      formalistic preconceptions.

DC   For me architecture starts with the position of the individual. This is fundamental
      to what I am interested in, what architecture does, how it places the individual, whether
      it is looking out at sea, eating your breakfast, cooking lunch, reading a book in the
      library, visiting your grandmother's grave, going to get a dog license in a law court,
      it starts in my opinion always with the human condition.
           What should it be like to be a visitor in a building, what should it be like to be
      working in an office, to visit a cemetery, a library or the law courts? Generally you can
      grab hold of something that you can start off with. To call it a spiritual idea is over-
      sentimental but an idea of what the spirit of the place should be is essential.

In the case of the public library for
Des Moines, the building form helps to create
a partnership between the interior spaces of
the building and the surrounding park. Only
by taking such an organic form could we create
an integration of park and building without
isolating the library within the park.

Des Moines Library, Iowa, USA

RN   The window always seems very important in your compositions.

DC   It's not only the window but the view. The elements I like are the ones that say things about the human condition or a person's relationship to the larger scale. Therefore what I am interested in is the connection between oneself as an individual and the experience of a building. So in the Ernsting office building in Germany, which is in fact very ordinary in many respects, it is reassuring that people love to work there. You sit there watching this landscape created by Jacques and Peter Wirtz. Every window is a picture frame. The building is successful because it is very humane. I pick on that because I do not think that office buildings are the easiest type in terms of what I talked about.

Progress such as the National Gallery in Rome and the Olivetti Project examine the sequence of volumes through the use of large-scale models. The museum project proposed a new sequence of non-orthogonal top-lit spaces. The sequence proposed a free-flowing plan where the spatial structure was imposed not by the walls but by a series of angular domes.

From left, National Gallery of Modern Art, Rome, Olivetti Bank Project

RN Jonathan Keates refers to the courtyard as an element that gives human scale to otherwise forbidding institutions, is that the same idea?

DC Yes, the courtyard is an element that imposes a human scale. It gives a sense of containment yet introduces spaces of a greater scale. In my opinion the courtyard is something that can create a bridge between the individual and the institution. It is a comprehensible element and turns the activity of circulation into something much more rewarding. Perhaps most importantly it creates a connection between architecture and nature. For an institution as intimidating as law courts the introduction of such elements could give back some importance to the individual. In Salerno, as well as in Barcelona, we can take advantage of the climate to use the courtyard as a fundamental circulation element of the project.

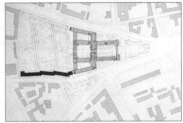

The projects for Grassi Museum in Leipzig and the Teruel Development in Spain (Aragon) investigate appropriate responses to strong historical conditions. In the case of Leipzig the addition of new storage, archive and laboratories continued the compositional process of wings, which at the same time exaggerated the idea of addition. In the case of Teruel, an alternative access to the city is provided by the discreet introduction of an elevator. Its role is given significance by the expression of a new portal and a white stone path that give scale to the new intervention without competing with the existing 19th-century staircase.

From left, Grassi Museum, Leipzig, Germany; Teruel Urban Development, Spain

RN   You just talked about the classical device of the courtyard but in the Des Moines library there are no such elements. Do you see this building as a new departure towards more organic or expressionist architecture?

DC   I think the idea is and has always been experiential. With the Des Moines library, we try to use not only architectural space but architectural form. The days of the big reading rooms are over, there is no big representational reading space anymore. Libraries consist mainly of shelving with a few clearings now and again allowing for reading areas. The reading areas have to be close to the open shelving. It is very difficult to see where your architectural concept is going to come from. The building is placed in the middle of a park so therefore we said the primary experience could be of reading a book in a garden. The space consists primarily of book shelving but the edges of the building with its expanded perimeter become interesting, so you could sit on the edges of the building and experience the garden. With a rectangular box your experience may be limited.
       When the building takes on a more organic shape, the interchange between garden and a building becomes more dynamic, you find yourself sitting on the prow of a ship with trees on one side and trees on the other side. I might be fooling myself completely in that I got there through an experiential idea and actually what I really was doing was creating a response to a current fascination with organic architecture. I think it is a little bit of both, I think that the general climate has opened up and there is a new level of expectation. Des Moines is a conservative Midwest town and yet when I presented them with four options, the organic one was universally more popular and given total support. I suppose I am not interested in breaking boundaries but enjoy the ones that have been broken, I think we can take advantage of this freedom without losing hold of the idea of what our architecture is about. Although it may not immediately look like one of our buildings, its shape is all about how you walk through it, how you sit in it, how you experience it . . . It is a building motivated by ideas of experience.

RN Many architects like to draw from the complexity of the program. You seem to wish to reduce the program to its simplest.

DC A lot of architecture tends to hide behind a programmatic task and justify form through an interpretation of function. I believe that the most interesting buildings are the ones where there is a synthesis of purpose, space and form.

I find the private house the easiest place to express those principles. Architecture is easy to play with when the program is simple and where the rituals of daily life can be the excuse to make the sort of architecture I am interested in. Sitting with a view to a garden or where the early light comes into the room is enough to create this type of dialogue. This type of process is sufficiently interesting. There is a dynamic between building programs were one is very much in control, pushing it around and re-interpreting. Building out of a sense of what the project should be about and what its character should be. In defining what a library should be, what a house should be, you are trying to collect together criteria you are building out of as an idea. You start with a kitchen, a bathroom, a bedroom and a dining table or sitting around the fire on a winter's night. You build out from a certain point until you turn around and you build in again as the site tells you this, or the tectonic idea tells you that, but the substance or the spirit of the project is something you build out from and in a way that is something one should be doing on every project. It is important to hold an opinion about what a law court should be like, it is a matter of critique of what law courts are like, or what a swimming pool should be like. I tend to start off saying what I don't like about libraries, law courts, cemeteries etc. You identify things that you don't like or think have negative qualities and that gives you the clue as to maybe what the qualities of a place should be, what a house should be like, what a cemetery should be like, what a law court should be like, what a library should be like and so on.

RN   You seem to want to suppress the authorship of the architecture, relying on an interpretation of ritual, physical and experimental responses, and context. Within this method, what is the role of language?

DC   You are right. What I am interested in is trying to establish what to interpret, what type of house or what type of building it should be, what the central issue could be, and in a way use architectural language as a method of completing that, so the architectural language is often mundane.

If you take something like Venice, the architectural language is nearly irrelevant. The first idea is the most important thing; the first idea is to make a courtyard or a string of courtyards enclosing spaces or gardens. I want the architecture to go away. I don't really want it to be exciting, I just want it to confirm the first idea.

I suppose that is how I try to create architecture. To have a strong opinion of what should happen inside the house, to have a strong opinion of what should happen on the outside of the house, how it responds to its context, and that meeting ground wants to be the building as opposed to a pre-conceived notion about what architecture should look like. It is an open process and in a way, I often find that extreme conditions are much easier to deal with than the non-extremes. A nondescript urban site or suburban plot where you get no clue or nothing to hold on to . . . a speculative office on a mundane site is a nightmare . . . where do you begin?

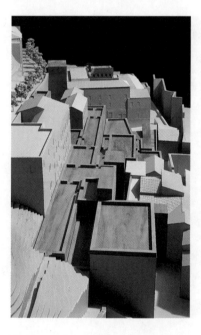

The proposal for upgrading the existing but derelict monuments in the historical center of the city relied on a reinterpretation of the competition brief. Rather than a restoration of the buildings and offering solutions for re-use, we identified a lack of public space and poor accessibility. Our proposal therefore was to construct a series of gardens and squares that connect the historical center with the main street above and the new town above.

Redevelopment of the Old Town, Salerno, Italy

RN   If your work depends on context and/or a strong interpretation of the building program, how do you deal with those conditions which are less inspiring?

DC   It is obvious that a strong natural site like that of the Corrubedo house is stimulating and provokes a response, and in the case of that house it was rather unusual to have an individual block as part of a larger physical form, (the elevation of the village). In other projects you have to work harder to find the idea. As I have already explained, for me the interpretation of the purpose of that building (I prefer the word purpose to function) often supplies this provocation. What I haven't discussed, however, is the role of composition, tectonic or constructional ideas. In my opinion these fascinations are part of the craft and are the 'words' that tell the story. It is dangerous when the craft becomes more important than the idea. This is not to suppress the importance of proportion, material and tectonic form, which are things that I believe that we remain very interested in. I am suspicious of architecture that relies on a sophisticated description to justify its form or idea. Too many buildings are clever but not intelligent. A good writer does not flaunt his interest in language but uses it to tell his story, the reader's enjoyment is surreptitiously assisted by the beauty of the language but is moved by the story.

Our proposal for a new museum in a residential
location within the city was to create a series
of volumes of small scale. These forms allowed
a transition between the domestic scale of the
surrounding buildings and the large institution
of the museum.

Dundee City Arts Centre, UK

RN A number of projects deal with complex historical settings which move us to a discussion of meaning and memory, how do you respond to a sensitive setting such as the Neues Museum in Berlin?

DC I am interested in the idea of continuity, both physical and historical. The modern movement was concerned with discontinuity and radical intervention. I think this impulse is no longer valid.

As far as the Neues Museum is concerned, the expected alternatives were either to recreate Stüler's building intact as a replica, which would have been easy to do, (essentially that is what happened with the Altes Museum, and the National Galerie during the DDR period) or the alternative was a sort of Old and New contrast. You restore the old bits, you build the new bits, and say that was the past and this is the future. It freezes both elements; it freezes the past as being a caricature of the past and freezes the new as a caricature of the modern. The typical solution is one of opposites. That is stone so this is glass. You always contrast the Old and the New. There are some very interesting interventions based on that idea. It does work quite well in a project where you are not trying to complete any more, you are just trying to place a roof over something, or you are putting a path through it . . . You do not want to touch the old. But we had too much destruction to deal with in the Neues Museum to do that. It would not have been enough to put a glass roof over the top, to be read as completely independent architecture. In the Neues Museum we had another responsibility, which was somehow to complete the building, not necessarily by reconstruction. It was important for me that we should not deny the idea of completion, in my opinion this was the only way to give back significance to the remains of Stüler's building. Furthermore the condition of ruination could not be ignored and therefore we had responsibilities, Stüler's original building, the ruin that has existed for nearly sixty years and a new functioning museum.

RN   When you talk about this Old and New, would you affiliate yourself closely to someone like Scarpa in the Abatellis Museum in Palermo?

DC   I think that Döllgast with his Neue Pinakothek in Munich is a better example of someone who is trying to make a 'third idea'. There is the original building, there is the intervention and a total idea, the 'new building'. This is what we are striving for in the Neues Museum. The first principle is that of re-establishing the original form (meaning volume, space and mass). In my opinion this is how we give sense back to the fragments, like a broken ancient vase, form is restored by means of an abstract material, but no attempt has been made to imitate the missing decoration.

The fact that we have worked on small interior projects for a number of years, making something out of nothing, has given us a certain confidence in the power of simple ideas, using materials to demonstrate their intrinsic qualities. These projects were a sort of laboratory for physical experimentation and composition.

From left, Circus Restaurant, London and Equipment Store, London

RN   You worked with the restoration expert Julian Harrap on this project. How important was this collaboration?

DC   Very important. Julian showed us how to achieve what he calls a 'soft restoration'. This means that we mediate and establish a position where damage is suppressed and original fragments are given significance by the re-establishment of some of the missing elements of the original design. The authenticity of the original elements is not compromised. It is a complex and highly subjective process. It requires us to respond to each condition separately while holding on to an overall ideological position.

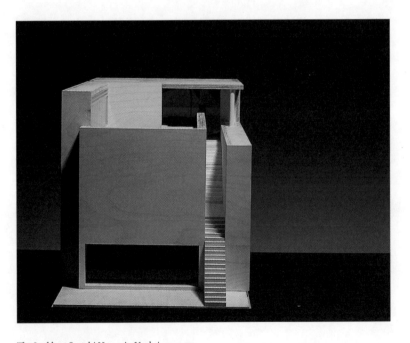

The Lockhart Saatchi House in Umbria was one of a series of projects that explored the design of introducing interior spaces around specific ideas of view or daylight. The dynamic between exterior form and interior space was monitored and developed through large-scale physical models. The villa in Berlin became the built consequence of this work.

Lockhart Saatchi House in Umbria, Italy

RN   Can you give some examples?

DC   The degree of damage through the building varies enormously, some rooms are in quite
      good condition with a substantial amount of their original decoration left, some spaces
      are empty shells, and some parts of the building are completely missing. Our ambition
      is to bring back some overall completeness to these pieces. This cannot be achieved by
      a series of rules. We trust the ruin as our context while responding to each condition.
      In working with Julian, a series of opinions are formulated about spaces and surfaces,
      the role they play, how they should be reintegrated and to what level should the damage
      be suppressed, etc. The extraordinary quality of this project is that we had to make small
      and big decisions at the same time. When you design a building you develop certain
      general ideas, intentions and gradually start working towards more detailed solutions.
      In the Neues Museum we have had to formulate ideas and respond to detailed issues
      in particular. What is overwhelming is the physical presence of the ruin. Under normal
      conditions you start with a blank piece of paper. In this case we started with a very
      complex piece of architecture in a complicated state of destruction.

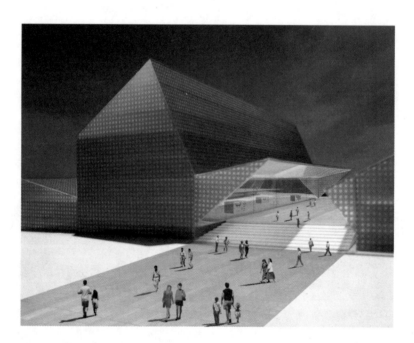

The design for the Museum of Natural History
in Los Angeles proposed to represent the
collections and laboratories (usually out of
public sight) as the centre of the museum.
An attempt to break away from the
conventional presentation of objects or the
new tendency of thematic installations that
rely heavily on sophisticated presentation
techniques. The objects of the collections,
the specimens should be the center of our
attention. The building proposes a 'light
filtered' barn full of these treasures.

Museum of Natural History in Los Angeles,
California, USA

RN   Would you not have preferred to build a new museum?

DC   If you had asked me that three years ago I would probably have agreed but now I think
      that I will never work on a more fascinating project than the Neues Museum. Over the
      last years we have got to know the building inside out. It has become something like
      second nature. The method that Julian Harrap has taught us allows us to respond
      in both an intellectual and an intuitive manner. Developing proposals, opinions,
      presenting and debating these ideas within the overbearing architectural and theoretical
      context of the Museum Island is thrilling and quite frightening at the same time.

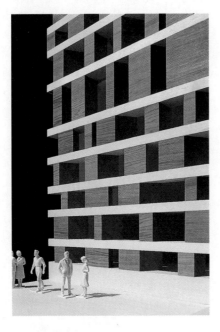

Many of our projects experiment with
composition or tectonic-like elements
seemingly stacked on top of each other.
The desire to achieve a solidity, which allows
views and light, helped to create the facade
for the Laban Dance Centre.

Laban Dance Centre, London

RN   The early work was characterized by a series of smaller projects, which culminated in some larger structures, such as the house in Berlin, the office building in Düsseldorf and River & Rowing Museum in Henley. Currently the office portfolio contains a number of projects, which are all about to be constructed. Do you believe they will maintain continuity with the earlier projects given their diversity in purpose and language?

DC   It is a fairly conscious strategy (probably born out of necessity) to encourage a diversity in the way we approach different projects, while not trying to make each project consciously different from the next. When I say probably born out of necessity I mean that it is fairly unusual for an architect to be building so many buildings without ever having established a body of work 'at home'. Working in such different locations has encouraged a sort of 'opportunism' i.e. what does this place/project allow us to do, that we couldn't do anywhere else? What materials could we use that we cannot use somewhere else? This opportunism is a positive response to the restrictions that we encounter. I learned very quickly that it was quite different to try to achieve the same in Japan as in London. On the other hand other things were possible in Japan that we could never achieve in London. This applies to both technical and cultural issues.

      This 'opportunism' has become a general approach to all projects. 'What could this be about?' is the introduction to our design method. At the same time, however, we look for continuity in the principles that direct our investigations. It is also inevitable that certain formal preoccupations continue through a series of projects. A sort of post and beam, 'Stick architecture' that developed from the Bristol Centre for Performing Arts, whilst paraphrased in a number of unbuilt proposals (Salle Philharmonique in Luxemburg, and Göteborg Centre of World Cultures in Sweden) and is now finally being realized in the Literature Museum in Marbach.

      It is fair to say that both the larger and smaller projects tended to enjoy solidity and permanence. Recent projects, such as Figge Arts Centre, Des Moines Library, the entrance building for the Museum Island in Berlin and the BBC Headquarters in Glasgow are dealing with transparency and translucency. We are investigating the ambiguity of glass, which is the most fascinating material, but probably a difficult one to invest with abstraction.

      However, at the heart of all of these projects I believe we still operate in the same manner, we still search for an organizing idea, the interpretation of a program that helps us to identify the ambition of the building.

RN   The current climate seems to encourage more spectacular projects and signature buildings. How can your 'modest' architecture stand up in this 'bolder' environment?

DC   These are interesting times. Architectural production achieves a high level and we are seeing architects producing buildings of great beauty and originality. There is more experimentation with both material and form. On the negative side, the city, or at least the conventional idea of the city, seems to be lost, in the pursuit of interesting and spectacular architecture the city seems to be the loser.

   Architecture is now as much admired for its publicity value as for its experimental qualities. Within this context I find myself quite old-fashioned still wanting to believe in the importance of the traditional city and seeing continuity as our responsibility. Although our office cannot claim to be radical, we benefit from this climate of experiment. What distinguishes our practice is that we are interested in disciplinary freedom, as opposed to an expressionistic representation of experimentation.

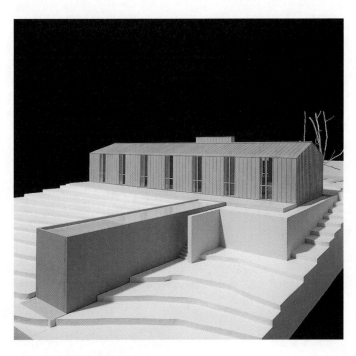

The context of the site in Martha's Vineyard is quite rural. The idea for the project was to create an 'elegant shed' as a minimal object in zinc, inspired by the simple agricultural barns of the island. The temptation to make a 'scenic' window was resisted in favour of full height doors establishing a column like pattern to the openings.

Martha's Vineyard, Massachusetts, USA

Projects

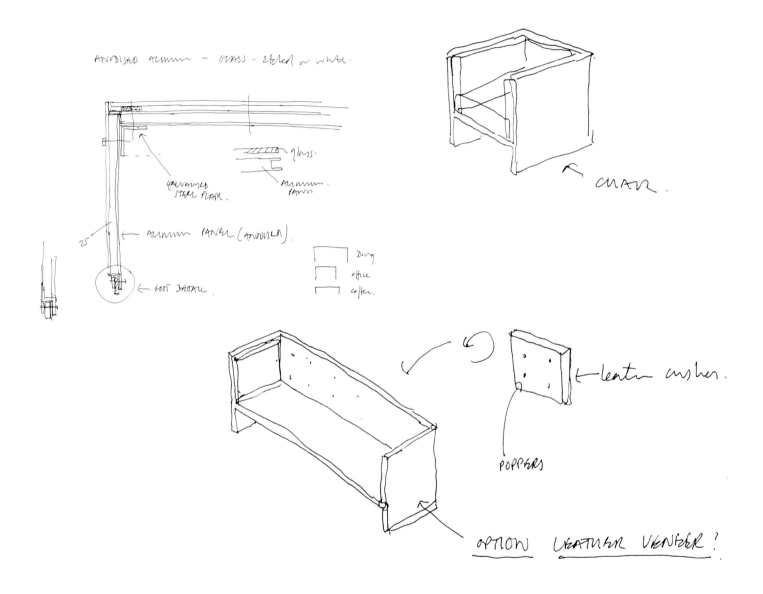

Air Frame furniture
1992–2002

Air Frame is a series of aluminum furniture designed for Cassina IXC in Japan. The material itself (strong yet extremely lightweight) was the starting point for the series, consisting of a honeycomb structure sandwiched between two sheets of anodized aluminum. In designing a range of pieces, the challenge was to find ways of modifying the material so as to make it suitable (both structurally and aesthetically) for use as a table, chair, or desk. The solution was to use the aluminum panels as both structure and surface, often with a single lateral support also in the same material, while secondary elements and detailing are kept to a minimum. The design and manufacture of the Air Frame

system also allowed for a number of different variations to be produced, such as birch veneers applied to table tops, or padded cushions to the aluminum cube armchair. In the tradition of the innovative furniture of the Modern movement (particularly those designs of Marcel Breuer, Eileen Gray, and Mies van der Rohe), the Air Frame range is an attempt to win back the simplicity of both design and construction.

Furniture commissions, like the Air Frame series, have developed in part through a close involvement with interior design projects, extending the architectural program inwards, to include the design of both the architectural space and objects and furniture contained

within that space. This involvement has resulted in close collaborations with furniture manufacturers, developing prototypes and exchanging ideas on materials. Among these, chairs have been produced with manufacturers B&B Italia, two sofa ranges for Hitch Mylius, a home office for Driade, lighting systems for Fontana Arte, brassware for Czech & Speake, ceramics and brassware for Ideal Standard and door furniture for Valli & Valli, each element of which has attempted to redefine ideas of system furniture or product design by creating pieces that can exist individually or as part of an interior collective.

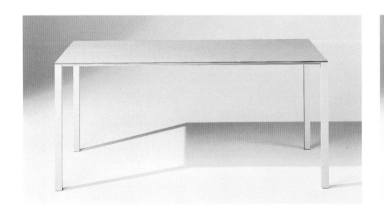

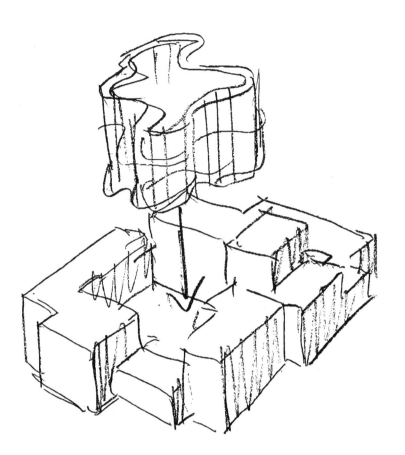
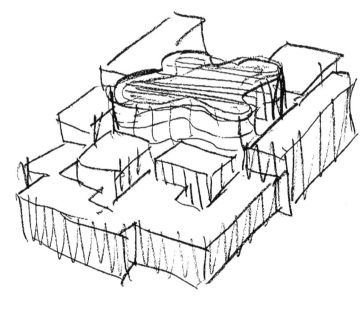

MUSEUM — BUILDING INSIDE THE BLOCK

Ansaldo City of Cultures, Milan
2000–2007

Won as the result of an international
competition, this proposal for a campus of
museums and 'City of Cultures' is located
within a block of disused industrial buildings
on the site of the former Ansaldo factory in
Milan. Inspired by the typical Milanese
condition of quiet, somber street facades
concealing beautiful, intricate courtyards,
the project looked to emphasize the inevitably
internalized quality of the existing site. As a
formal intervention within an informal
industrial complex, the proposal built upon
these inherent characteristics through both
the restoration of the existing industrial
buildings and the introduction of a new and
distinct central building as a focal point for

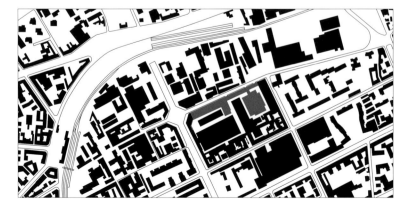

the network of connections that the perimeter of the site encloses.

The program for Ansaldo forms a mixture of both public and private facilities. Housed within the newly restored factory buildings will be Milan's Archaeological Museum (relocated into a single structure from the buildings it currently occupies in the city center), new premises for the Milan CASVA (Centre for Advanced Study of the Visual Arts), and a workshop for the traditional Colla Brothers puppets.

Alongside these existing buildings will be the new Centre for non-European Cultures. Containing exhibition galleries, an auditorium, a restaurant, workshops, archives and a study

center, the building is distinguished by its free-form, organic central hall, forming an internal courtyard for both the Centre and site as a whole. Due to the tight surrounding context of the factory block, the surfaces of this new building have effectively been inverted: that is, the spaces they enclose and adjoin are turned inside-out and outside-in, so that the representational space of the building is a more random assemblage of volumes reminiscent of the other industrial structures located within the complex. The spaces in between, therefore, become part of a formal sequence of external courts and passages, intertwining new and old architectures within the inner world of the Ansaldo block.

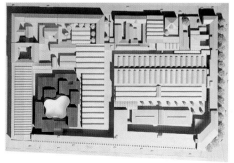

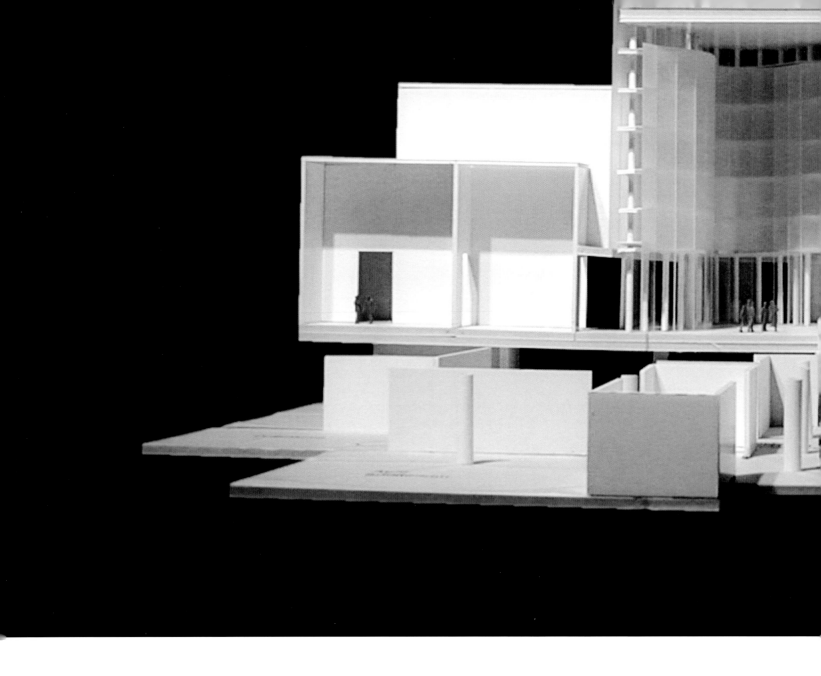

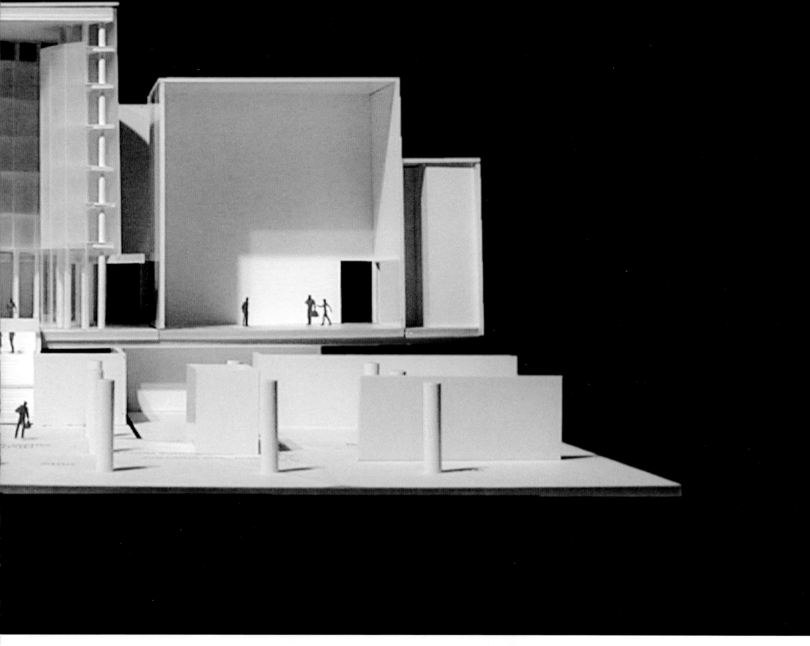

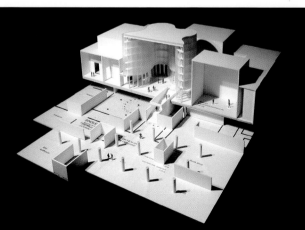

Above and left, study model showing the external form of the Centre for non-European Culture, its below-ground spaces, and access to the central atrium.

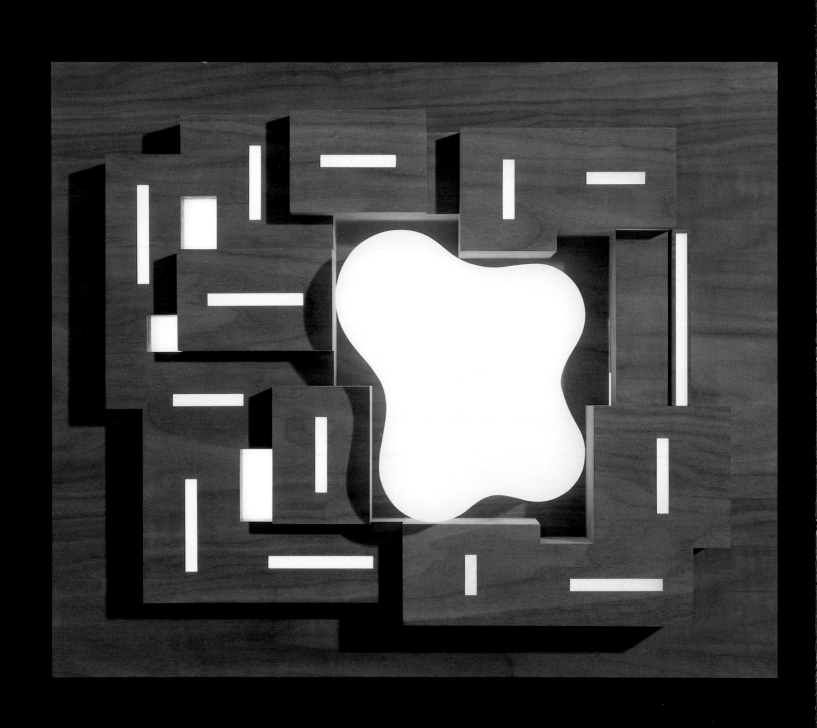

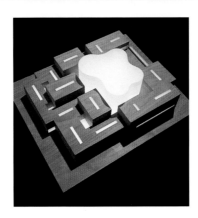

Views from inside the central atrium and surrounding display spaces.

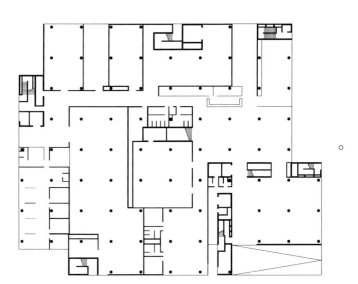

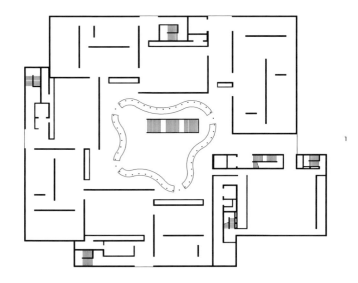

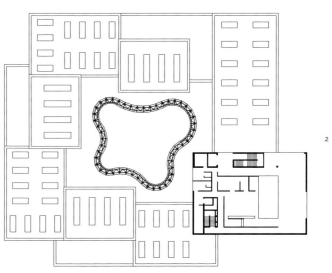

Longitudinal section

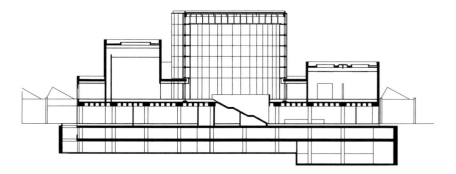

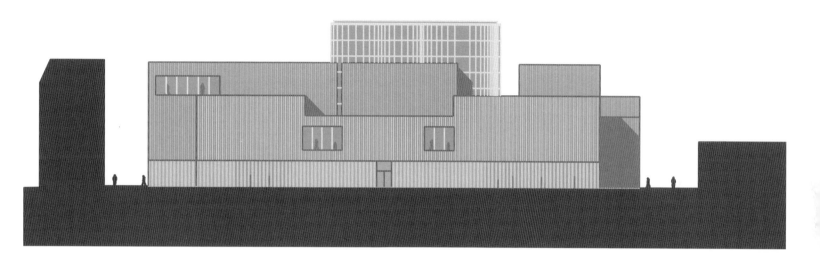

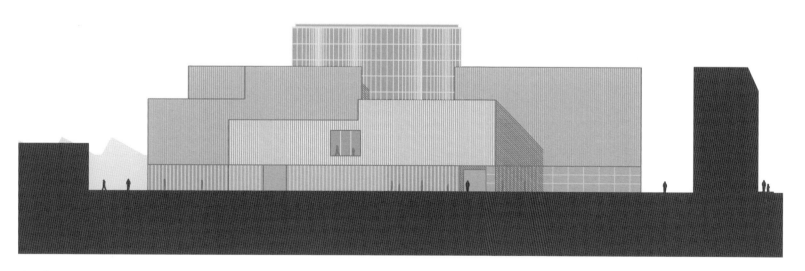

Above from top, east elevation, west elevation

Apartment in Kensington, London
1997–1999

This remodeling of a large second floor apartment overlooking Hyde Park sits within an existing 1960s block, originally designed by Richard Seifert. Arranged over two floors, the apartment features a large 18 m by 6 m double-height living space, library, kitchen, and dining areas, linked via a gently curving spiral staircase to the bedroom, bathroom and office spaces above. Each of these areas has been designed not as separate compartments but as an evolving sequence of spaces, articulated to take advantage of the endlessly shifting qualities of natural light and the existing views of the park.

In certain ways the apartment, in terms of the clarity of its spatial organization and quality of detailing, is typical of many of the projects carried out over the last fifteen years – a standard intensified further by the client's commitment to achieving the highest possible level of design and construction, according the apartment a particular importance. This commitment is revealed by the simple but elegant materials that extend across the apartment's surfaces – polished plaster on the walls and ceilings, gray *pietra serena* stone flooring, travertine-walled bathrooms, and American black walnut shelving. Complementing these materials, the apartment also features specially designed furniture pieces – dining tables, chairs, sofas, and daybeds.

The result of this thoroughness and attention to detail is a home environment totally designed, from door hinges to ceiling lights. Yet despite the extent of this architectural involvement, the apartment is robust and adaptable enough to be personalized, disrupted and generally lived in. The desire, in this way, to produce a space of dramatic proportions and qualities while at the same time elaborating the domestic rituals of daily life – eating, sleeping, bathing, cooking – lies at the heart of this and other residential projects.

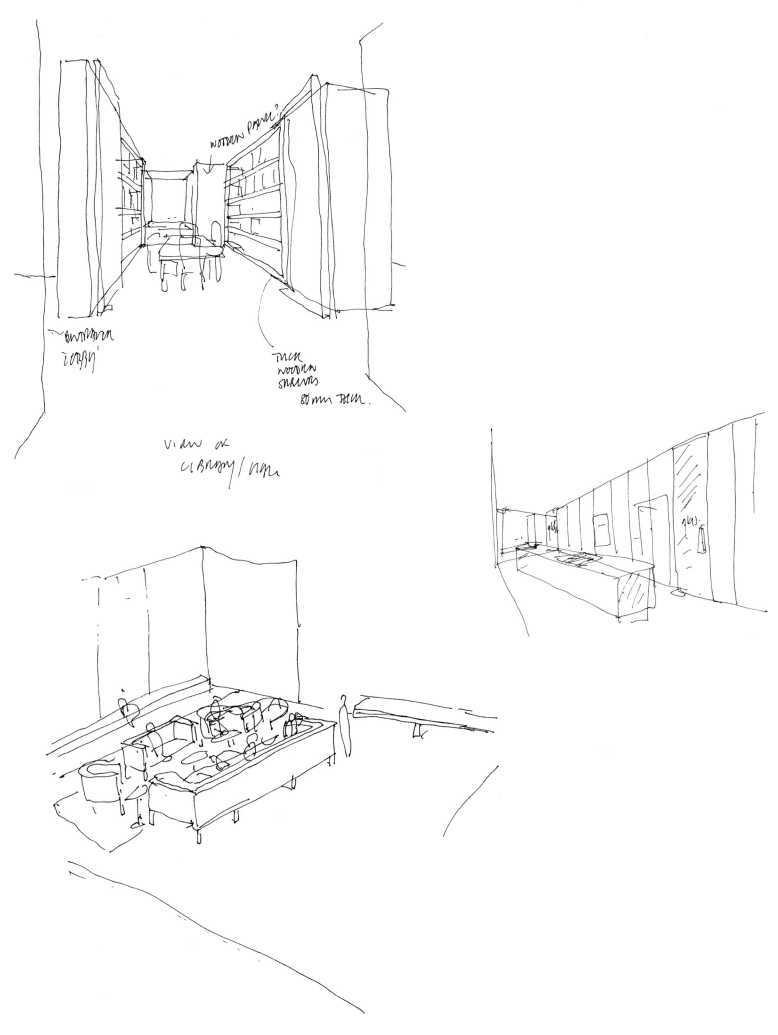

WOODEN PANEL?

ENTRANCE
LOBBY

THICK
WOODEN
SHELVES

80mm THICK.

VIEW OF
LIBRARY / ...

Above, views into the kitchen from the living room and entrance hall, and left, the first-floor bathroom.

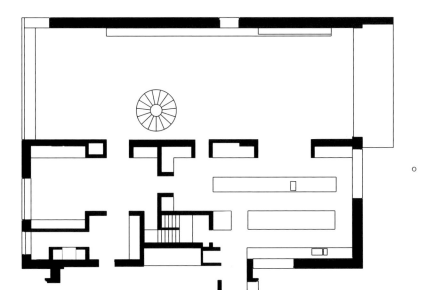

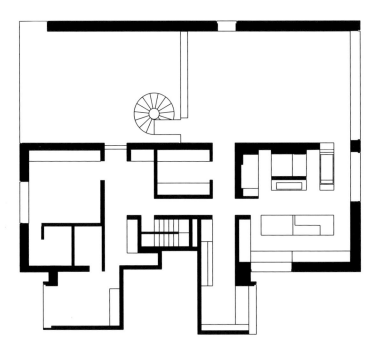

Longitudinal section

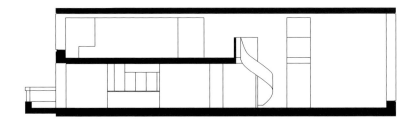

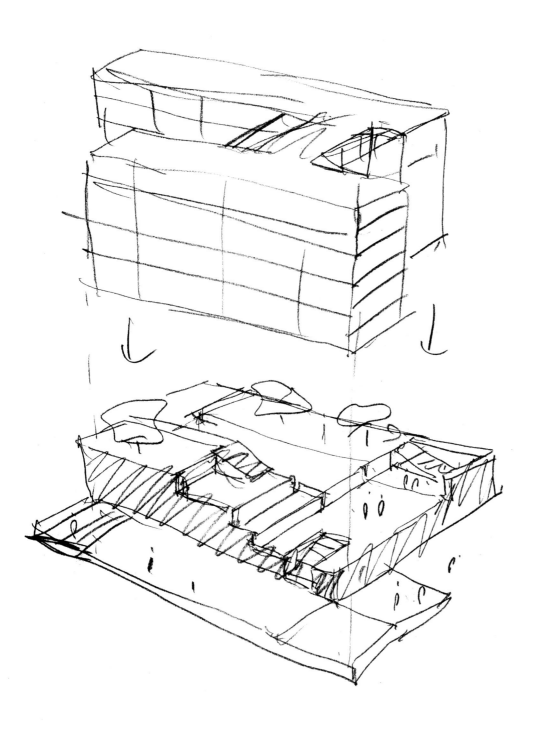

BBC Scotland, Glasgow
2001–2005

This project, developed from the winning proposal in the architectural competition for the new BBC Scotland headquarters in Pacific Quay, Glasgow, is located alongside the abandoned Govan docks on an exposed plot of land dominated by the expanse of the River Clyde and the mountains of the Scottish Highlands to the north. Faced with this open landscape, the design of the building had to find ways to establish its own sense of place and satisfy the demands of the BBC for a contained yet publicly accessible building.

The resulting proposal looked to create a building distinct from conventional offices; more industrial, loft-like in feel, it gives equal importance to collective work areas, individual work stations, and public spaces. Accordingly the central atrium is configured as a tiered sequence of platforms and terraces, visible through glass walls from the outside. Circulation and communication through the building and between office floors is promoted by this giant staircase, which not only offers informal meeting areas, but encourages movement between spaces, giving powerful visual representation to the public aspect of the building.

In terms of the formal design of the structure, the most immediate problem posed by the project brief lay in the compositional relationship between technical elements such as studios (that had to be solid) and office space (that to enjoy the surrounding views had to be transparent). In particular, the juxtaposition between the solidity and size of the principal television studio (Studio A) itself four storeys tall and the adjoining office spaces was the most difficult formal issue raised by the program. The response throughout all of the design decisions was to integrate each of the building's elements, avoiding a back-of-house atmosphere for technical areas, and the compartmentalization of common spaces, so that the building as a whole can absorb and reveal the diversity of its uses.

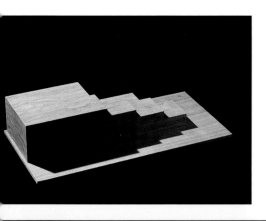

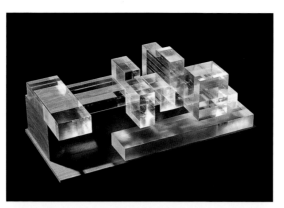

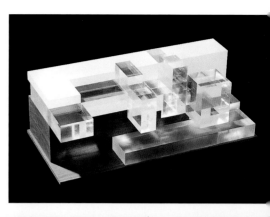

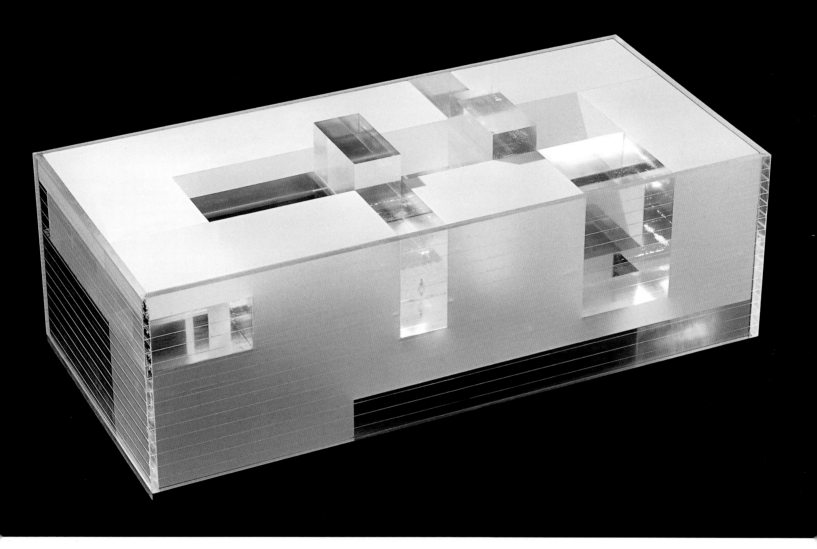

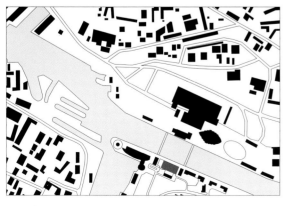

Above, study models revealing the articulation
of the building's central staircase and
adjoining studio and office spaces.

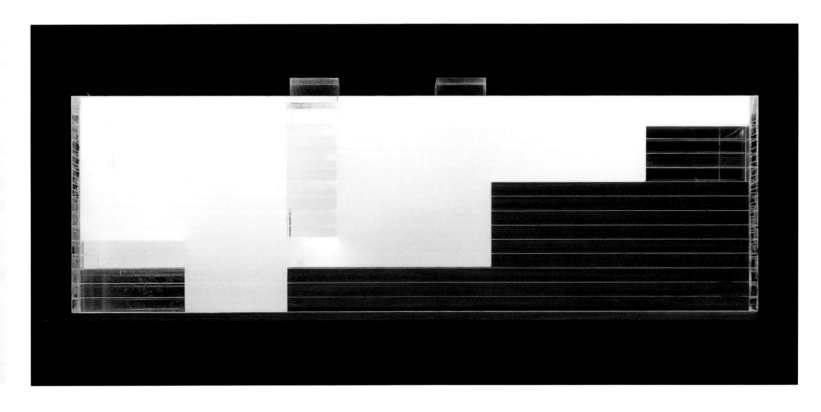

Longitudinal section

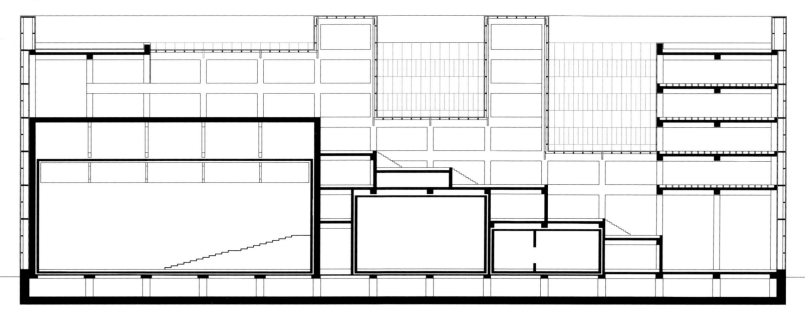

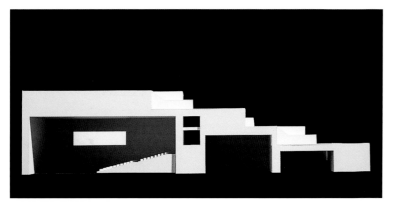

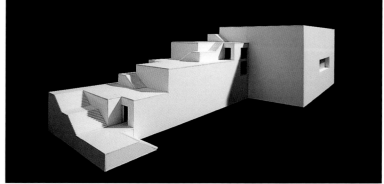

N

50 m

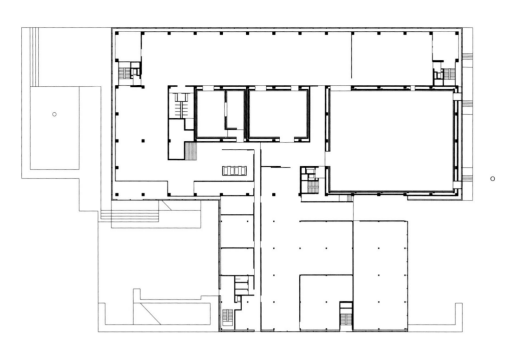

0

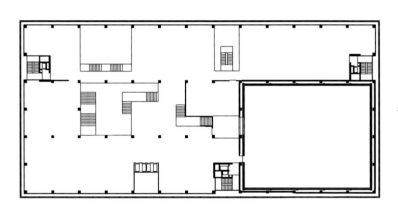

2

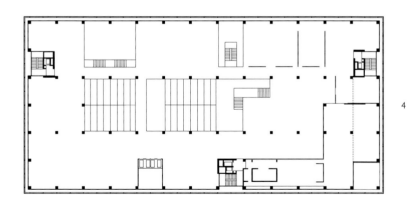

4

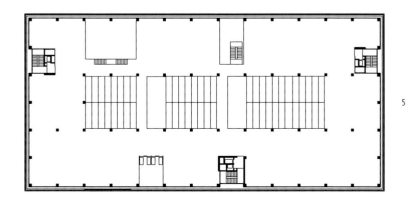

5

BFI Film Centre, London
2001–2007

Located somewhat ambiguously within an evolving masterplan for London's South Bank, this competition stage design for the new center for the British Film Institute is situated immediately alongside Jubilee Gardens. Given the imprecise physical conditions of the brief, the design looked to blur the boundaries between cinema and architecture with an architectural idea that could ideally form part of any more defined future development for the British Film Institute.

The culture of film itself provided a clue to this blurring, being made up of two diametrically opposed forces – the transience and ephemerality of the medium (projected light passing through celluloid) and the

solidity of its traditional container (the cinema – an enclosed, dark space). The design looks to offer some kind of simultaneity between these twin forces, particularly through its use of light, as the external surface of the structure is punctured by a series of openings so as to envelop and define each of its various interiors through a constantly varying palette of natural and artificial light.

In resolving the organisational challenges of the brief, the proposal also promotes a strong sense of movement and visual connectivity. As the essential vehicle to this idea, the foyer of the Film Centre is structured as an internal extension of a street, providing an open, visible route through the building

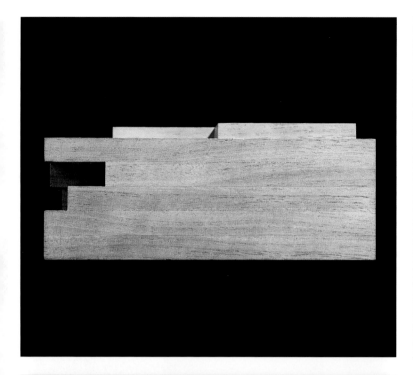

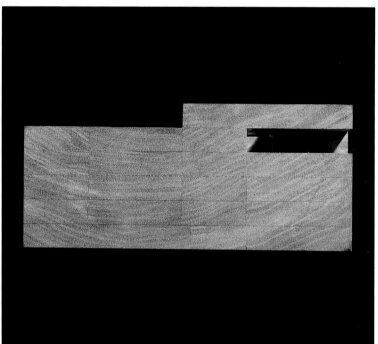

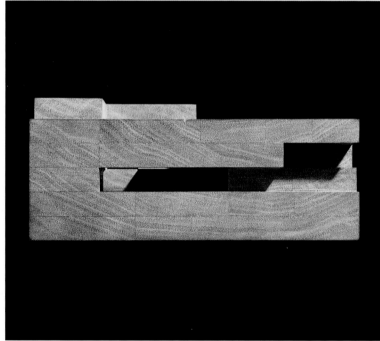

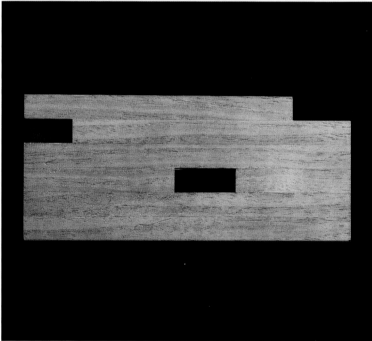

so as to offer glimpses of each of the Centre's elements (the National Film Theatre, the Museum of the Moving Image, BFI offices, exhibition and education spaces, café, and shop), and a continuation of movement to and from the public external spaces of the surrounding area. Not a singular pathway, this circulation system would offer choices of direction, while each channel would reveal itself as more than just a corridor but as a habitable, active space. As an interlocking sequence of spaces, as a light and dark filled canvas, the BFI Film Centre would be revealed and more clearly understood as an organization that effectively integrates and promotes all aspects of film and television culture.

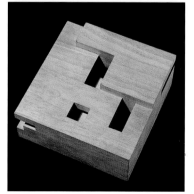

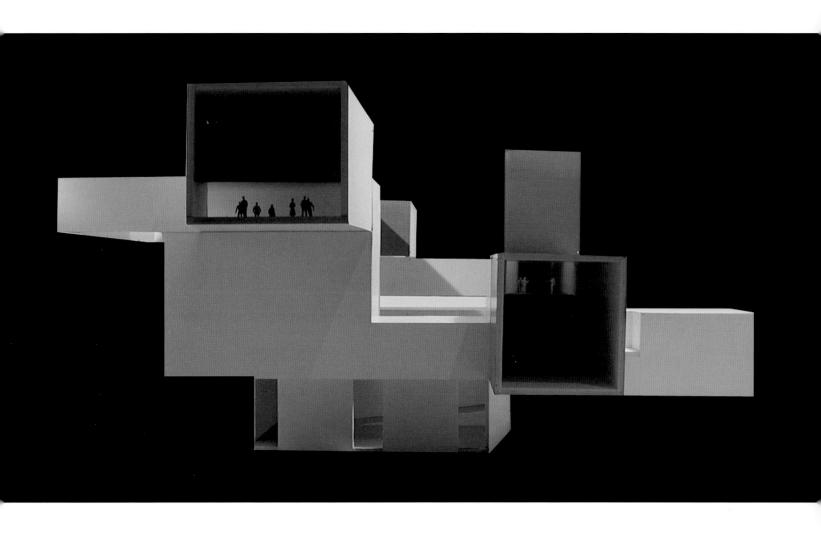

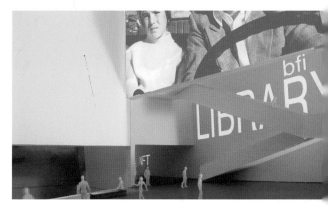

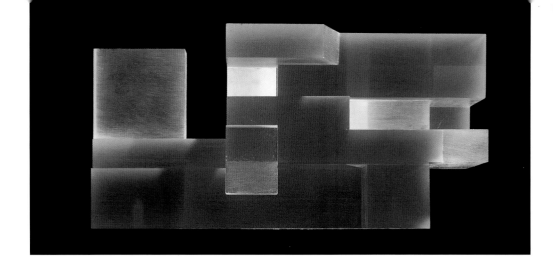

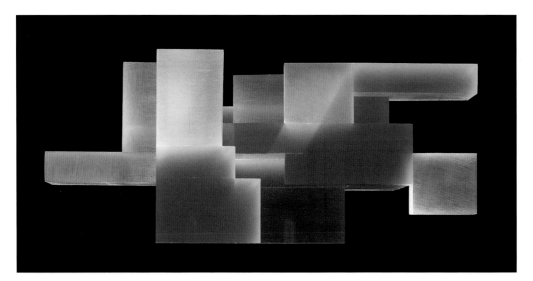

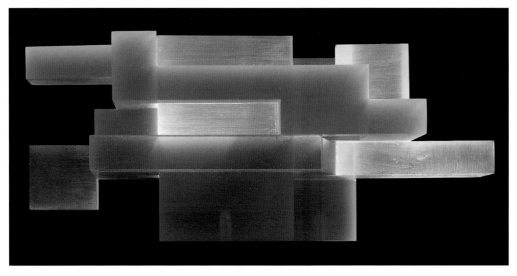

Inspiring the design of the building's internal spaces were the light installations of artist James Turrell, in particular *Blue Walk (night)*, 1983 (far left) and *Red Around (night)*, 1983, left.

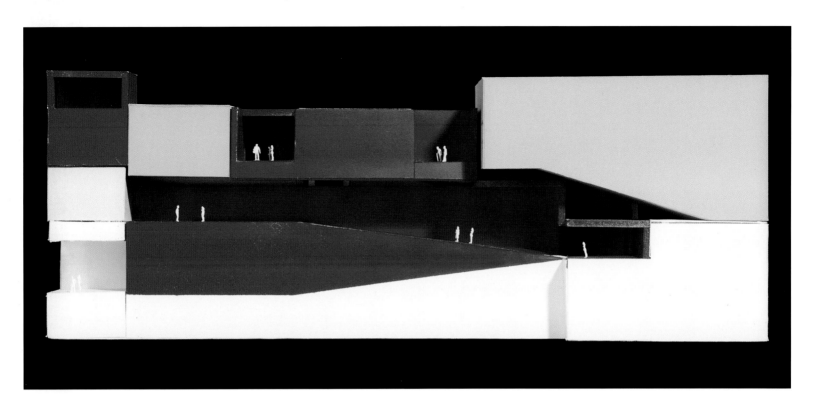

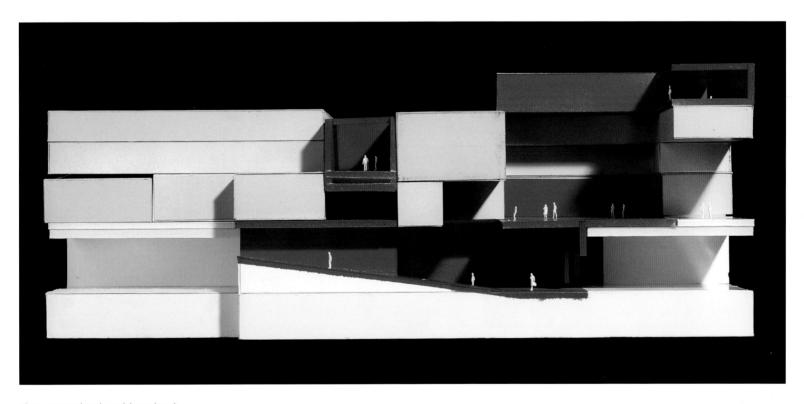

Above, sectional study model revealing the foyer of the building as an internal extension of a street.

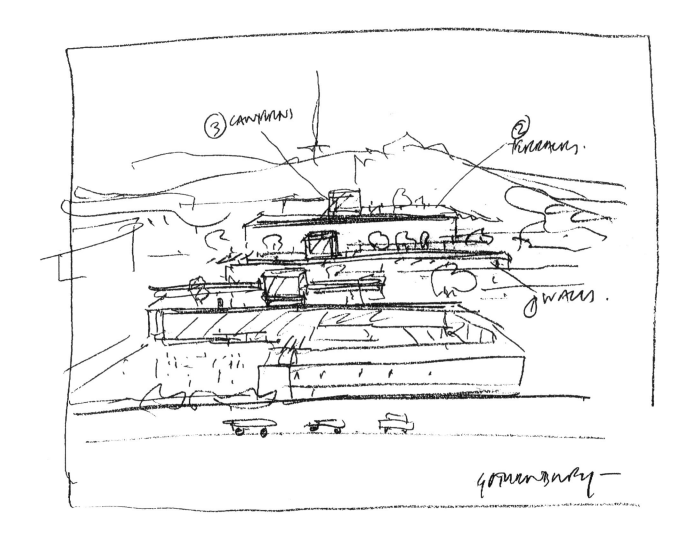

Centre of World Cultures, Göteborg
1999

This competition proposal for an ethnographic museum was located in Göteborg, close to the urban fabric of the city center on an open, undulating site dominated by the nearby Liseberg Hill. Providing flexible exhibition, office, and public spaces, the project was articulated around the idea of situating a museum within a strong topographic context (that is, building on a hill), yet at the same time, it also had to address the more regular, even landscape of Göteborg's urban streets and blocks. The project, in this way, was to act as an interface between nature and the city, between a hill slope and a flat plain.

Initial studies for the Centre defined the spaces of the museum within a series of abstract walls running parallel to the contours of the hill. These tectonic interventions were seen as a sort of landscape terracing, underneath which were provided all of the necessary exhibition spaces. Rejected due to the lack of spatial continuity they afforded and the problems they posed in terms of natural lighting, the wall was subsequently replaced by the idea of the platform. Instead of being revealed from within enclosures, therefore, the museum sits on top of a tiered series of stone granite plinths, stepping up from the flat area of the site into the incline of the hill.

The actual museum spaces, uninterrupted by room divisions, are contained within laminated timber 'cages', providing a light

and open landscape of galleries, terraces, stairs and balconies. Like the platforms, the wooden frame changes levels, reflecting both the internal volumes of the building and the gradual stepping up of the terraces. These cages are in turn wrapped by a glass skin and a system of louvers. Inside, more environmentally controlled spaces are housed within pavilions that sit in the open continuum of the galleries, allowing the translucent glass walls to provide a soft daylight background for all of the internal spaces of the museum and establish a continuity of orientation through the clarity of the enclosing architectural structure.

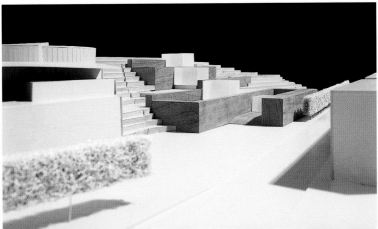

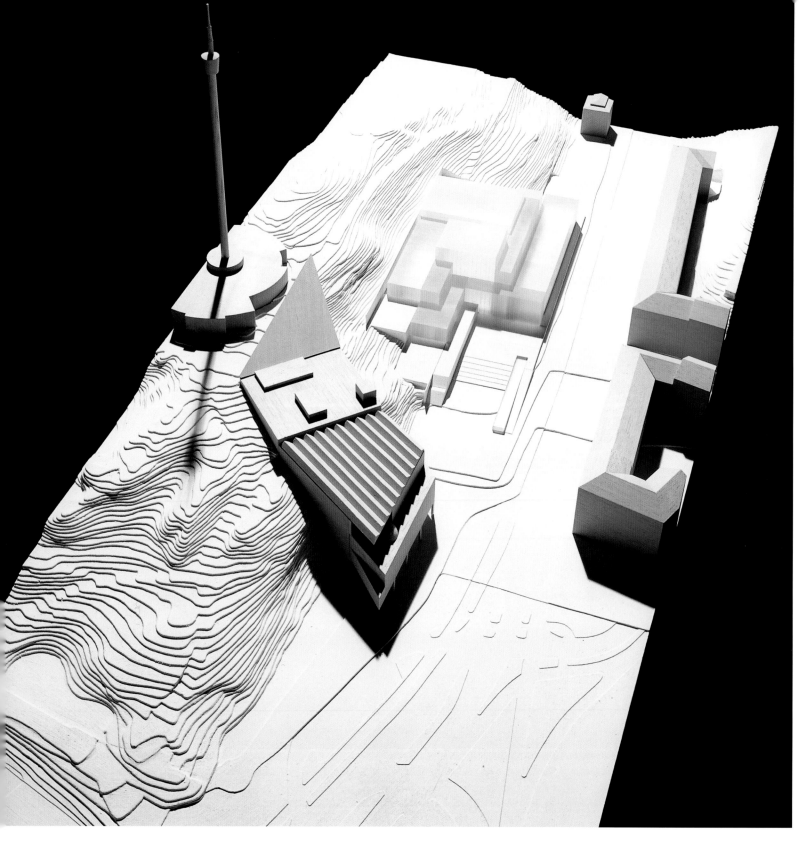

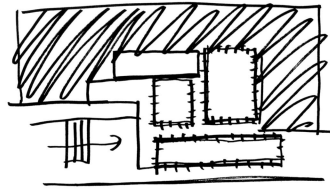

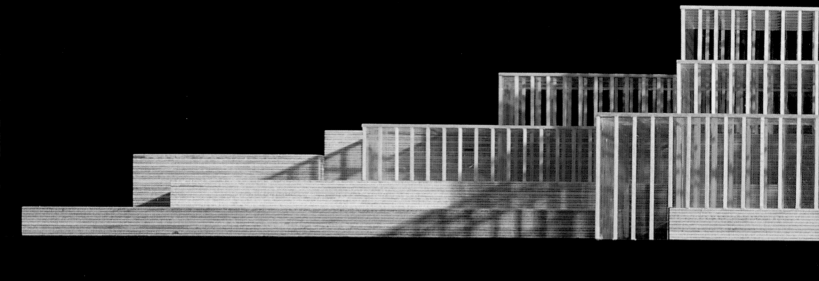

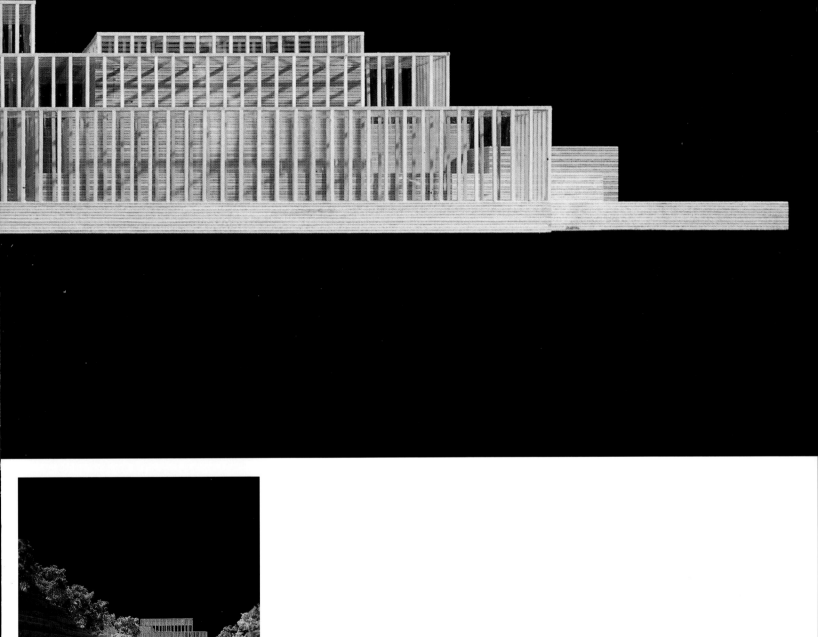

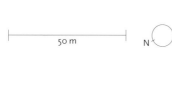

50 m   N

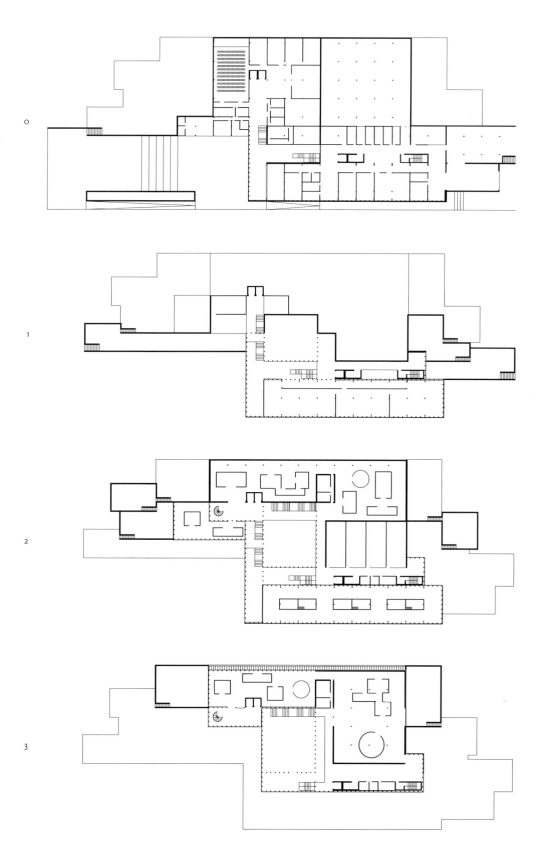

Below, north elevation

Dolce & Gabbana shops
1999–

Over a number of years Domenico Dolce and Stefano Gabbana have distinguished themselves as designers of great style and originality, producing consistently innovative clothing that challenges our ideas of material, form and colour. The redesign of the Dolce & Gabbana worldwide identity and its subsequent realization in shops from Osaka to Los Angeles developed from the often overlooked idea of positioning these clothes as the most important elements within each shop.

Rather than competing with the clothes, the shops were all conceived with the idea of maintaining a contrast between these extravagant, sometimes fantastical costumes

and a sparse, minimal architectural setting. Unifying this calm, even backdrop, gray basalt stone extends across the entire floor area of each shop, enveloping stairway and perimeter benches that run in ascending heights throughout the spaces, and providing an atmospheric, monochrome surface against which the clothes appear. In contrast to this dark stone, wall and ceiling spaces maintain a more ethereal sense of lightness – pristine white walls and laminated silk glass screens act as a canvas for special display items and delineate the sales floor from the fitting room areas. Additional material elements feature rich burgundy velvet curtains in the fitting rooms and specially designed polycarbonate

luminaires giving an even distribution of light across these spaces.

These contrasts between lightness and darkness, contemporary and antique, textured and smooth surfaces, extend into the furniture used throughout each store. Developed at the same time as the architectural space, and manufactured by B&B Italia, the display systems have been designed almost as domestic objects – easily repositioned and able to be moved around each shop – and feature both wall-mounted and free-standing teak pieces, together with illuminated glass cases containing black stained oak accessory drawers. These modern furniture elements are placed alongside signature Dolce & Gabbana

pieces (baroque chairs, paintings, zebra skins, Mediterranean plants and sculptural Sicilian urns) so as to blend the character of the spaces with that of the clothes, and highlighting Dolce & Gabbana design as distinct from all others.

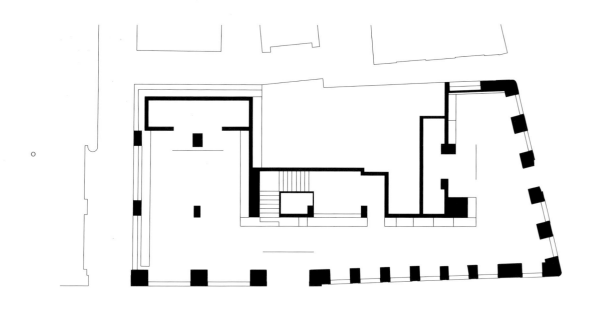

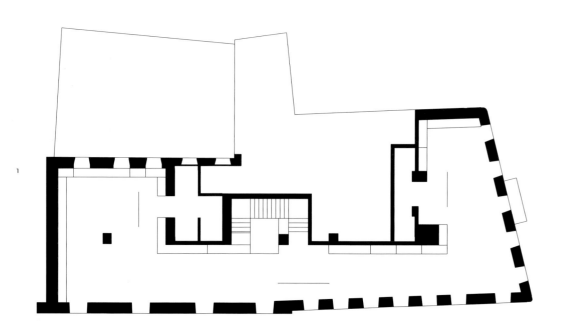

This page, Villa della Spiga, Milan
Right, longitudinal section

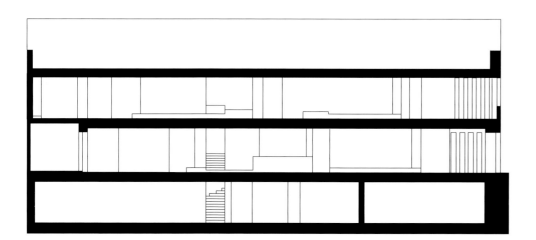

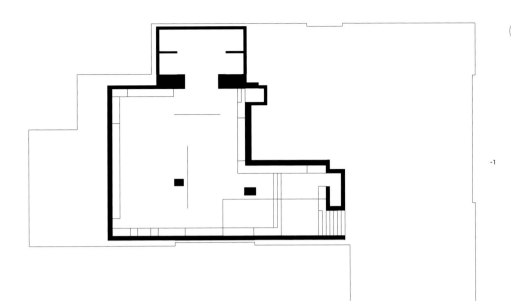

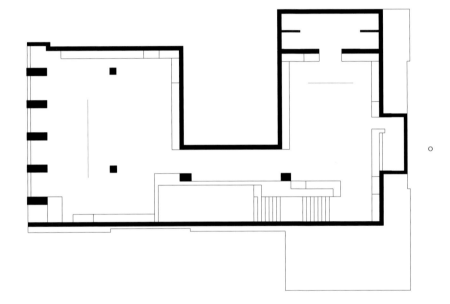

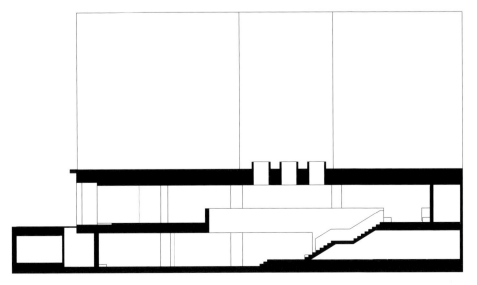

This page, Old Bond Street, London
Left, longitudinal section

Ernsting Service Center, Coesfeld-Lette
1998–2001

This building, located in the small town of Coesfeld-Lette, just west of Münster in Germany's Nordrhein-Westfalen region, is the new headquarters for the German clothing retailer Ernsting. Designed on a greenfield site, the structure stands alongside two existing distribution centers, one of which was designed by Fabio Reinhardt & Bruno Reichlin and Santiago Calatrava in the 1980s and the other by Schilling Architects in the late 1990s. This third building completes the Ernsting compound and provides office space for business and retail managers together with a research and development department.

The concept for its design was to break up the form of the two-storey building so as to

allow each of its spaces a closer interaction with the surrounding landscape and to provide a more open than usual relationship between inside and outside. This notion of fragmenting the internal mass of the structure was also influenced by the demands of the client who sought to define each of Ernsting's various business holdings within a singular building envelope. These conditions allowed for the opportunity to design internal courtyards which provide a hub from which all of the programmatic elements of the building could radiate, and which simultaneously afforded all of the office areas light and open space. The sense of openness is further emphasized by a colonnade and balconies around the periphery

of the structure, and by two atrium spaces, the
larger of which acts as the main lobby and entry
point for the building, and accommodates the
principal area where people inside the building
can meet. Inside, the office space is open-plan,
with very few of the more conventional cellular
office compartments dividing up the space, so
as to provide views into the courtyards and
across to the surrounding countryside from
both sides of the interior of the building.
Complementing this strong sense of lightness
and horizontal detachment, the building is
raised slightly off the ground plane so as to
appear to float, and vertically further looking to
maintain a lightness of touch within the weight
of architectural presence.

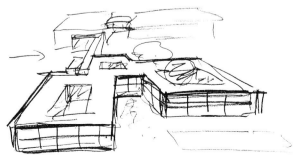

N
50 m

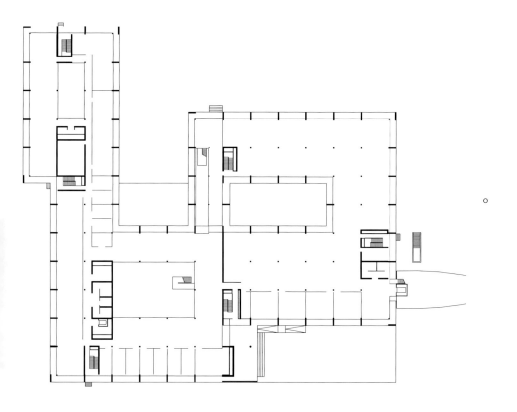

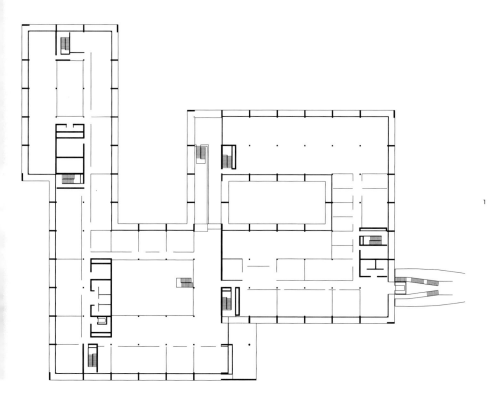

Left, northwest elevation
Bottom, section

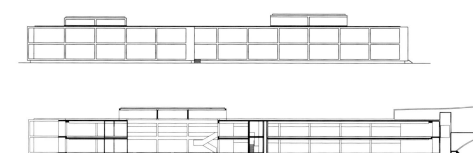

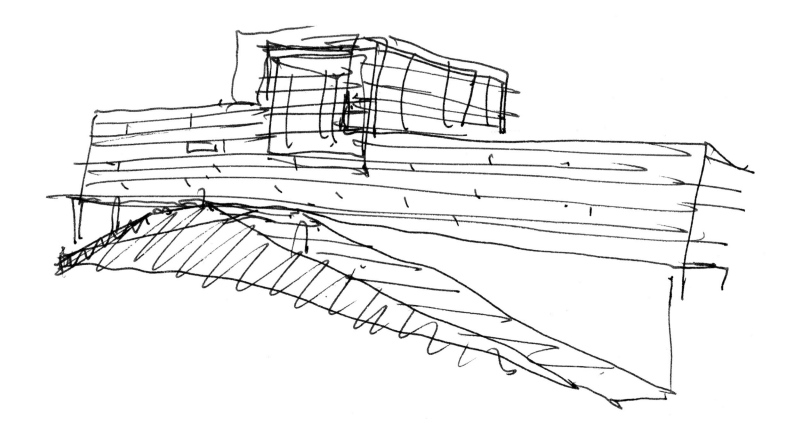

Figge Arts Center, Davenport
2000–2004

The center of Davenport, located on the banks of the Mississippi on Iowa's eastern border, suffers from many of the problems endemic to a number of American cities. Over the years the area has witnessed the departure of much of its residential and business communities leaving downtown Davenport with little of the vibrancy normally associated with urban life. In an attempt to reinvigorate this area, and recreate a connection to the river, the city identified the relocation of the Davenport Museum of Art (renamed the Figge Arts Center) as the catalyst in a programme of urban regeneration. The museum will rehouse the existing permanent collections – American, African, Haitian, Mexican, European, as well

as an important Grant Wood archive.

Seeing in the brief a wish to create an emblematic building for the new city, the design of the Figge Arts Center was conceived as a monolithic glass structure that would powerfully yet simply landmark Davenport's redeveloped waterfront. Its architecture was developed around the idea of a simple volumetric block enveloped by opaque, transparent, and translucent surfaces. These glass surfaces are fritted with horizontal banding that varies in density so as to define each of the Center's formal elements. In urban terms, the design looked to support the old city grid by filling one half of a previously empty city block, yet while maintaining a

strong and singular outline, the design of the Center reveals itself as more varied than its urban footprint would suggest – different frontages reflect differing site conditions and define each of the building's facades with distinct approaches; city plaza, street entrance, and riverside terrace.

Inside the building the program for its design and layout is based largely on the existing Davenport Museum of Art with its rich mix of exhibition and non-exhibition functions but also including educational spaces, drawing and study studios, lecture and library facilities. The proposed design encourages the overlap of these functions and for a public route through the building, giving visitors

an awareness of the activities of the Figge Arts Center, and students and artists an immediate relationship with the collection of paintings and objects that it houses.

Above, Grant Wood, *Fertility*, 1937, from the Figge Arts Center's Grant Wood archive.

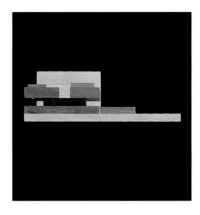
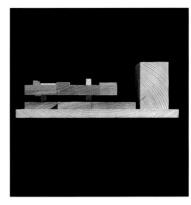

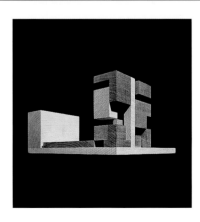

A series of study models exploring various formal strategies for the building.

Model showing the fritting of the building's
external glass surfaces.

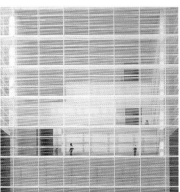

20 m

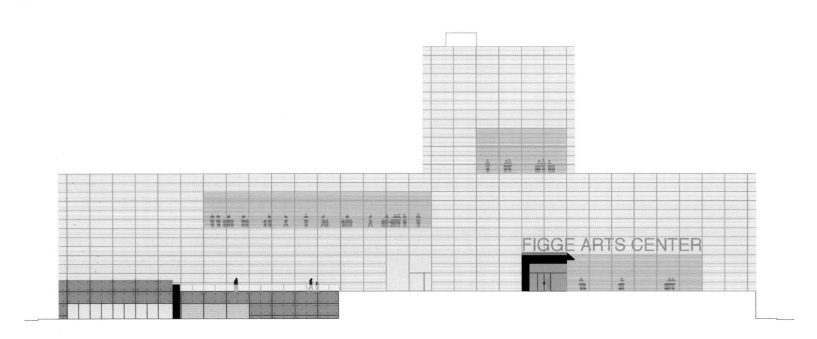

FIGGE ARTS CENTER

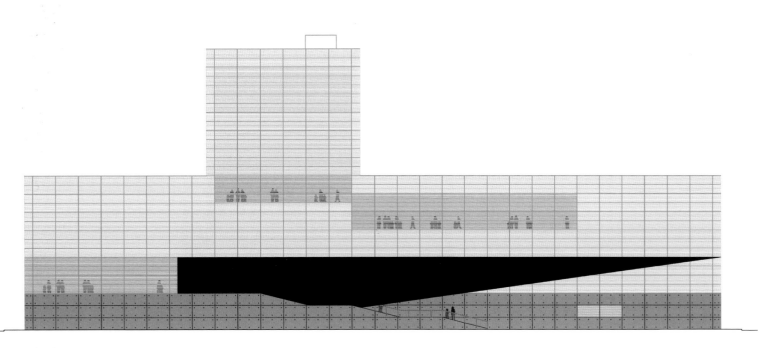

Top, street elevation
Bottom, river elevation

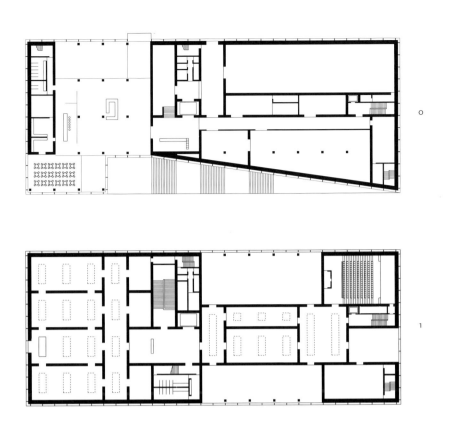

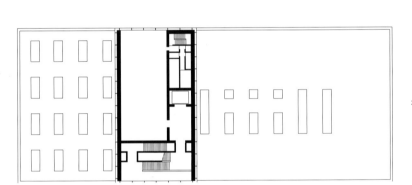

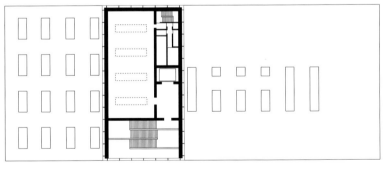

N

50 m

0

1

2

3

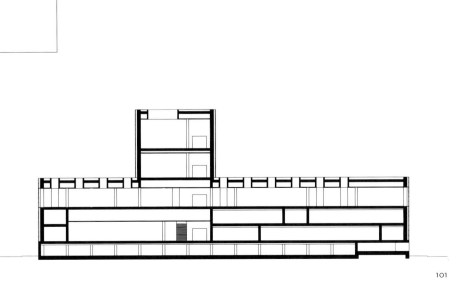

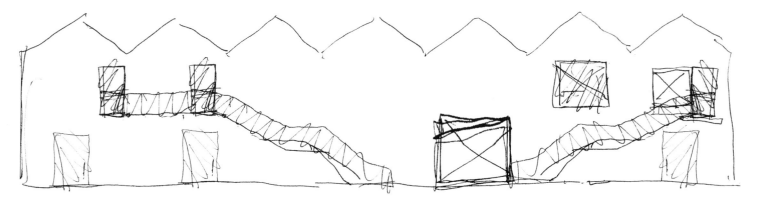

Gormley Studio, London
2001–2003

This design for a new studio for the English artist Anthony Gormley is located amid the industrial buildings, warehouses, and rail yards north of London's Kings Cross station. Attempting to create light and open spaces for the diverse and specific ways in which Gormley works, the building provides studio space for drawing, painting, sculpting, welding, casting, and photography.

A former Turner Prize winner, and an artist whose work has been exhibited in museums and as installations all over the world, Gormley has created some of the most ambitious and recognizable sculptural works of the past two decades, including *Field*, *The Angel of the North*, and *Quantum Cloud* on the

River Thames in Greenwich. With the increasing interest in his work, Gormley required a space that would be large enough to construct his often huge installations, yet at the same time would also be somewhere intimate and personal enough in which he could conceive his next artistic projects.

Looking to satisfy both of these requirements, the design of the proposed studio references and abstracts the large scale, industrial architectural vernacular of the surrounding buildings, and also the smaller, more domestic model of the artist's studio as illustrated, amongst others, by Le Corbusier in the space he created in 1924 for the painter Amédée Ozenfant. Like Ozenfant's studio the

building is distinguished by the silhouette of its pitched roofs and its bright but even interior light. Located to the rear of its site, the studio building itself is approached across a large yard, left open for the assembling of bigger pieces. A pair of galvanized steel staircases connect this yard to the domestic-scale studio and office areas on the upper floor of the main building. Operating as both a workshop and as a kind of paired down, white-walled studio space, the building will become the focus for all of Gormley's artistic production, and will sensitively yet pragmatically edify a collaborative effort between artist and architect.

Anthony Gormley, *Untitled (for Francis)*, 1985. Image courtesy of the artist.

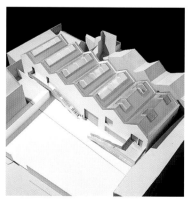

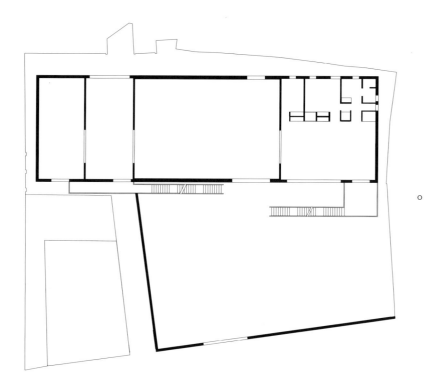

0

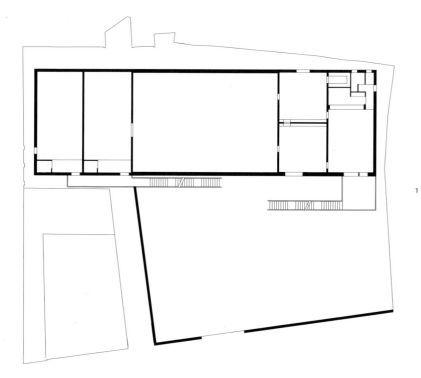

1

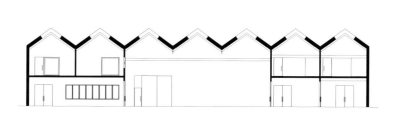

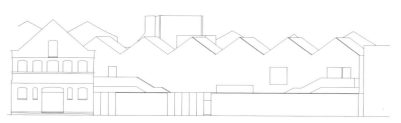

Gotoh Museum, Chiba
1988–1991

This museum, situated in a small residential suburb in Chiba, north of Tokyo was the first of three buildings completed in Japan in the early 1990s. Designed to house the client's collection of art works, the building also provides a number of student apartments, rented to the local university and integrated into the structure so as to help subsidize the running costs of the museum, as well as maintain a vibrancy and continuous life in the building.

In an attempt to locate the museum culturally, the design of the project was concerned with a number of themes that were considered in some way Japanese. Foremost among these was the play of internal and external space, and the ambiguity of certain types of spaces like colonnades and courtyards which, while not fully enclosed, still constitute an integral part of the architectural form. This ambiguity also reveals itself in the spatial allocation of the building's programmatic elements. Due to height restrictions, nearly all of the building's public areas (including exhibition galleries, a café, and museum offices) have been constructed underground (approximately 5.5 m below ground level); yet because of the generosity of their proportions and their light and airy interiors (illuminated by light wells and windows onto a basement courtyard) one is never really conscious of being underground.

Circulation routes through the building also maintain a strongly Japanese character. Rather than being organized around the shortest distances possible, movement through the museum follows a more involved path. For example, from their own cloister-like entrance, students living at the top of the building can only access their apartments after first passing through the public spaces of the museum and across balconies and over terraces. The way one moves through the building, therefore, elaborates and extends all journeys through the museum, so that, like much contemporary and traditional Japanese architecture, one has to pass through outside areas in order to move between interior space.

In this and other spatial manipulations, the museum established a model not only for later Japanese projects but for much of the architecture subsequently produced by the office.

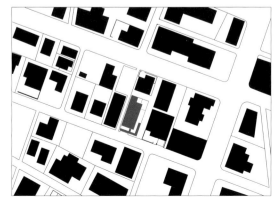

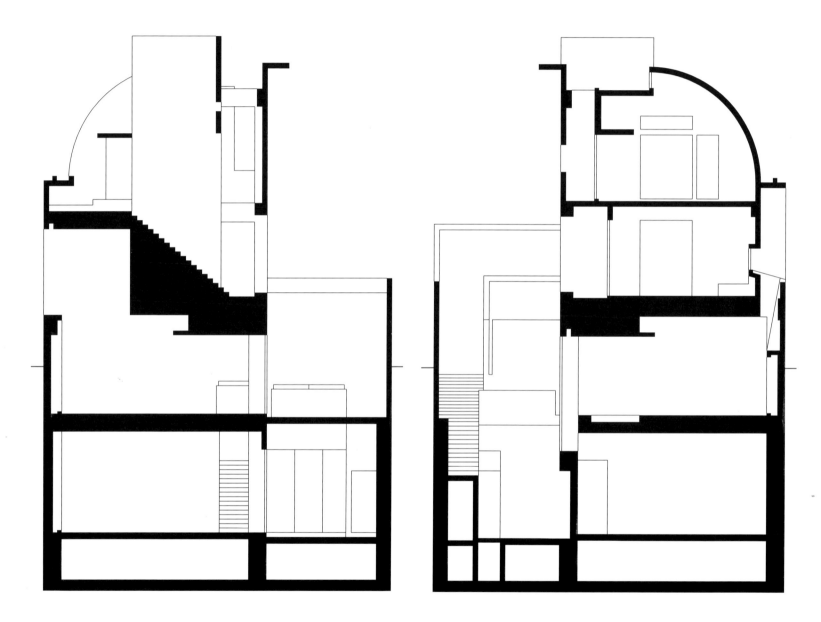

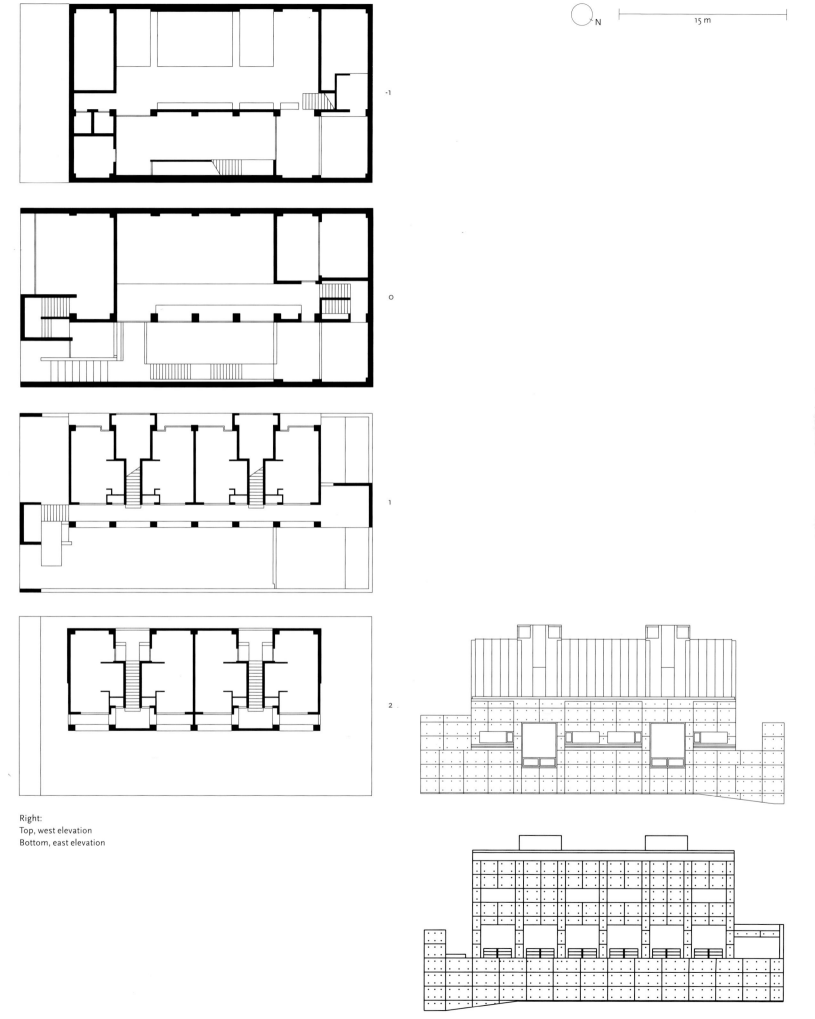

Right:
Top, west elevation
Bottom, east elevation

House in Galicia, Corrubedo
1996 – 2002

The house occupies a gap in the main street of the small Galician fishing village of Corrubedo. Sitting at the northern edge of a large protected bay on Spain's northwest Atlantic coast, the site offered dramatic views out over the harbor and to the sea beyond. Unlike the other buildings along the harbor side, which turn their backs to the sea, facing instead the enclosed spaces of the village, the house exploits the views afforded by its location and orientates all of its internal spaces towards the ocean.

From the sea, the collection of individual and apparently random buildings in Corrubedo form a kind of village elevation – a thin ribbon of buildings that although made up of houses of varying heights and geometries, still presents itself as a unified and solid arrangement. The introduction of a new house with different priorities had to take into consideration its place within this wall. Looking to provide a sense of continuity, therefore, the house sits on a solid stone and concrete base, and its upper mass, like the neighboring houses, is punctured by small windows. Placed like a shelf between these two conditions, a large panoramic window, extending the full width of the house, provides all encompassing views across the beach and harbor.

In this way, rather than resisting the surrounding geometries, the house takes them into its own form. This strategy is most apparent on the street side of the building where the colliding geometries of adjoining houses extend across the building, dictating its formal composition. Internally this pattern is repeated with stairs, bedrooms, and living spaces articulated according to differing geometries, while on top of the house, introducing its own more organic outline, a large roof terrace allows panoramic views of the sea. Looking out from this terrace over the surrounding rooftops, the house can clearly be seen to maintain a sense of continuity with the rest of the harbor side, while at the same time its silhouette, angular spaces and white walls also offer something striking and new.

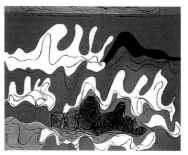

Left, *Mar del Orzán*, 1973, by Galician artist
Luis Seoane.

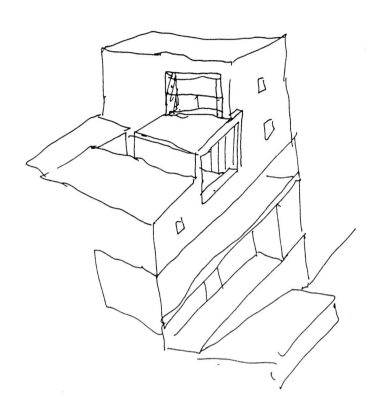

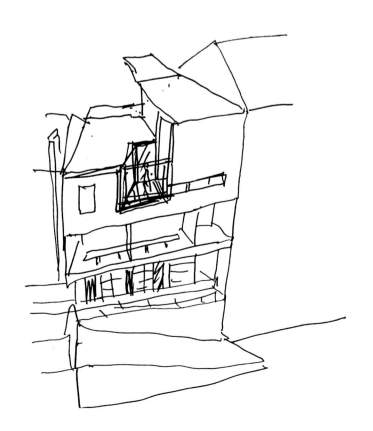

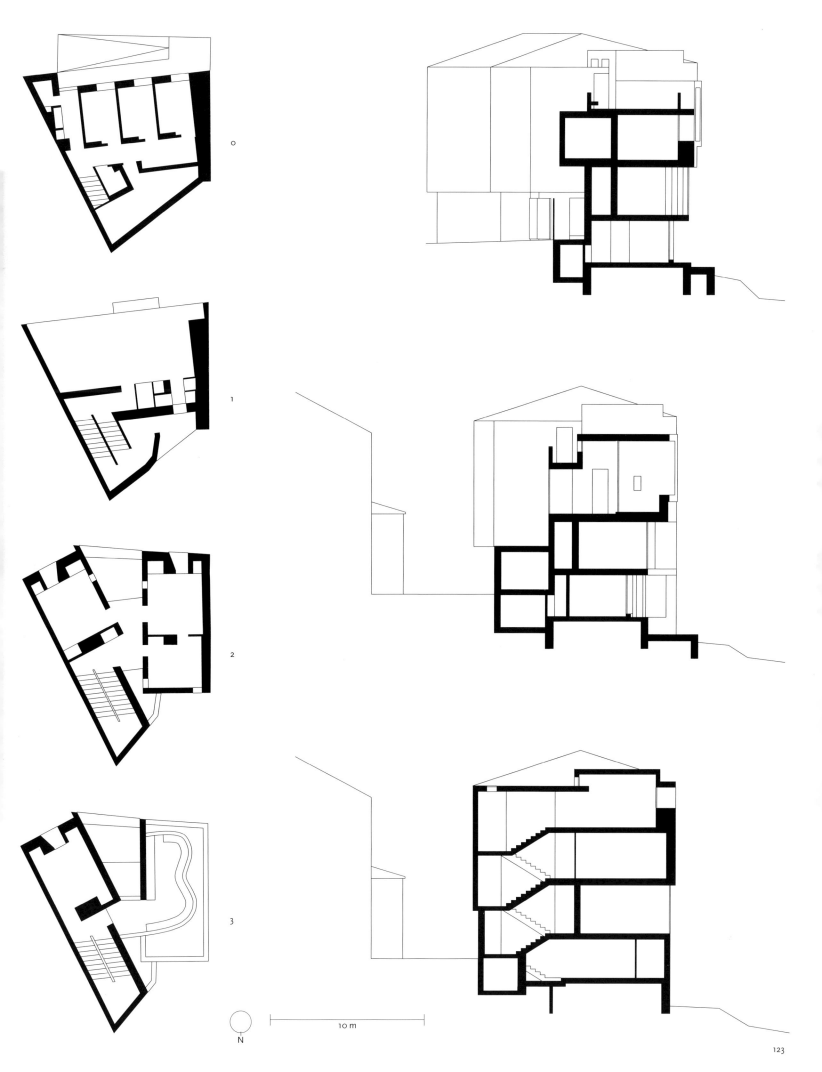

0

1

2

3

N

10 m

123

Joseph, Sloane Avenue, London
1997

Converted from a 1960s former office building, the store is located near the Brompton Road in London's South Kensington. After completely stripping away the extraneous arched detailing on the outside of the block, together with all of the internal room divides, the project itself consisted of two parts – firstly to insert a new two-storey shop, housing men's clothing and accessories, over the ground and first floors of the existing office building, and secondly to refit the upper levels of the block so as to provide office, showroom, and stock areas.

This dual aspect to the project brief was reflected in two separate surface finishes for the facade. Extending over the ground and first floors are a series of 2.5 m by 6 m glass panels,

opening up the interior spaces of the building as much as possible, while the second floor is concealed behind a stainless steel mesh screen, abstracting the office floor into the overall composition of the building. Revealed through the glass skin, the lower levels of the building demonstrate an open idea of display and create a vista all the way through the shop. The clarity of this view is heightened further by the relatively limited palette of materials used – *pietra serena* floor tiles, dark *wenge* wood display cabinets, stainless steel stands, and natural white plaster finished walls.

Acting as a kind of sculptural piece within this open space, a spiral staircase connects the ground and first floors of the shop.

Constructed from a set of steel ellipses, and then clad in timber and rendered, this stair maintains the even gray and white tones of the rest of the shop. In the consistency of this backdrop, not allowing the architecture to compete or attract attention away from the clothes, this building for Joseph anticipated many subsequent fashion shops produced by the office.

N

10 m

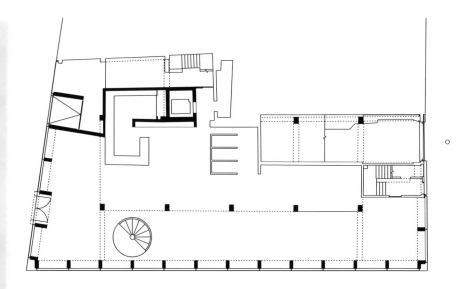

o

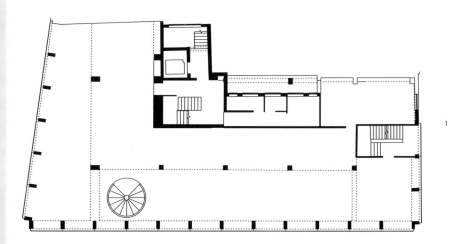

1

Below, west elevation
Right, south elevation

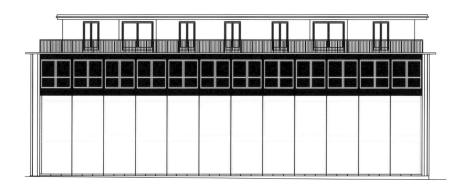

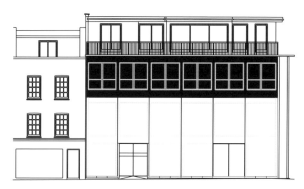

Kaistrasse Studios, Düsseldorf
1994–1997

This building forms one end-point to a river-front series of new and renovated buildings in the port area of Düsseldorf, Germany. The area still retains a number of elements from its more industrial past – shipping cranes, cobbled streets, and simple unadorned warehouse buildings – but increasingly this atmosphere has been lost beneath the over-sized forms and uniform cladding systems of more recent commercial developments. Looking to reverse this trend, the studios have been designed in such a way as to return to the scale and materiality of the older, dockland vernacular.

The building itself is conceived of two interlocking forms – an in-situ concrete mass

placed alongside and over a black steel frame. This double aspect to the structure was designed to allow for the creation of large, studio-like windows while maintaining an overall impression of mass and solidity. These distinctions between structure and surface, and between the lightness of interior space against the weight of its architectural presence, are heightened further by the rough finish given to the concrete; a texture that not only establishes a powerful contrast to the smoothness of the adjoining steel frame, but also references the aesthetic and materiality of the building's harbor site.

Commissioned as a block of studio spaces for sculptors and painters, the building is

conceived as a series of light, double-height lofts and mezzanine floors, forming a repeating pattern of singular and double-height windows alternately expressed on the side and front elevations of the building. Terminating the studios at the top level is an enlarged triple-height loft, while at the bottom, a restaurant looks out over the raised entrance terrace and to the River Rhine to the west. With the quality of its studio spaces, together with the accessibility of these ground level public spaces, it is hoped that the building will become a focal point for the area, reinvigorating and repopulating once again Düsseldorf's river side.

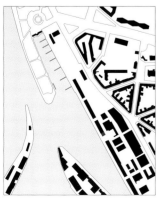

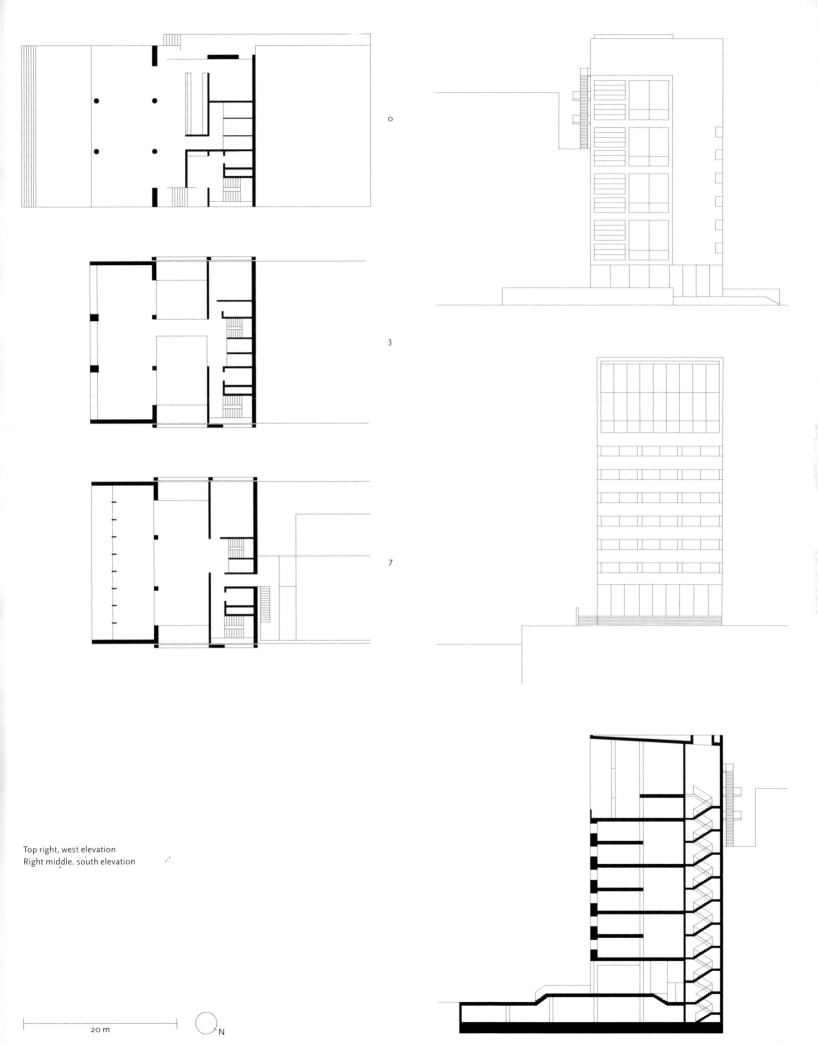

o

3

7

Top right, west elevation
Right middle, south elevation

20 m

N

Knight House, Richmond
1998–2001

In 1998 David Chipperfield Architects completed a house for the photographer Nick Knight and his family in Richmond, Surrey, extending and reworking an existing 1950s suburban house. Over the last ten years, however, with the photographer's family expanding, this first house consequently needed to be extended, providing additional living, working and storage space, as well as the opportunity to enlarge the rear garden.

Early designs for this second building initially explored the possibility of extending the architectural language of the first 1990 house, but this approach was soon rejected as the unity and coherence of the original project became obscured. Finding an architecture that would exist on its own and in tandem with the older house was complicated further by the resistance of local residents – having approved one ostensibly 'modern' house for traditional Richmond they were reluctant to approve of a second.

In response to these reservations, the architectural concept for the new addition placed an archetypal house form (with a pitched roof and two gabled ends) alongside the original house. This new element was then connected to the existing house via an abstracted glass box. Clad in translucent fiberglass shutters, this connecting piece provides a link to the older house at both floors, as well as containing a bathroom and storage spaces. Accessed through this channel, within the main body of the new house are provided a master bedroom, workspace and archive, arranged as two continuous rooms, one on top of the other – giving a sense of openness exaggerated further by the large bedroom window which slides vertically to transform the upper room into a balcony. In this way, the themes established in the original project – of space, light and view – are continued in this addition, retaining the spirit of the existing house while pursuing and introducing a different figurative idea.

Above and left, views of the first house for Nick Knight, extended by the construction of the second building, far left.

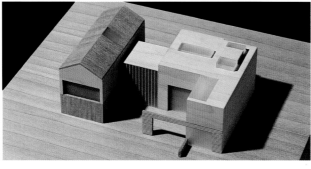

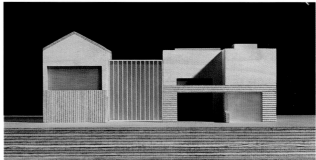

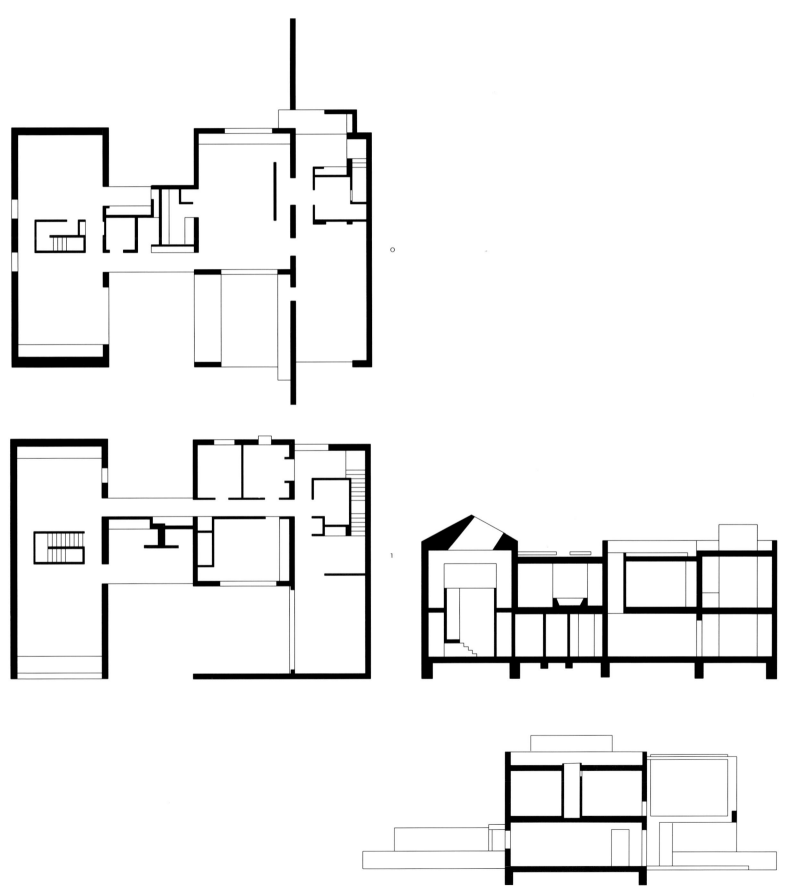

Landeszentralbank, Gera
1994–2001

This new headquarters building for the Landeszentralbank is located near Leipzig in the former East Germany. Situated on the periphery of the historic town of Gera, the building has been designed to take advantage of its prominent position and to create a series of internal and external spaces that facilitate the complex program of security and money handling.

The main building form (containing the banking hall, office, and administration spaces) is organized to form on one side an edge to the busy Am Stadion street, and on the other, a protected courtyard enclosed by the bank vault building and a housing block for staff. Each of these elements has been

designed to create a consistent and coherent whole, but at the same time they each also comply with the strict technical and security requirements dictated by the Landeszentralbank.

The homogeneity of the various built elements of the bank is in part created by the way each of its surfaces has been clad with the same gray/green concrete finish. Distinguished by its horizontal banding, the seemingly irregular pattern of these facades allows for a flexible system of openings within the bank's architectural compound – from the windowless bank vault block to the more open, public areas of the offices and banking hall. These more accessible parts of the

building are distinguished further by the generosity of their internal spaces (particularly the three-storey stair hall, and double-height banking hall), and by their lighting (flooded by natural light from windows and roof lights). Providing some kind of emblem to these areas, advertizing their accessibility, English artist Michael Craig-Martin was specially commissioned by the Landeszentralbank to produce a series of wall murals – everyday images of chairs and musical instruments presented on bright, saturated purple and sky blue backgrounds – that play with our traditional heavy associations of bank buildings with colour, humor, and a certain degree of frivolity.

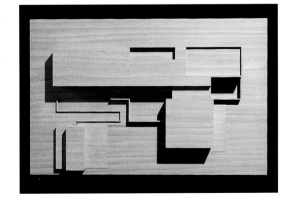

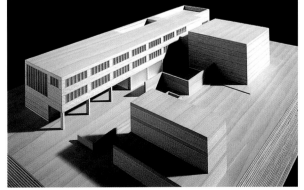

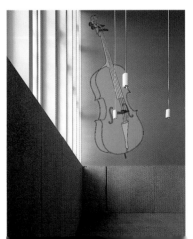

Above, one of a number of wall murals by
English artist Michael Craig-Martin

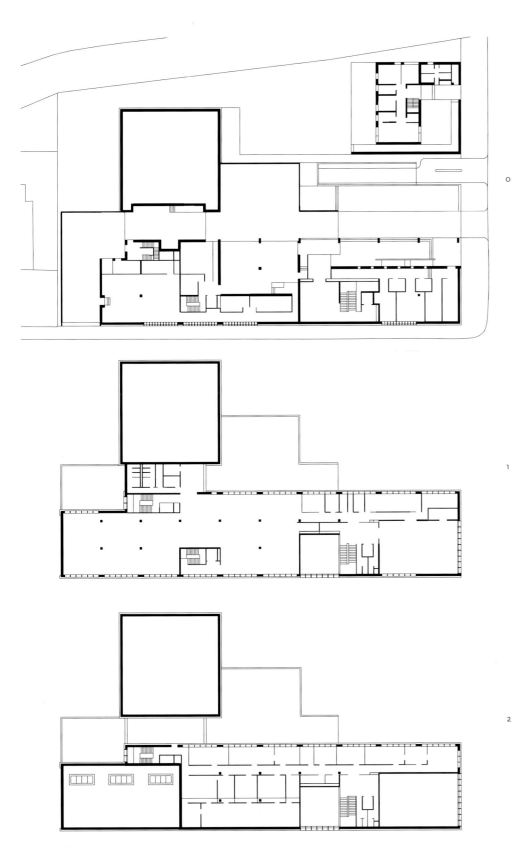

Below, west elevation

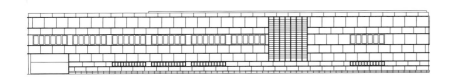

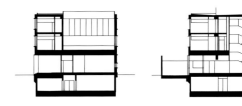

Literature Museum, Marbach am Neckar
2002–2005

This museum, which will be completed and officially opened on the 200th anniversary of German dramatist Friedrich Schiller's death (9th May 2005), is located in Marbach's scenic park, on top of a rock plateau overlooking the picturesque valley of the Neckar River. As the birthplace of Schiller, the town's park already holds the German Literature Archive, the National Schiller Museum, and a monument to the writer, immediately alongside which the new museum will stand. Displaying and archiving works of 20th-century literature, notably the original manuscripts of Franz Kafka's *The Trial* and Alfred Döblin's *Berlin Alexanderplatz*, the museum will also provide panoramic views across and over the far

distant landscape.

By means of a sequence of terraces, the architectural concept for the museum proposes to connect the lower park level to the forecourt of the Schiller Museum. In this way, by utilizing the steep slope of the site, the terraces allow for the creation of two very different characters – an intimate, shaded entrance on the brow of the hill, and a grander, more open series of tiered spaces facing the valley below. Entered from its highest point, the pavilion-like interiors of the museum therefore reveal themselves the more one descends through their display and archive spaces.

Inside, the exhibition floor is made up of

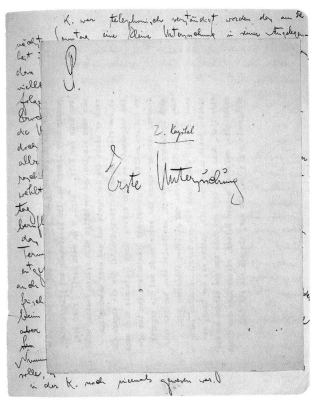

a mixture of halls and galleries of varying proportions and alternating ceiling heights. Housing and displaying manuscripts, transcripts, and catalogues, the majority of these spaces, because of the fragility and sensitivity of the works on display, are contained in the lower part of the building, in timber-paneled rooms illuminated only by artificial light. At the same time, each of these environmentally-controlled spaces borders onto a naturally lit gallery, so as to balance views inward to the composed, internalized world of texts and manuscripts with the green and scenic valley the other side of the glass.

Above, original manuscript pages from Franz Kafka's *The Trial (Der Prozeß)*, 1914, from the collection of the Literature Museum.

Sections showing relationship between
galleries and site levels.

Image of internal gallery and viewing window.

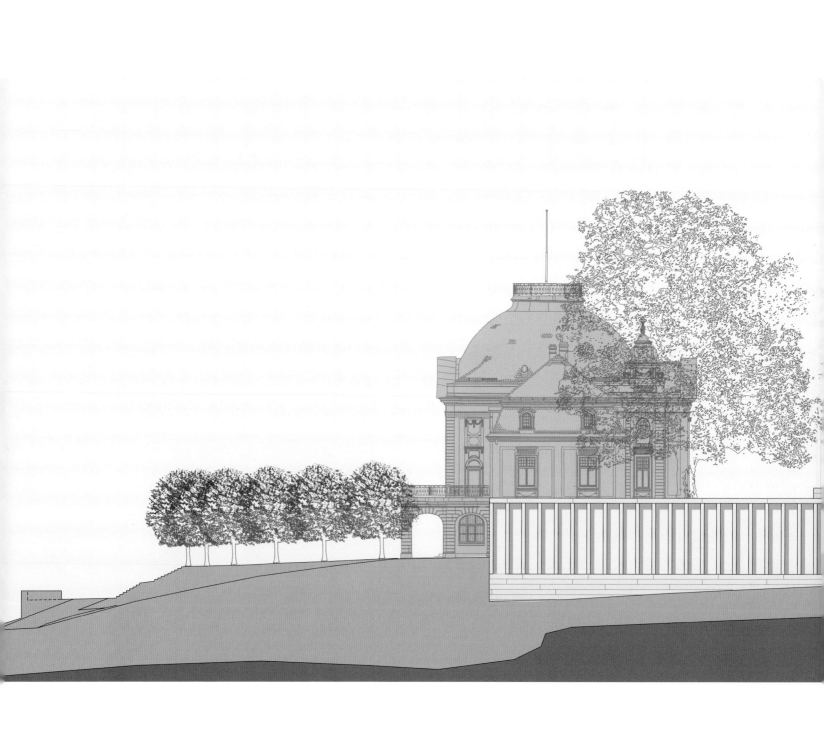

Museum of Modern Art, Bolzano
2001

This competition proposal for a modern art museum was located in the city of Bolzano in Italy's northerly Trentino Alto Adige region, not far from the Austrian border. The site for the scheme was situated close to the city center, and played a potentially important role in Bolzano's *Via Culturale* – the sequence of museums and cultural institutions that stretches its way through the heart of the city parallel to the Adige River. Surrounded on three sides by the back of surrounding buildings, the museum looked to form a bridge between the irregular and enclosed geometries of its neighboring buildings and the more open spaces of the meandering riverbank. The ambiguity created by the site's

public and private aspects was reflected in the design of the building as a structure made up of both formal and informal facades. The museum, in this way, takes on the characteristic of a series of different shapes joined together, some of which are formally related to the main street and the river, while others informally reference the surrounding buildings.

This ad hoc arrangement of volumes was also carried through into the interior of the museum's gallery spaces. Requiring a high level of flexibility, the Bolzano Museum of Modern Art stipulated a framework of open exhibition space in contrast to the more rigid, clearly defined gallery spaces of most modern

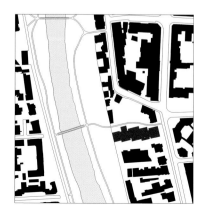

museums. Within the design are proposed exhibition areas that have enough volume and flexibility to allow for subdivision and reorganization yet that are sufficiently specific to have an interior character – a sense of identity further revealed by the natural and artificial light that illuminates the spaces. Clad, externally, in a skin of translucent glass, in front of a series of red-colored panels, the varied lighting of the museum's interior is mirrored on the outside by shifts in the building's surface color. Changing with the seasons, the museum would then cast itself across a spectrum of reds, from the pale pinks of winter to a warmer, richer crimson of the north Italian summer.

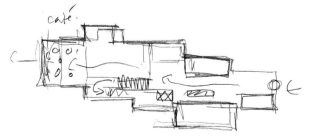

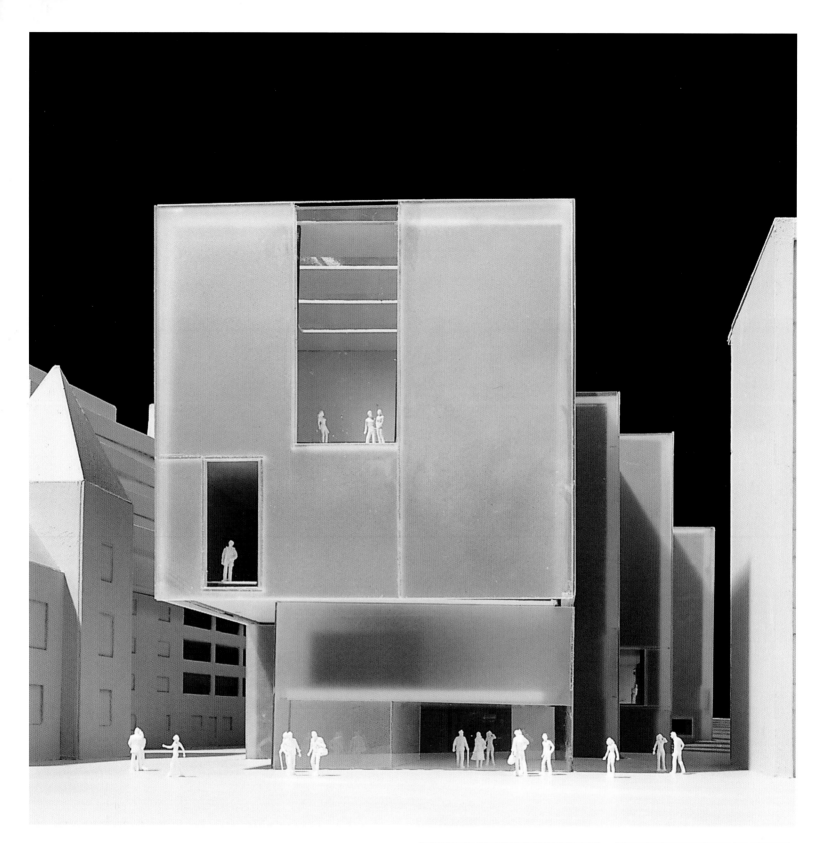

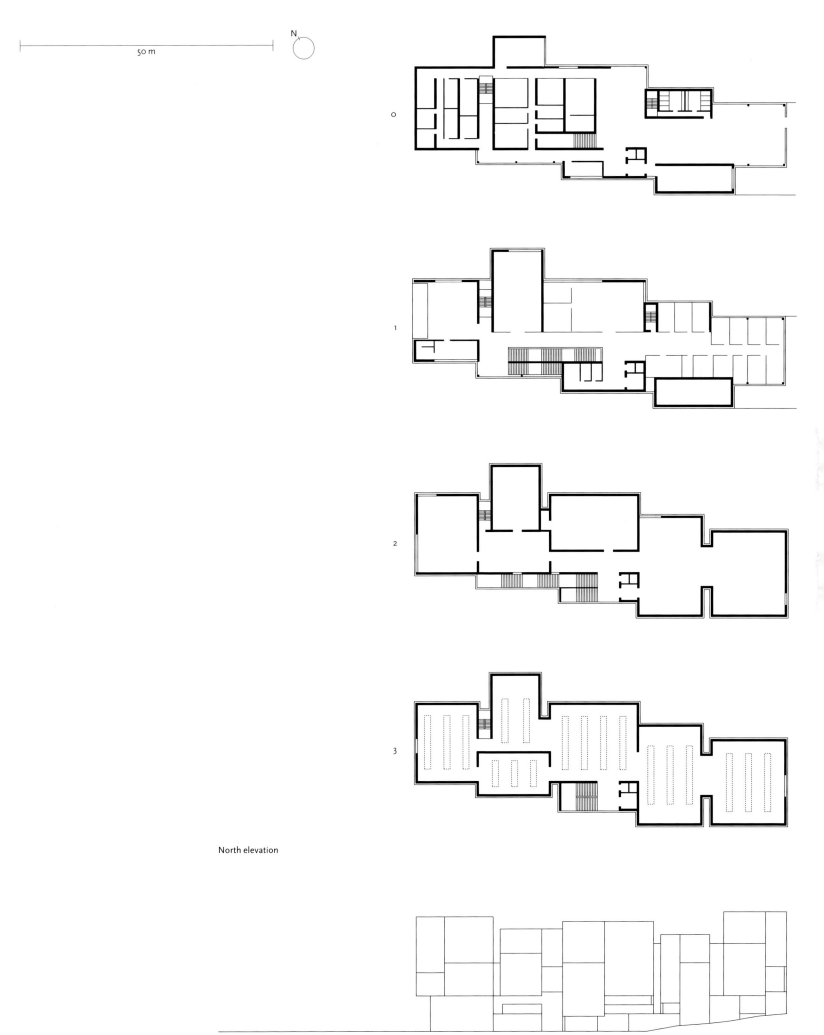

50 m

N

0

1

2

3

North elevation

Neues Museum, Berlin
1997–2009

In 1997 David Chipperfield Architects won an
international competition for the restoration
of Friedrich August Stüler's 1859 Neues
Museum in association with the restoration
consultant Julian Harrap. Located on the
Spree Island, in the heart of the former
East Berlin, the building had initially been
constructed to extend the space of the Altes
Museum, built immediately to the south by
Stüler's teacher Karl Friedrich Schinkel.
The original Neues design had formed part of
an overall architectural concept for the Spree
Island, prompted by Friedrich Wilhelm IV,
of a series of art and archeological museums
styled so as to promote a greater appreciation
of classical Antiquity. Among these museums,

and in terms of its construction and rich
interior decoration, the Neues Museum was
considered the most important monumental
Prussian building of its era.

Seen today alongside the four other
reconstructed museum buildings on the
island, Stüler's Neues Museum is the only
structure still ruined from the war – a contrast
that demonstrates ideas of history and decay
in a compelling and powerful way, although
throughout the building the degree of
destruction varies greatly. Certain interiors
have survived almost completely, with
elaborate finishes and ceiling frescos still
intact, while other building elements exist
only as the enclosures of a gaping void.

The power of the ruin stems not least from
this exposed brickwork shell, investing the
building, 150 years after it was first imagined,
with the indelible presence of a picturesque
classical ruin.

Given this evocative yet inaccessible
space, the restoration of the Neues Museum
followed a principle of conservation rather
than reconstruction – that is, the design gives
back only enough context so that the
significance of the whole structure and the
sequence of spaces contained within it are
legible. Accordingly, the missing northwest
wing and southeast bay are rebuilt, the
enfilade of rooms is restored, and the stair
and courtyard spaces are designed so as

to maintain elements of the building's own decay. In this way, the new Neues Museum and its collection of Egyptian antiquities should navigate carefully between de-historicised reconstruction and monumentalized preservation.

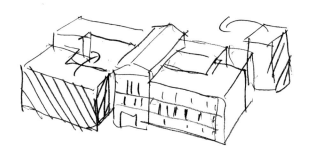

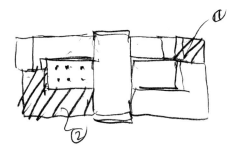

RE-ESTABLISHMENT OF FORM + FIGURE

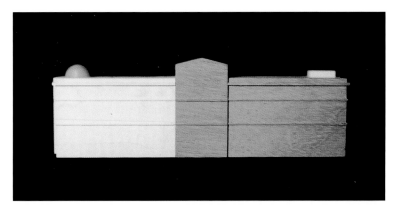

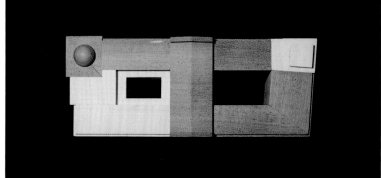

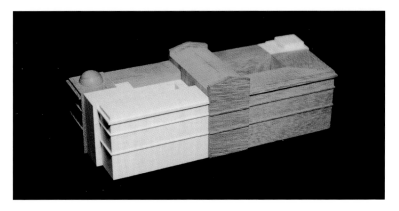

Above, concept model showing a re-established
Neues Museum form and figure.

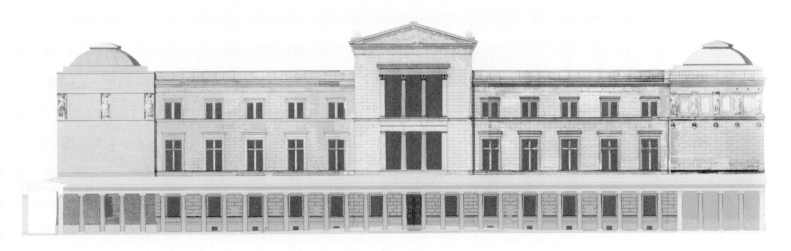

Top, west facade; bottom, east facade

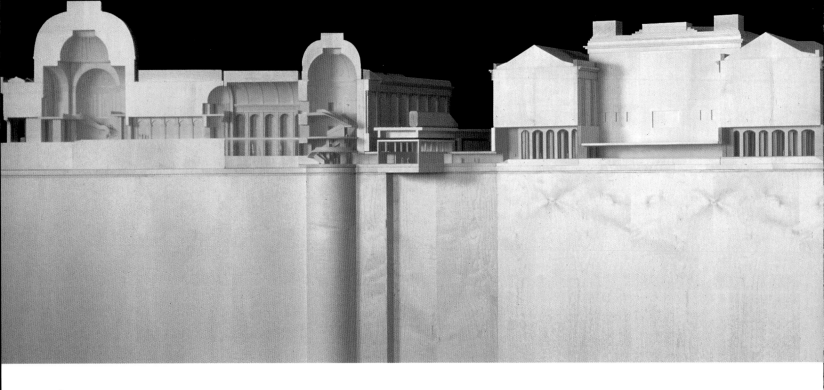

Above and left, sectional model and photomontage showing the 'Archeological Promenade' – a main component of the masterplan for the Museum Island. The masterplan was compiled by the Planungsgruppe Museuminsel of which David Chipperfield Architects is the coordinating planner. The other members are: Atelier Heinz Tesar (Bodemuseum), Hilmer & Sattler (Altes Museum), O.M. Ungers (Pergamonmuseum), and Levin Monsigny Landschaftsarchitekten (landscape architects).

Above, the current state of the museum's central stair hall.

Existing spaces within the Neues Museum,
from the top, in the Niobidensaal, the
Römischersaal, and the dome room ceiling.

Above and left, restoration studies, developed with Julian Harrap Architects, of the building's east facade and the west wall of the Bacchussaal look for a way of providing a setting for the conserved fragments of the museum without negating their state of preservation. The strengthening of these architectural frames repairs the damaged appearance of these surfaces while increasing the legibility of the historic fabric. These separate studies, although revealing a progressive restoration, are not to be read sequentially, but rather they offer a spectrum of repair and change from which the restored surfaces of the Neues Museum will be tailored.

Left, photographs showing the original stair hall.

Above and right, model studies of the
Egyptian courtyard.

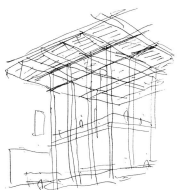

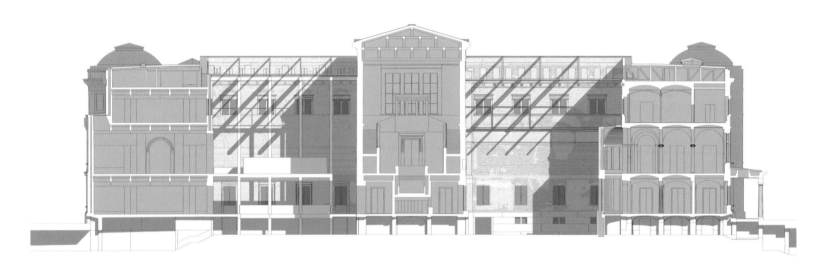

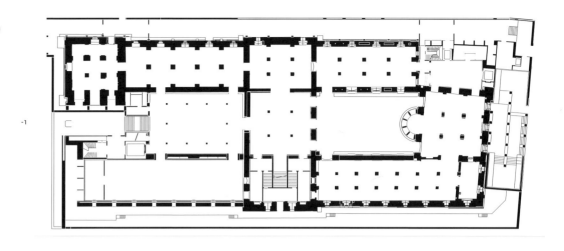

50 m

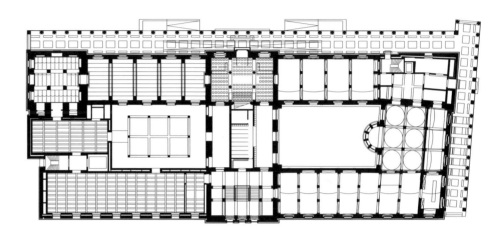

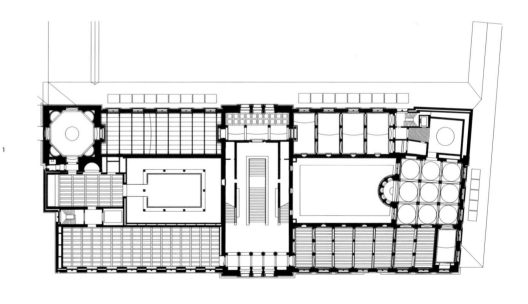

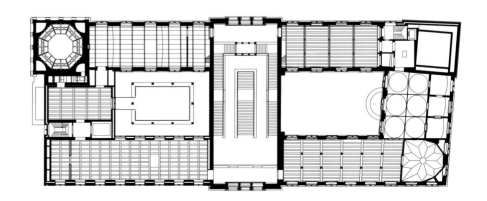

New Entrance Building, Berlin
1999–2009

The New Entrance Building adds a new building block to the architectural formation of Berlin's Museum Island, initiated in 1825 by Karl Friedrich Schinkel's Altes Museum. Playing a key role in the overall reconstruction of the site, the building will form the principal entrance point to the island, and to the 'Archeological Promenade' – a sequence of new and existing spaces connecting four of the five museums together. It is the first new building on the island since the completion of the Pergamon Museum over seventy years ago, and extends its collection of structures to a sixth building.

The link to the Pergamon Museum forms the core of the building's design – a central

focus given visual representation by a stair hall linking its ground floor to a basement level. On the floors above, the building contains all of the public services that have come to be expected of modern museum spaces, so as to relieve the necessity of squeezing these services into the historic museums themselves. Below these levels, visitors can directly access the main tour of the Pergamon Museum, together with the Bode, Neues, and Altes museums via the promenade, allowing the different collections of the island to be experienced as a spatial continuum.

Schinkel's Packhof building, which originally stood on the site, offered an important starting point for the scale of

the New Entrance Building. Like Schinkel's building, the design will be constructed as a free-standing structure and orientated towards the southwest to provide easy access from Unter den Linden. Composed of abstract, sculptural volumes, covered uniformly in a skin of translucent glass, the surface of the building will be satinated so as to reduce the reflective severity of conventional glass facades and appear instead as an independent body, absorbing rather than reflecting the different colors of its surroundings. The overall effect then will be one of a monolithic, somewhat ethereal block, boldly yet unassumingly providing a gateway to a unique and tightly packed constellation of museums.

Left, Karl Friedrich Schinkel's Packhof building, immediately in front of the Neues Museum, originally stood on the site of the New Entrance Building before being demolished due to subsidence in 1938.

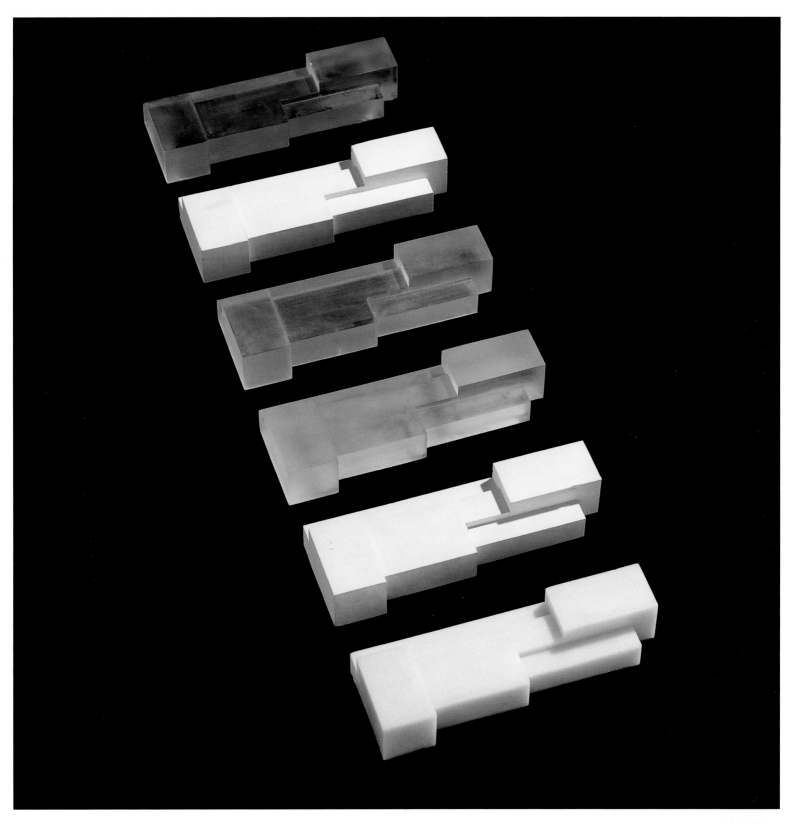

Above, study models developing the formal and material articulation of the building.

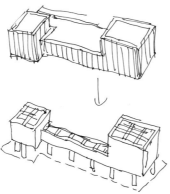

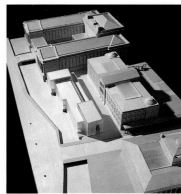

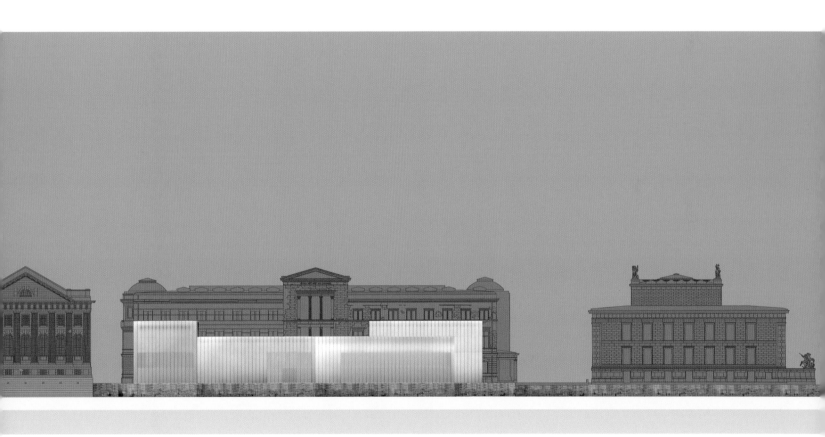

Southwest elevation of the New Entrance
Building showing relationship of Bode
Museum, Pergamon Museum, Neues
Museum and Altes Museum.

Photomontage showing main staircase to
the Archeological Promenade.

Above, model studies showing the
New Entrance Building's lower hall areas,
and left, exhibition spaces.

Section through the New Entrance Building
and the Pergamon Museum to the west.

50 m   N

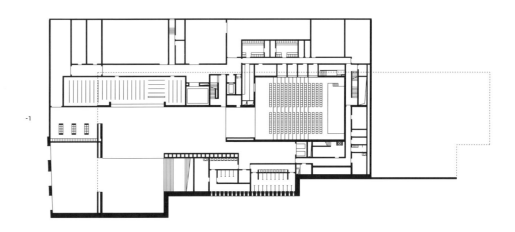

-1

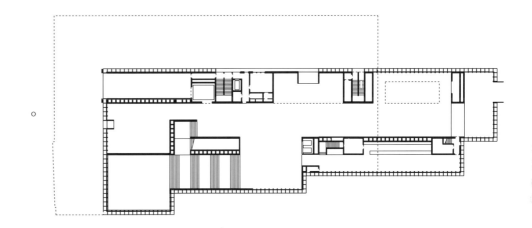

0

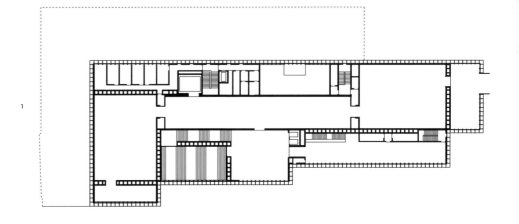

1

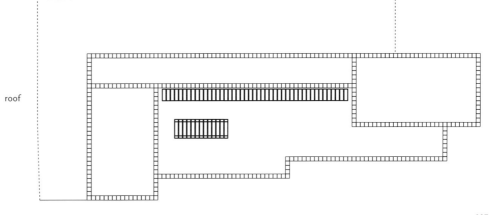

roof

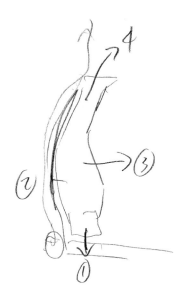

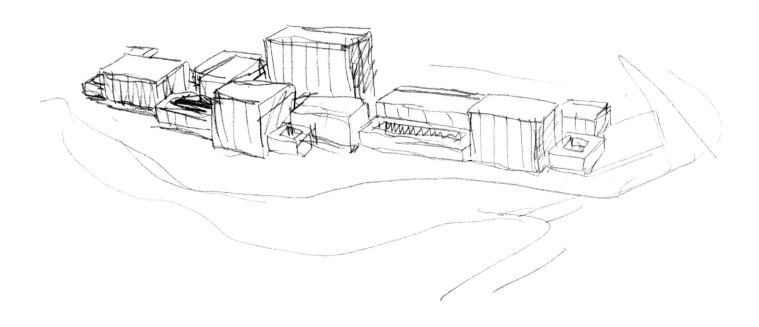

Palace of Justice, Salerno
1999–2004

The location for this design for a Palace of Justice in Salerno, southern Italy, is a former railway goods yard, peripheral to the city center, in an area highlighted for renewal and regeneration as part of Spanish architect Oriol Bohigas' masterplan for the city. Won in competition, its solution to integrate the massive program of the law courts into the existing urban fabric was to conceptually structure the site as a series of responses to its immediate context – principally the new boulevard that extends along the site's eastern side, the railway siding to the west, and the tail of the site looking south towards the sea.

Within this site, and central to the development of the new law courts, was the idea of creating a judicial building which was not intimidating but expressive of ideas of justice rather than authority. The building's design concept, in this way, developed as a reaction to the existing typology of a law court, traditionally understood as an imposing, portico-fronted singular structure. In contrast to this conventional image, the proposal fragments the large institutional model by dividing the volume of the law courts into a composition of smaller buildings. Each of these smaller, individualized structures is articulated as a simple block, finished in pre-cast concrete panels with terracotta aggregate, and punctured by a series of openings designed to emphasize their vertical aspect in contrast to the horizontality of the services plinth out of which they emerge.

To reinforce this idea of an open and accessible structure (in both a physical and social sense) the design is presented as a public space that exploits Salerno's ambient climate by connecting each of its various blocks via a series of gardens and colonnades. This revealing of the internal spaces of the courts and clustering of individual buildings not only offers an original architectural take on the judicial court, but also maintains a sense of organic growth, vital for the Palace of Justice and for the redeveloped city of Salerno as a whole.

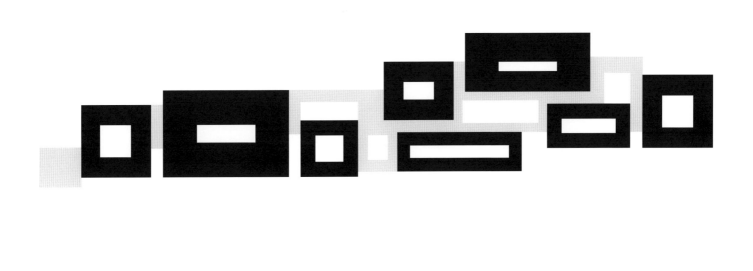

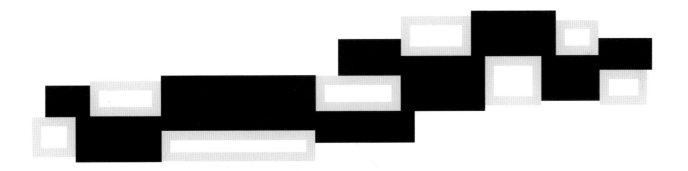

Above, diagrams showing the formal evolution
of the design.

From top, competition, *preliminare*, *definitivo*.

Above and right, photos of models from
competition stage.

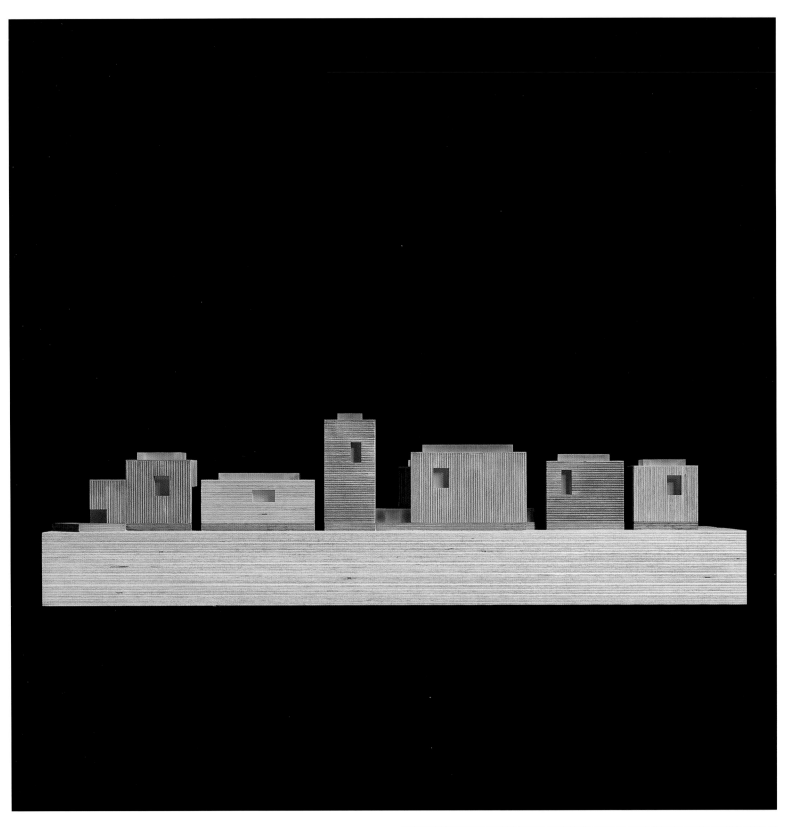

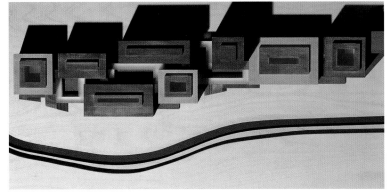

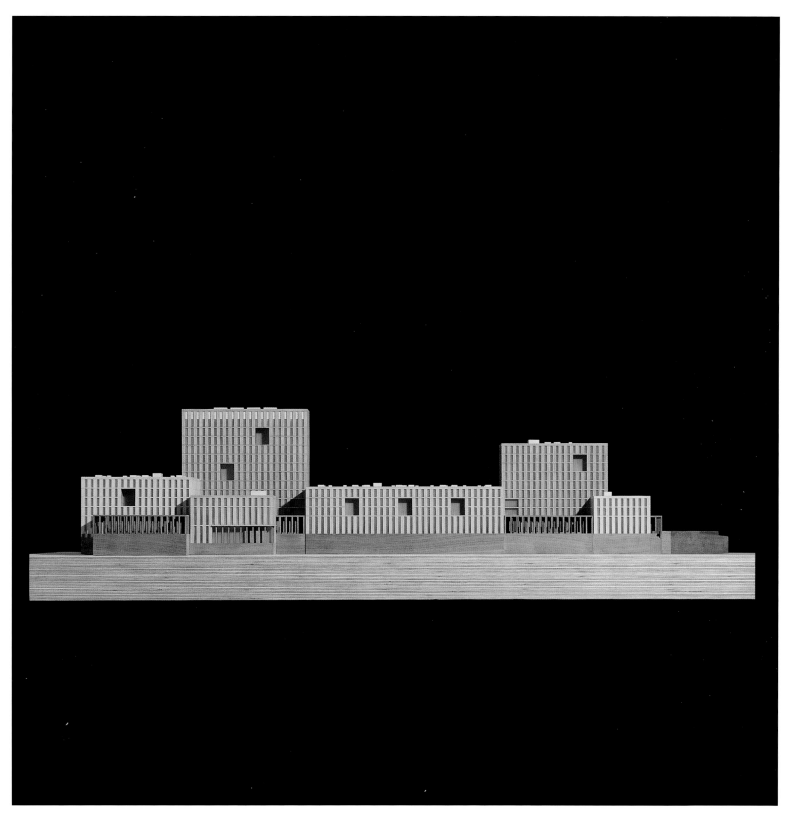

Above and following pages, model of
final project.

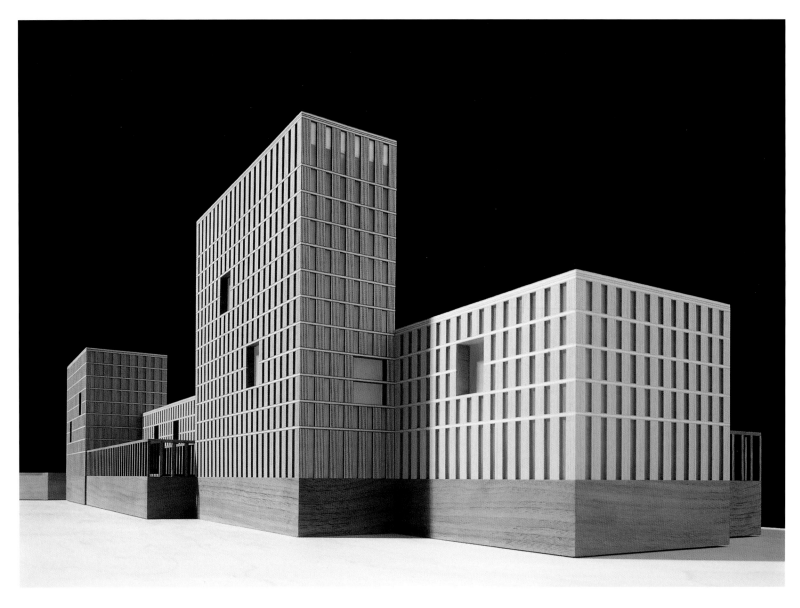

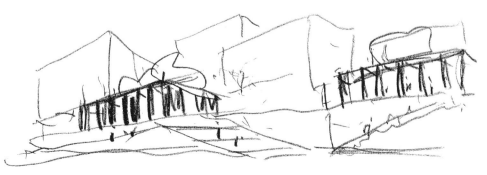

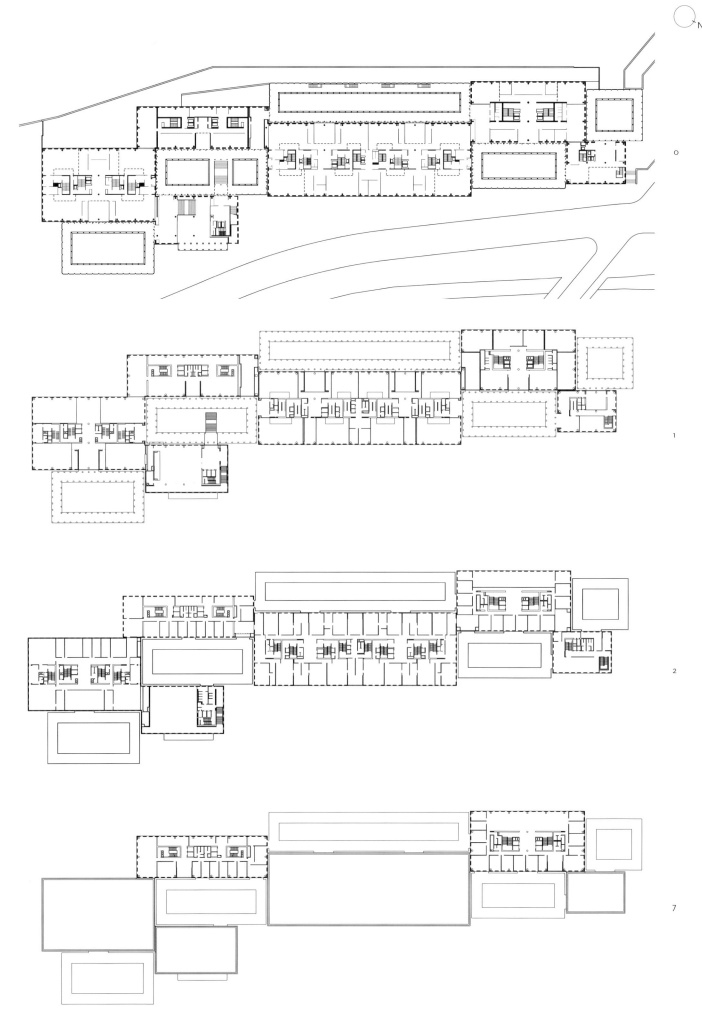

N

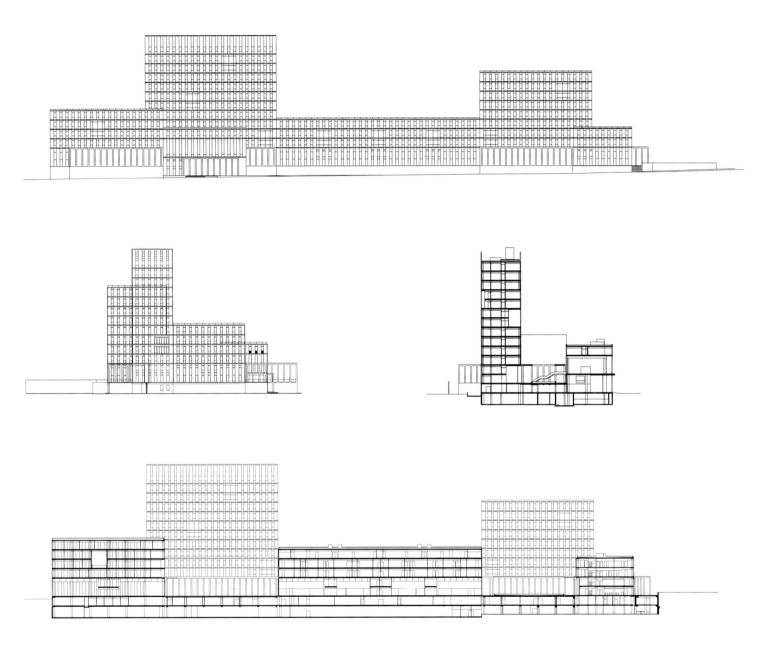

Top, east elevation
Middle, south elevation, section
Bottom, east section

Pasquale Bruni showroom, Milan
2000–2001

Jewelry designer Pasquale Bruni first commissioned this design for a showroom displaying his jewelry collection in 2000. The interior space, formerly occupied by a fashion house, is tucked away virtually out of sight in an old courtyard in the centre of Milan. Rejecting conventional approaches to jewelry display, in which the decor of the architecture is embellished as much as the pieces it is displaying, the showroom instead is presented as a clear and unornamented space.

Central to the way in which this space was imagined was the idea that no part of the architectural intervention should puncture or touch the existing building elements –

the marbled columns, ceiling and wall moldings. In this way, the screens and displays act as a conduit between the small scale of the rings and necklaces and the large scale of the space, so that the Bruni jewelry floats within the translucent display cases, which themselves appear suspended within the existing space of the courtyard.

The new elements within the showroom are made up of a series of red, green, and yellow jewelry screens and cabinets (developed in association with museum display specialists Goppion). These cases have been manufactured using a colored etching process and integrated lighting and can be arranged in any configuration above the

seamless black resin floor. Blurring slightly
the hardness of the glazed cabinet and screen
edges, a gossamer-fine silk fabric is
sandwiched in between their glass surfaces,
visually providing a colored and see-through
divide between sales areas within the
showroom and those for jewelry display.
By coding each of these cases and screens
through their materiality and colour, the
design establishes some sense of identity not
only for this specific Milanese space but for
the Pasquale Bruni brand in subsequent shops
and showrooms all over the world, so that the
tricolor red, green and yellow becomes a
stable backdrop to the fast moving fashions
of jewelry design.

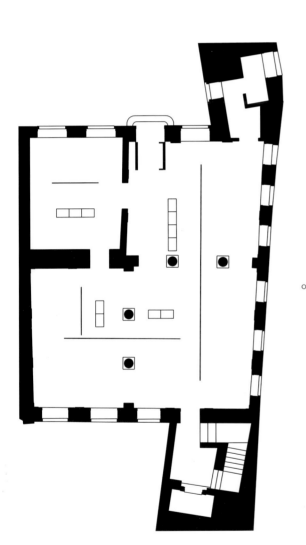

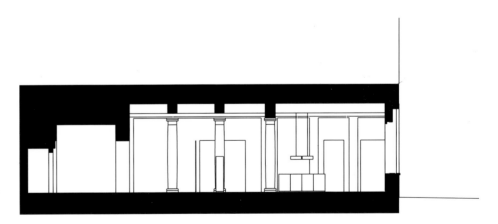

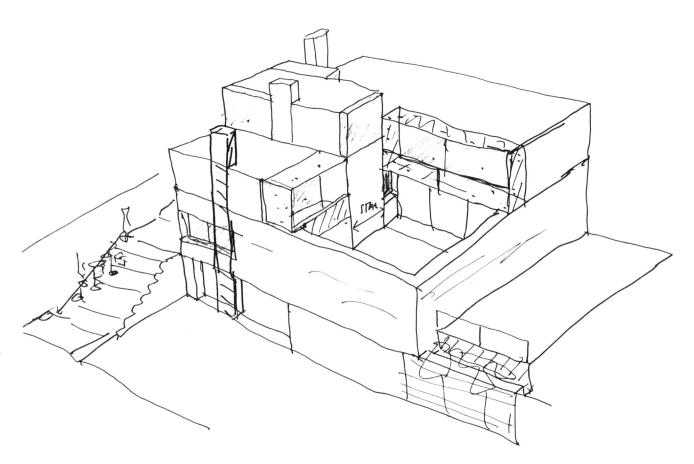

Private house, Berlin
1994–1996

This house, organized around a south-facing courtyard overlooking a large rear garden, is situated in a leafy suburb in the southwest of Berlin. Although designed so as to reveal a distinct sequence of rooms and to forge a clear relationship between inside and outside space, it was the building's material that became the foremost determining element in its architecture. The house, entirely enveloped by brick, is lent by its skin a physical solidity reminiscent of the early Modernist houses of Erich Mendelsohn and Mies van der Rohe (particularly Mies' three brick house projects of the late 1920s – Wolf, Esters, and Lange). The irregularity of this textured, hand made brick finish also effects a powerful contrast

with the smoothness and regularity of the steel-framed glazing, so that the house really expresses differences in its own materiality.

Constructed around its courtyard, the plan of the house builds up a series of simple, internal spaces, with each room carefully considered in its sequence and composition. This spatial structure establishes a series of volumes that present both abstract and physical qualities, so that the spaces themselves dictate the hierarchies within the building rather than one imposed upon them by the functional dictates of each room. The result is that spaces within the house enjoy the manipulation of various ceiling heights – a vertical compression and

expansion that reveals itself in the articulation of the building's exterior surfaces, where once again the game between physical restraint and abstract freedom is played out.

Defined by its brick surfaces, the house appears from the street as an assemblage of opaque layers, ambiguously expressing the brickwork both as a massive physical presence and at the same time manipulating it to respond to abstract and formal compositions. The resultant building, constructed from a rigorously limited palate of materials, presents itself as a completely interlocked composition of material and form, internal and external space, vertical and horizontal dimension, abstract space and domestic program.

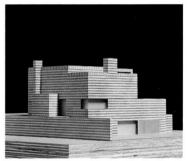

Left, view of basement pool with artwork
by Ed Ruscha.

Above, view of living room
Right, entrance hall

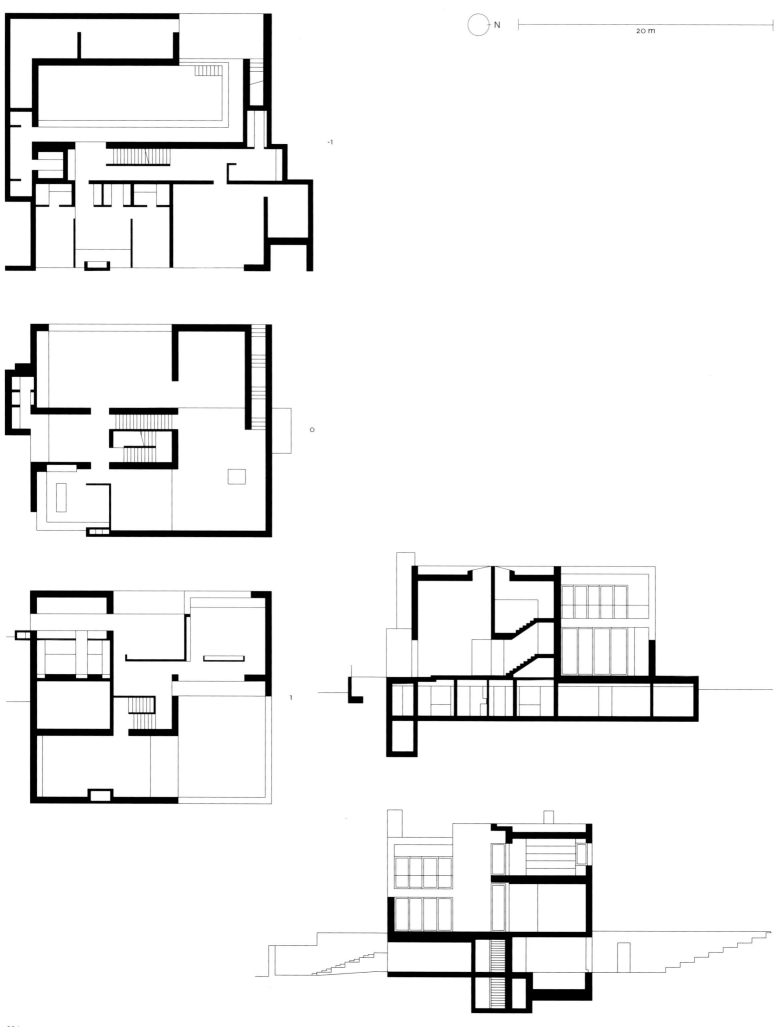

N   20 m

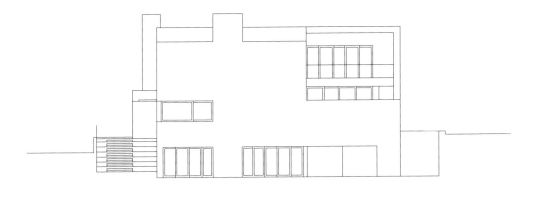

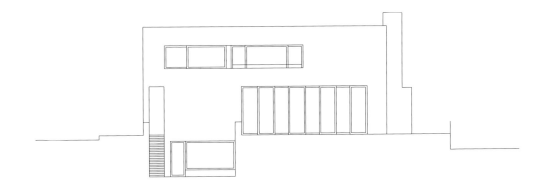

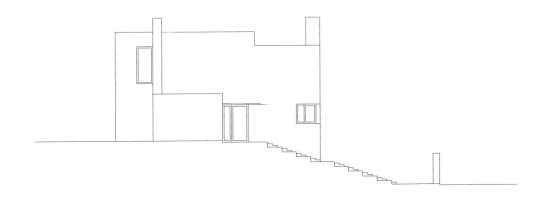

From top, street elevation and garden elevation

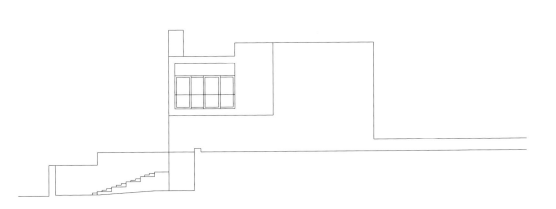

**River and Rowing Museum,
Henley-on-Thames
1989–1997**

David Chipperfield's very earliest sketches
for the museum at Henley-on-Thames were
inspired by local river boathouses and the
traditional wooden barns of Oxfordshire –
a simple and clear architectural idea that
could easily be understood in context with
its immediate neighbors. Looking at the
completed building today, it is a carefully
crafted manifestation of these first sketches,
with long, parallel, oak-clad forms and steeply
pitched lead-coated roofs. It is clearly a modern
building, but one that resonates at the same
time with a vernacular architectural past.

The practice was first appointed architects
to the project in 1989. After almost seven years
of delays, the museum was finally opened by

HM the Queen in 1998. Sitting in water
meadows on the south bank of the Thames,
close to Henley's town centre, the museum
houses a significant collection of rowing
boats, cataloguing the history of the sport, the
River Thames, and the town of Henley.

Considered in two parts, the museum is
made up of a transparent and open entry floor
space (containing public areas and elevated
off the ground because of the periodic
flooding of the river) and a sequence of first
floor galleries, enclosed and lit from skylights
above. Each gabled boat hall has direct
external access doors at ground floor level
so as to allow the hulls of the eights and
single-scull boats to be brought in and

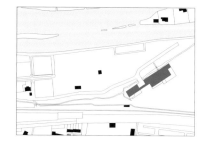

displayed. The whole of these upper spaces is clad with untreated green oak timber – a wood that hardens and effectively weathers with age – so as to further align the building with a local vernacular. In this way, by carefully negotiating the conservative aesthetic sensibilities of rural England, the River and Rowing Museum merges figure and abstraction, appearing behind its screen of poplars to reveal both convention and invention.

Study models exploring the timber cladding
that envelops much of the building's exterior.

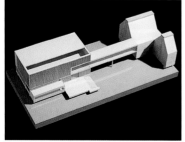

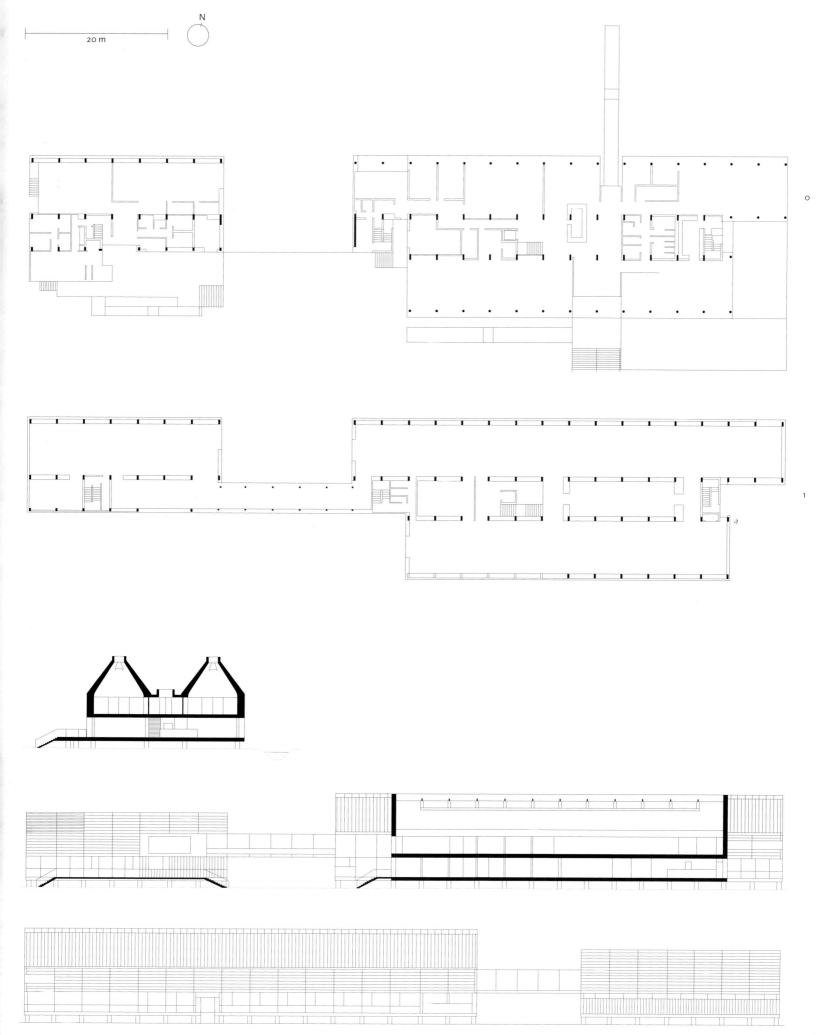

N

20 m

0

1

Royal Collections Museum, Madrid
1999

Built on top of a steep ravine overlooking the Campo del Moro gardens, the Royal Palace of Madrid was completed in 1764 as the official residence of Bourbon King Philip V. Constructed almost entirely of granite and white limestone, and designed in an Italianate neoclassical style, it was seen as Spain's own version of the Palace of Versailles. Today the building no longer serves as a royal residence but as the focus for public galleries and tours. Given the palace's ever increasing popularity, however, and the difficulty it was having in displaying all of its royal collection of works, an architectural competition was organized requiring designs for a new museum located within the interstitial space between the palace and the Almundena Cathedral on the south side of the plaza.

Looking both to interact with this rich architectural context and its extraordinary landscape, this proposal was organized as a museum of descent – playing with ideas of ground by creating a series of ramped spaces that define both a museological trail and the topographical condition of the site. Visitors would enter the museum from the cathedral plaza (simultaneously both floor and roof to the project), into a glazed pavilion space looking out towards the valley below. Two main staircases then intertwine with the external ramp system, providing access to all of the subterranean gallery spaces, together

with a route into the Royal Palace itself.

The pieces on display include tapestries, paintings, decorative arts, musical instruments, and a collection of royal carriages, relocated from a separate museum in the palace's former stables. Each of these works have been arranged in vertical succession throughout the building, and are lit by light filtering down from the glazed plaza floor and by more controlled electrical lighting. During the day, therefore, the museum would only register through its light, elemental frame, while at night it would appear more pronounced as an illuminated block radiating a glow onto the palace, cathedral, and gardens below.

Opposite page, Alonso Sánchez, *Monasterio de las Descalzas Reales*, Madrid; Antonio Joli, *View of Madrid from the far bank of the Manzanares*, 1754, from the collection of the Royal Palace.

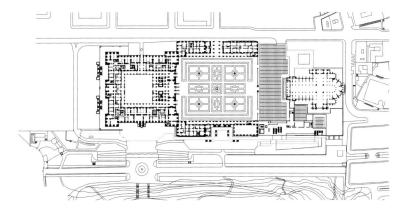

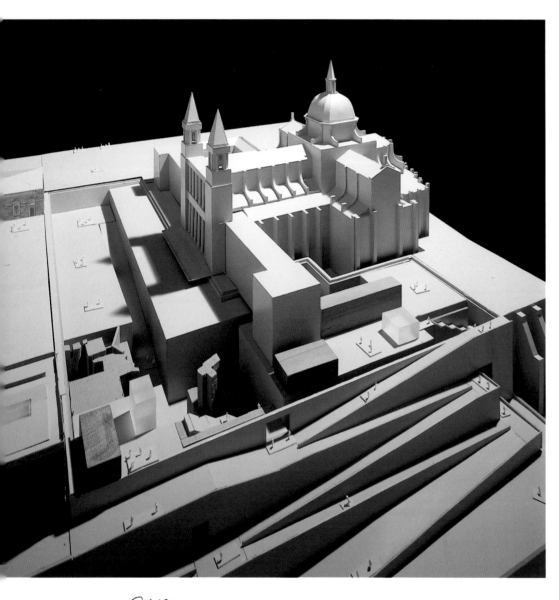

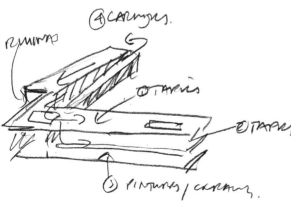

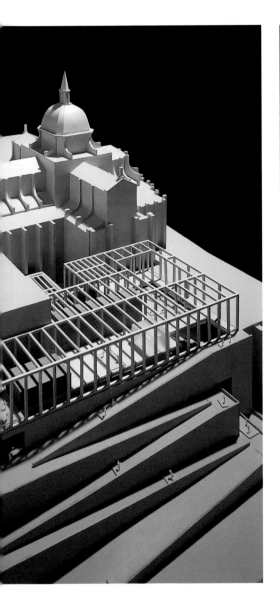
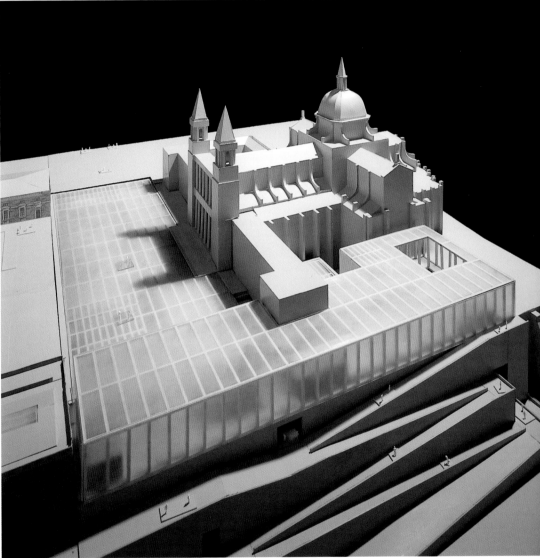

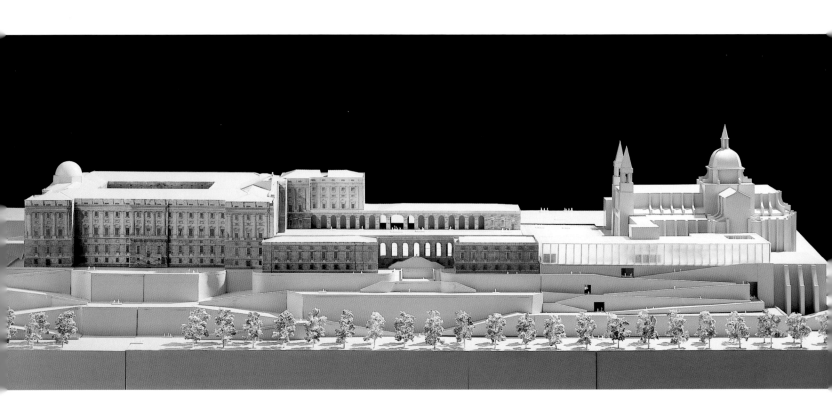

cafeteria

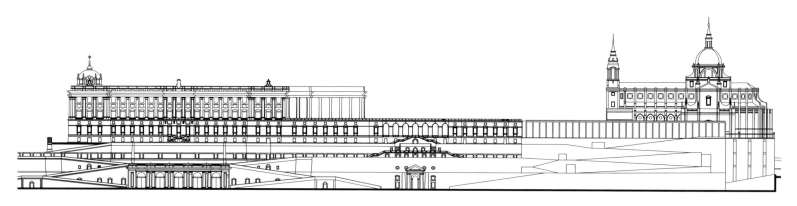

Above, west elevation

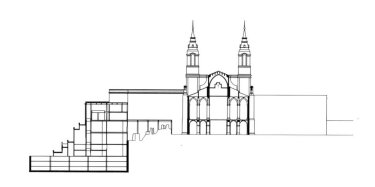

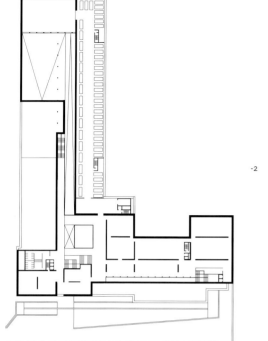

-2

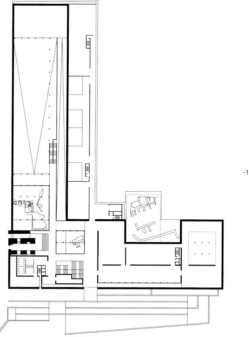

-1

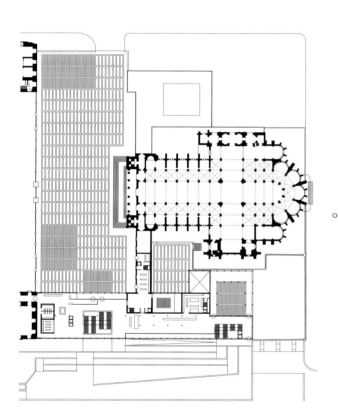

0

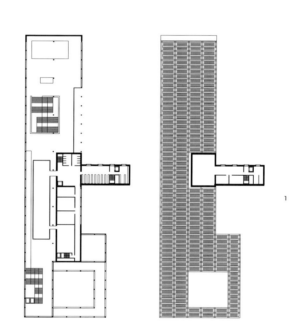

1

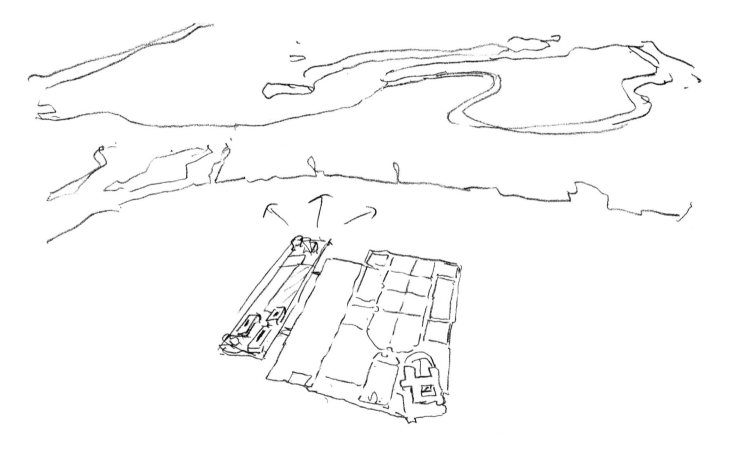

San Michele Cemetery, Venice
1998–2013

Following an international competition, this proposal for the redesign of Venice's principal cemetery was selected to develop and extend the island of San Michele. This historic site, located in the Venetian lagoon and enclosing a fifteenth-century church and convent, has been in continuous development for over four hundred years but has recently evolved to a point where the romantic image of its outer face is in stark contrast to the somewhat dour municipal character of its interior. Looking to address this apparent imbalance, the proposal sought to redefine some of the cemetery's former tectonic and physical qualities.

The project itself comprises two phases: in the first, the burial grounds of the current cemetery are complemented through the construction of a series of new courtyards, an ossuary, a cinerarium, a crematorium, and a chapel. In contrast to the existing rows of tombs, the proposed scheme offers a new arrangement of buildings, walls, tombs, and landscape. Rather than distributing the new elements in a uniform manner (which through their regularity creates something of a rigid, repeating pattern of walls and tombs) an organizational structure has been developed which groups the buildings together to form a greater sense of settlement and enclosure. Informed by the principles of *scorci* (views), *giardini* (gardens), and *corti* (courtyards), this spatial organization hopes to create a

more varying and yet clearly defined San Michele landscape.

The second phase of the project involves the construction of a new island, running parallel to the existing cemetery but separated by a 15-m-wide channel. This new island, composed of platforms on different levels will feature four tomb buildings (designed as simple, sculpted blocks) together with a series of gardens at water level. Unlike the remainder of San Michele, built higher above the water line and with its perimeter wall, this new island looks to create an open, accessible structure so as to provide a greater sense of place not only for the cemetery but for the lagoon and Venice as a whole.

Top right, Arnold Böcklin, *Die Toteninsel*, 1883
Left, competition sketch showing courtyard
concept

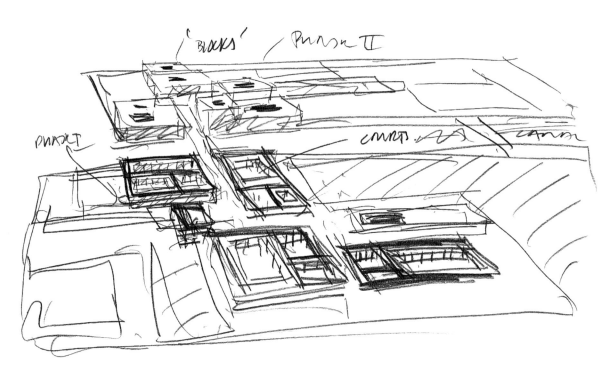

Sketches showing development of
courtyard concept

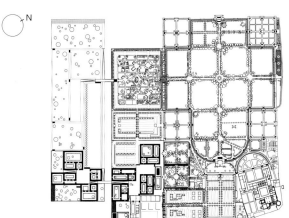

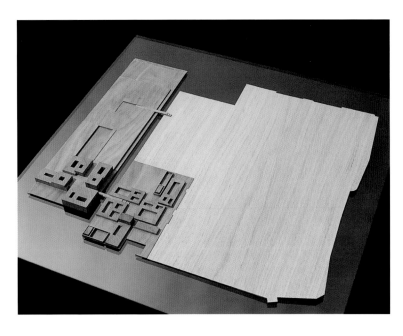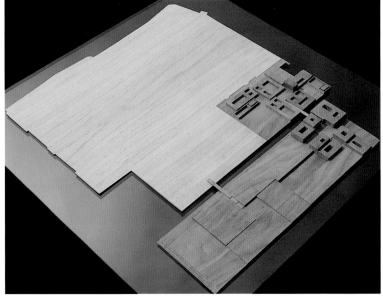

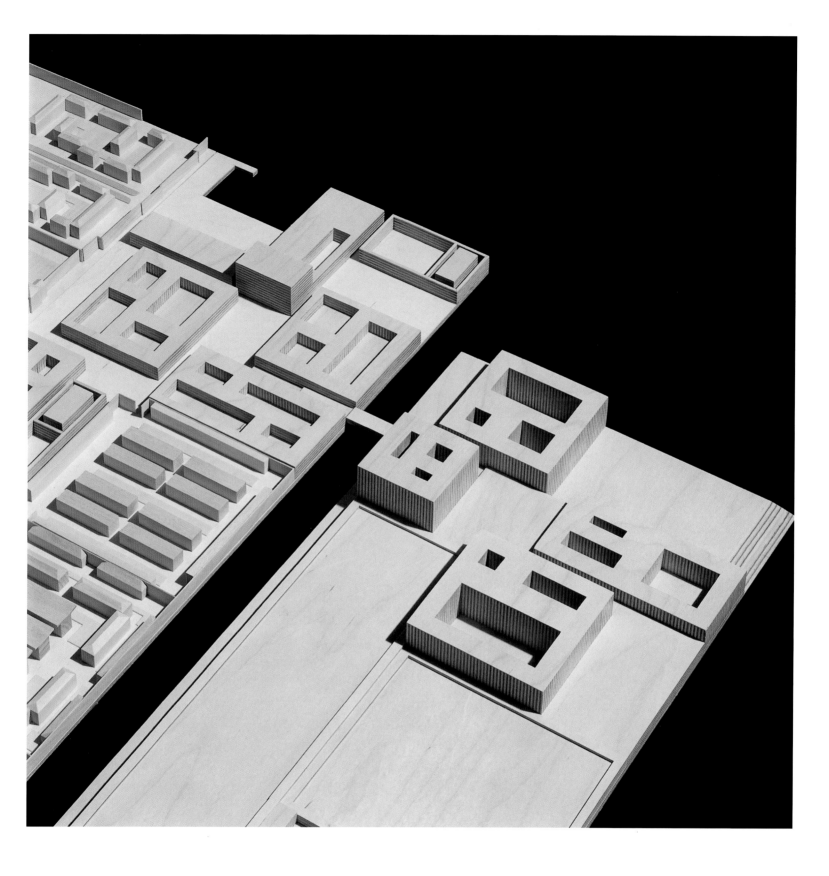

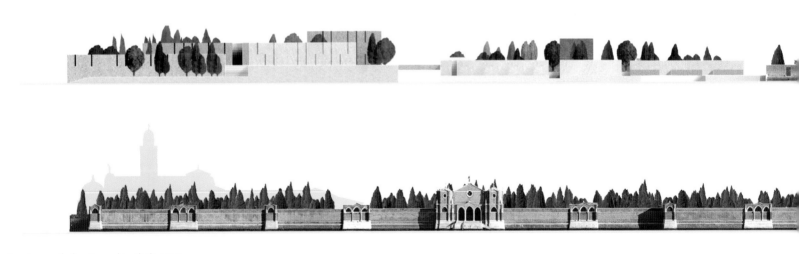

From top, north elevation and south elevation
showing the new island

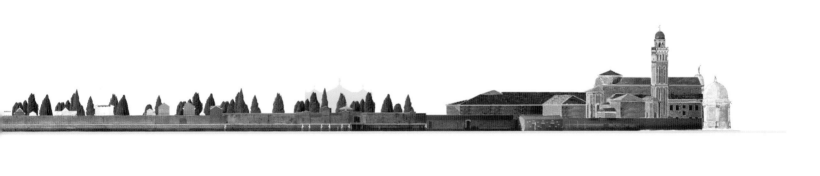

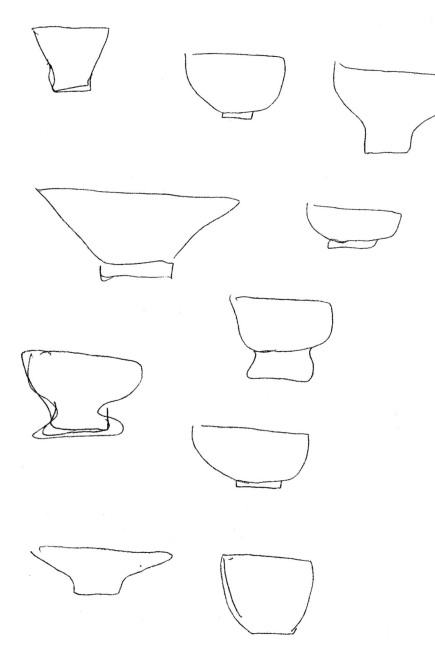

**Slegten & Toegemann ceramics
1996**

In 1996 Bernard Slegten and Oliver Toegemann asked a number of artists and architects to design a series of everyday, largely domestic, objects that they would produce. Each of these designs were to be manufactured in limited numbers, to a high standard, and to somehow straddle the associations between domestic, functional pieces and art objects. Among the designers approached, John Pawson produced drawings for a jam jar, Claire Bataille looked at silverware and crystal glasses, and Anish Kapoor designed a vase. As an invited member of this group, David Chipperfield Architects chose to produce designs for a simple plate, bowl and cup.

Chipperfield himself has long held a fascination for vernacular ceramics, in particular for eating bowls, collected in the main from trips to Korea, Japan, and China. These cheap, simple and somehow familiar objects helped form an approach infused with ideas of the ordinary and the normative – why should one attempt to reinvent something as timeless as a plate or a cup when it seems more valuable and interesting to do the existing well. In this sense, the responses to this small commission for product design mirrored the practice's approach to much larger architectural projects, playing with simple ideas of the existing, of the vernacular, and materiality,

rather than the dismantling of an established type.

The actual pieces produced – a large dinner plate, bowl, and cup – were all made with a fair-glazed ceramic finish and manufactured in the Netherlands by Cor Unum. Acting as some kind of touchstone to their design, the still-life paintings of Giorgio Morandi inspired each of the pieces' muted colours – white inner faces set against dove grays, creams, and pale terracottas. Like Morandi's images, these kitchenware objects advertise their own uniqueness (of plate-ness, bowl-ness, cup-ness), confirming in the process a design methodology far removed from the architectures of reinvention or imitation.

Giorgio Morandi, *Still Life*, 1955

**Social housing, Madrid
1999–2004**

Commissioned by the Empresa Municipal de la Vivienda, the location for this design for a social housing scheme is plot 203 of a new development in Verona, in the Villaverde district of southern Madrid. Comprised of 176 one, two and three-bedroom apartments, the scheme responds to an overall masterplan for the site which requested a single U-shaped block, 15 m deep, and with a footprint of just over 2,000 m². Like other buildings within the same development, it also required that the block be eight storeys high and have the appearance of a pitched roof.

Within the confines of this brief, the design attempted to manipulate these architectural restrictions so as to abstract the normative idea of an apartment block. So whereas other neighboring buildings adopt a symmetrical, double-pitched silhouette, here the traditional relationships of wall and roof are abstracted into a low, single pitch for the bulk of the block, and a small secondary pitch bevelling the building's front edge. The increase in floor area achieved by this reduction in roof volume also allowed for a more sculptural approach to the building envelope – carving back the sides of the block, away from the orthogonal, to create a more varied outline to the building's elevation. Further distinguished by its choice of materials – earthy-pink concrete facade panels, slate-blue concrete for the courtyard portico, and a dense band of landscaping in between, the effect is a rich tricolour of colors radiating outwards.

Like the building's overall form, the surface of the block also evolved from a predetermined set of limitations. These emerged from the desire to create both a hierarchical facade (with larger rooms expressing themselves on the outside with more windows openings) and one in which this fenestration does not repeat itself over the building's eight floors (so that each window placement appears unique). As much, then, as a three dimensional study into mass and form, the design of plot 203 represents a two-dimensional, almost mathematical, exercise in patterning.

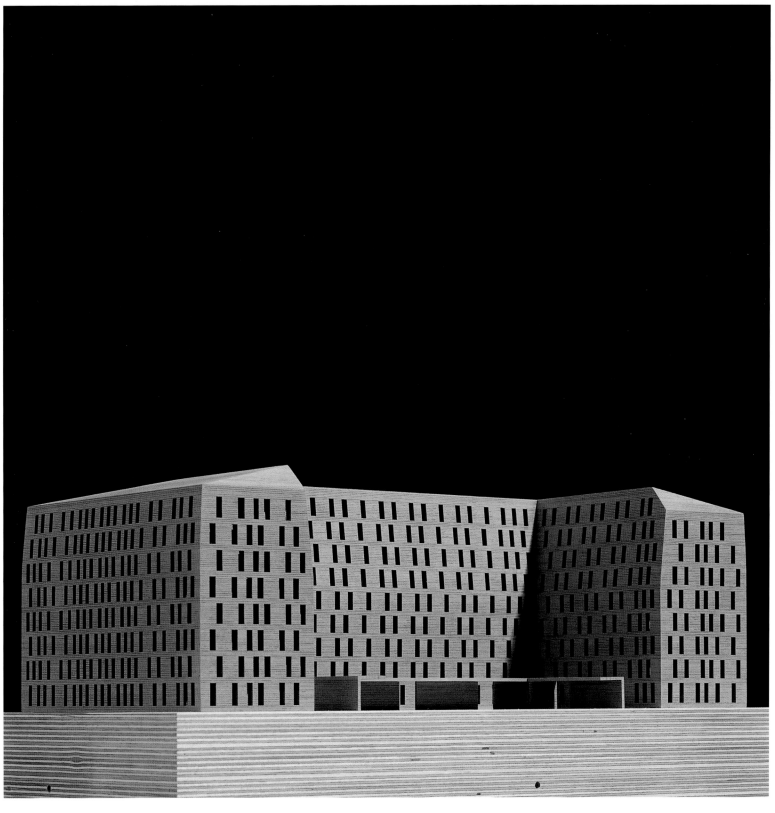

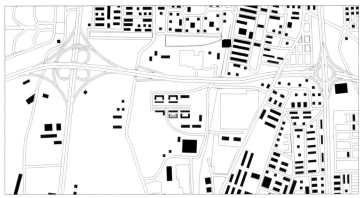

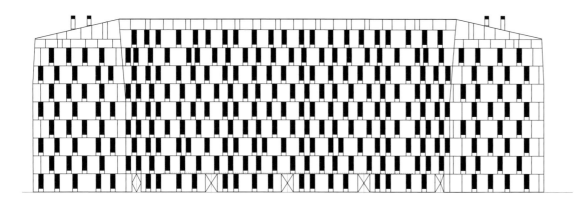

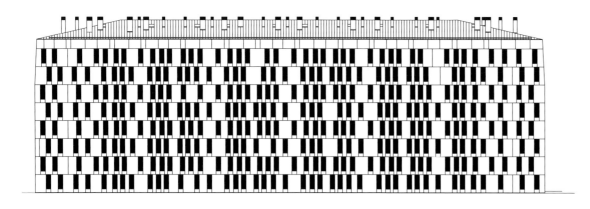

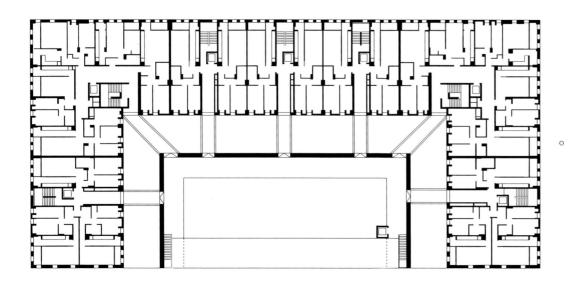

From top, north elevation and south elevation

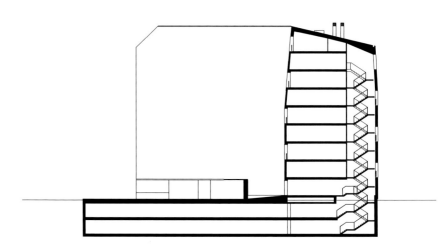

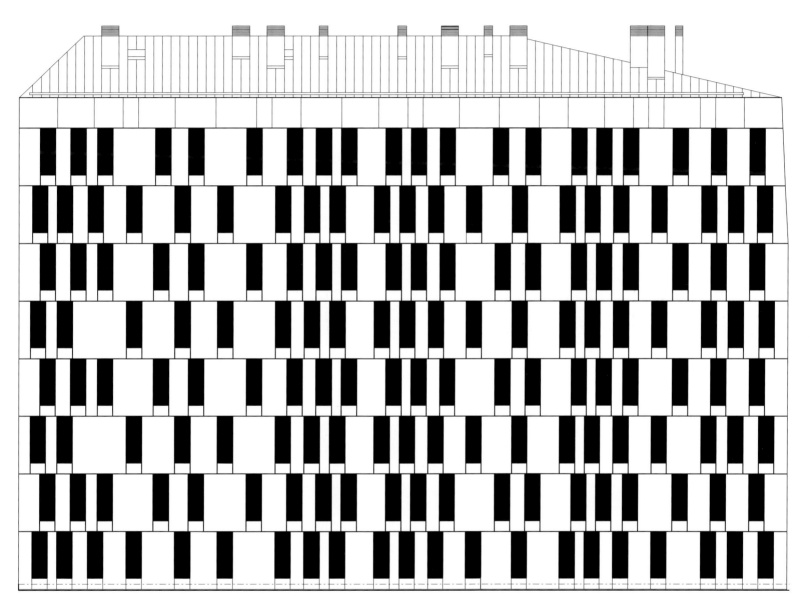

Above, west elevation

Spreedreieck, Berlin
2001

In 2001 the Berlin newspaper *Der Tagesspiegel* invited five architectural practices (David Chipperfield Architects; Bothe, Richter, Teherani; Eisenman Architects; Gerkan, Marg and Partner; and Nalbach + Nalbach) to submit study proposals for a skyscraper project, situated along the city's Friedrichstrasse on the southwest corner of the River Spree. Unlike other, more infamous, newspaper-sponsored architectural competitions – notably the *Chicago Tribune* Tower competition of 1922 – no building was ever intended to be realized; rather the study simply acted as a gentle provocation for Berlin's planning authorities and the newspaper's readership.

Rather than the *Chicago Tribune* competition, however, the historical associations of this architectural brief resonate more strongly with an earlier Berlin project. On this same site in 1921 Ludwig Mies van der Rohe produced his famous scheme for a glass skyscraper. Like his later glass tower proposals, his wax crayon perspective envisaged an almost featureless high-rise structure, faced entirely in glass, rising above its Friedrichstrasse neighbours. In its abandonment of conventional architectural forms, and focus upon ideas of transparency rather than solidity; eighty years later the project still remains radical.

Given this architectural heritage, Mies' glass skyscraper unavoidably became the

starting point for the David Chipperfield Architects' submission, with the design presented as a continuation of his tradition of crystalline towers. As with the Mies project, the building, clad completely in glass, rejects the classical architectural standard of base, shaft, and capital in favour of a singular, sculptural tower. Enveloping this continuous form, the building's facade offers a shifting, geometric modulation of vertical and triangular surfaces, tailored in part to maximize the views over the Reichstag government buildings and the Tiergarten. The glass skin of the skyscraper, and its 47 floors, are supported structurally by a central core, freeing up the surface of the building

to express a striking silhouette, and to respectfully but not imitatively maintain Mies' innovative architectural legacy for Friedrichstrasse.

Opposite, Ludwig Mies van der Rohe, Friedrichstrasse Office Building project, 1921.

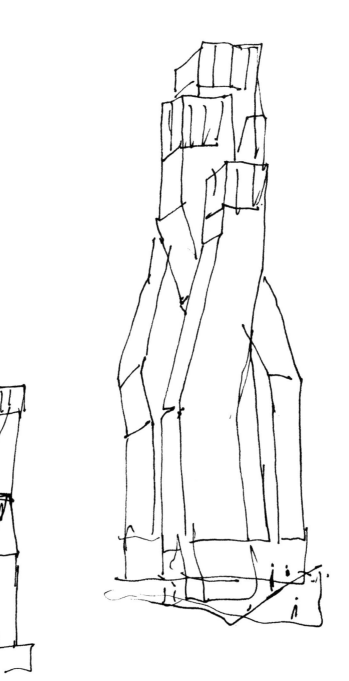
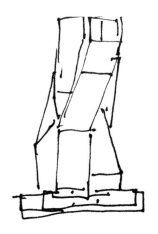

Early concept sketches of the
Spreedreieck tower exploring different
formal configurations

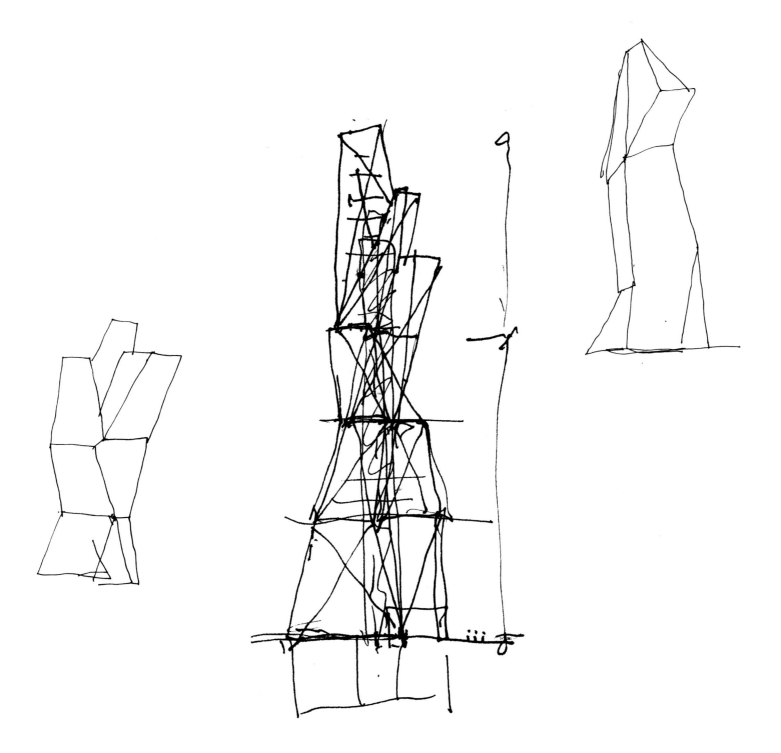

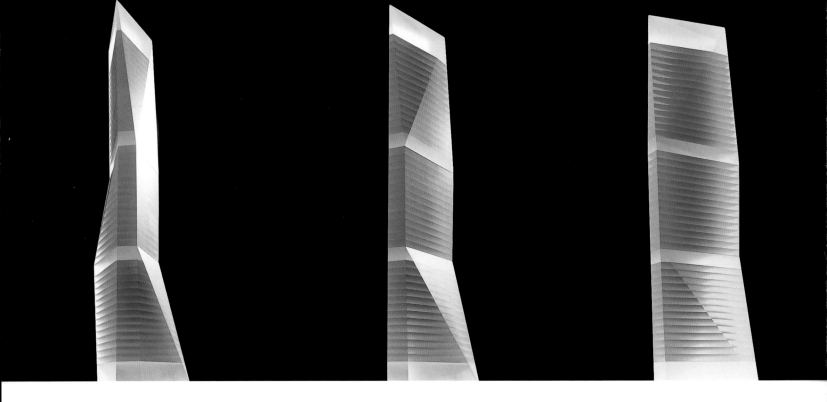

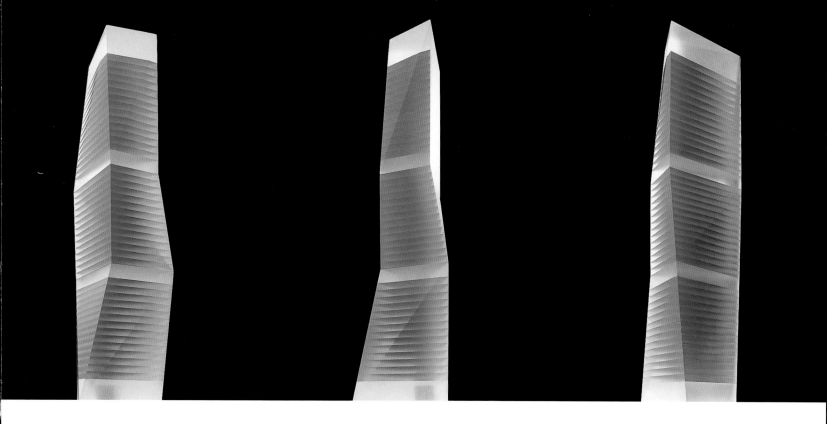

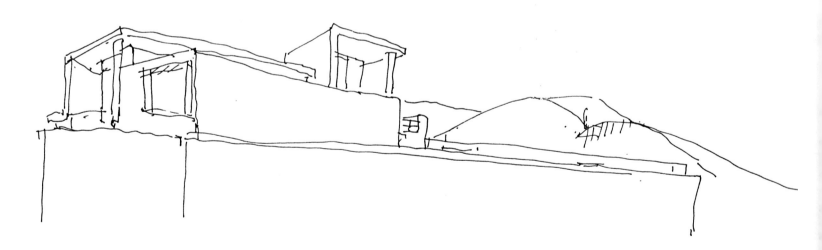

Toyota Auto, Kyoto
1989–1990

Occupying a deep site in Kyoto's Higashiyama district, the Toyota Auto building was the second of three projects completed in Japan in the early 1990s (alongside the Gotoh Museum in Chiba and the Matsumoto Corporation Headquarters in Okayama). Inspired in equal measure by Kyoto's medieval labyrinth of passages and courtyards, and by the picturesque hills that encircle the city, the building looked to engage with its context by incorporating both of these defining Kyoto elements into its architecture.

Accordingly, the building's principal facade is turned ninety degrees to the street, maintaining the irregularities and set-backs within the city's street pattern. Outlining this facade, the main concrete volume of the building rises the full ten metres allowed by local regulations above two neighboring, traditional houses, and forms one side of a pierced and layered outer box. So as to soften the impact of the solid concrete screen, this pale gray 'shoebox' is then set inside another loosely compartmentalized black stainless steel box, which itself rises out of its enclosing layer to form a small rooftop pavilion.

Animating many of the intricacies of the building's overall form, the client had first presented the project to the architect as a multi-use building conceived and presented as if it were a private house. What would be the garage at ground floor level is therefore in reality a Toyota car showroom; the lower level dining room is a restaurant; the library and dressing rooms upstairs are a bookshop and clothes shop; and the roof-top pavilion with its panoramic view of Kyoto's hills is a client entertainment apartment. Each of these spaces maintain a sense of coherence through the richness of their surfaces. Everywhere there are reminders of the building's locale – a *shoji* screen grid of glass blocks; expanses of smooth white Kyoto plaster; and pale Japanese sen oak. The building, in this way, marries tradition with innovation, the domestic with the corporate, and achieves in the process a highly sophisticated expression of architectural simplicity.

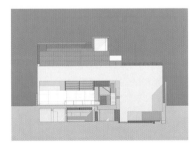

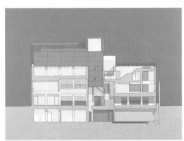

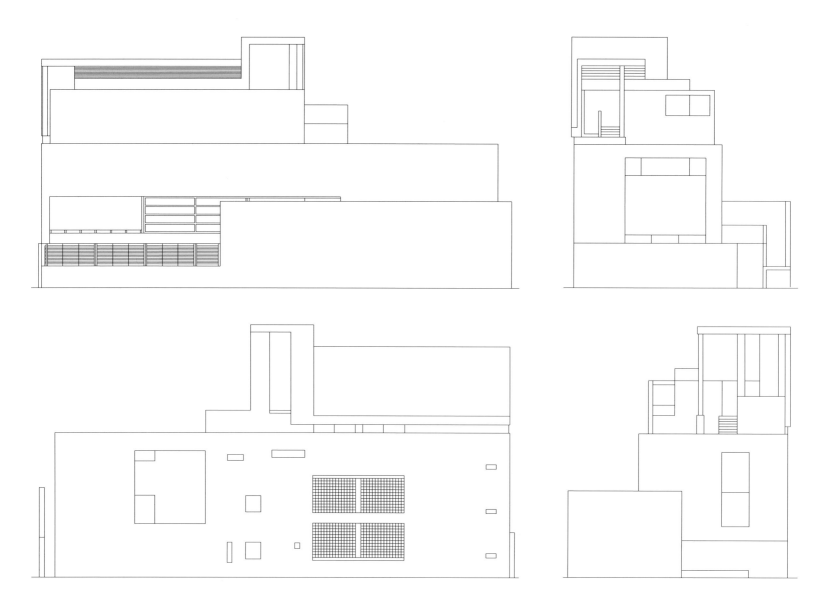

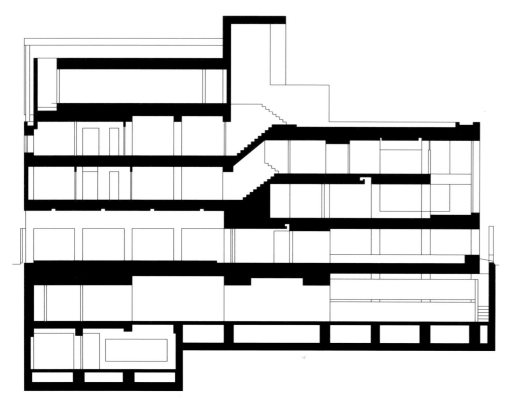

Clockwise from top left, east, south, north and west elevations

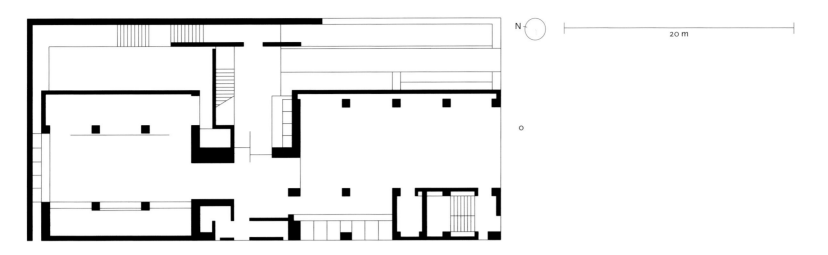

N ⊢————————————————⊣ 20 m

o

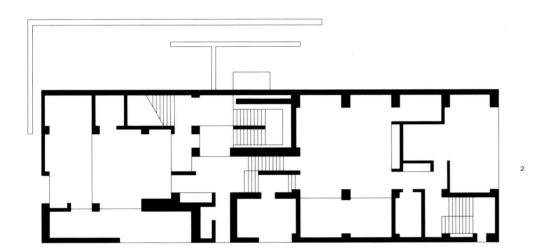

2

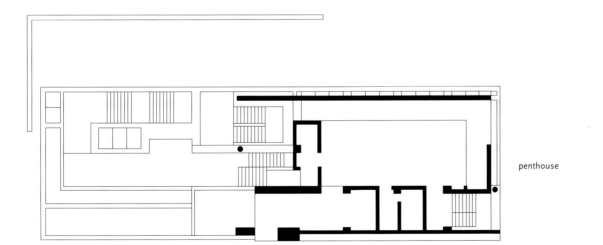

penthouse

Essays
by Jonathan Keates

In the detailed introduction to his *Lives Of The Most Eminent Painters, Sculptors and Architects*, the Renaissance artist and theorist Giorgio Vasari sets out the criteria for the construction of an ideal palace. The building, he says, must seem to rise above the ground 'to protect it from earthquakes and other accidents of fortune', as well as to emphasise the grandeur of its occupants. It should represent the human body, whether entire or in part, and its facade 'should be divided as is the face of a man', with the door for a mouth and the windows for eyes. The staircases must be well-lit and furnished with the appropriate magnificence, as these are the arms and legs of this architectural body, while coherence must be observed between the various rooms on every floor because 'if the whole composition were broken up, one thing high, another low, this great and that small, it would represent lame men, halt, distorted and maimed'.

To some, this deliberate personification of a building may appear no more than the wishful thinking of a writer with practical knowledge of the dichotomy between noble ideals in art and the various circumstances limiting their ultimate realisation. To others, the notion of the house as a body will be only a further variant of a quaint old cliché, part of our natural desire to humanise the inanimate, to find, as Vasari's near-contemporary Shakespeare puts it, 'books in the running brooks, sermons in stones and good in everything'. Besides which, experts in Renaissance aesthetics will point to similar ideas better expressed in Filarete's *Trattato dell'Architettura* of 1464 or in the works of Leone Battista Alberti.

Yet the desire to invest the spaces and structures in which we live with an articulate identity of their own is rather more deeply rooted than as a canon of artistic theory in an age with a taste for emblem and allegory, let alone as a purely banal excursion into fantasy. It is easier perhaps to believe in the numinous or even vocal quality of houses if they are invested with a suitable burden of age. Tennyson's poem 'Mariana', an extraordinary pre-Freudian study in sexual frustration, shows its heroine actively persecuted in her loneliness by the mansion in which she lives assuming a menacing life of its own:

> Old faces glimmer'd through the doors,
> Old footsteps trod the upper floors,
> Old voices called her from without.

The contemporary house, on the other hand, must contend with the architect's determination to impose terms and imperatives on it, so that the occupants are threatened with becoming mere 'vile bodies' in a controlled experiment. We recall, in this case, half-legendary stories from the annals of English country house design, like the Duchess of Marlborough's complaint to Vanbrugh that her dinner at Blenheim was always cold because it took so long getting from the kitchens to the dining room, or Lord Portman telling Richard Norman Shaw that he would agree to living at Bryanston only because, once completed, it would be too expensive to pull down and start again.

Theory and system as the fountainhead of architecture, a set of canons demanding abject conformity, or the idea of beauty as something preconceived rather than evolved from a process of collaboration with the immediate circumstances, are all conditions which David Chipperfield's work, by its very nature, would seem to reject. Ideology, by no means always supported by an armature of morality, may have inspired many of modernism's most forceful statements, just as an alternative dogma seems to have developed from the British reaction to them led by the Prince of Wales. In this case, however, the challenge to orthodoxy is not from a counter-culture of historicism and pastiche, but from the acknowledgement, among architects of Chipperfield's generation, that the inherent differences between one project and another, brought about through a whole range of forces – the versatility of the space, the character of the locality, the sense of an accent or a dialect within already extant buildings – will prescribe the terms more usefully than an inflexible array of calculations and formulae.

This pragmatic quality, which I prefer to call accommodating as opposed to compromising, often noted in Chipperfield's work and frequently attributed to that spirit of improvisation in the face of circumstance somehow regarded as typically English, emerges at its strongest in his response to a variety of commissions for private houses. Indeed, if we wanted to isolate and present a section of his achievement as the one which most characteristically proclaimed its creator, we should surely look among projects of this kind, where the architect's dialogue with his surroundings, with his materials and with the human dimensions shaping each building is at its liveliest. So too is that governing awareness of outline and profile which Chipperfield always uses as his point of embarkation. Among all the images connected with individual works, the sectional drawings, the site plans, the models, the front and rear elevations, the computer imaging and photographs of buildings from various angles, it is his initial sketches, often tiny doodle-like scratchings, which have the greatest power to move. Later, I write of 'seeing what this might become' as perhaps the most enviable faculty any architect possesses. That prophetic grasp of a reality not yet existing but certainly attainable is what these first thoughts convey more vividly than the most meticulously constructed models and plans which develop from them.

In the case of Chipperfield's various house projects, the initial tracing of the line which defines the building's character results in a singularly eclectic range of solutions. There is no typical Chipperfield domestic idiom, no trademark or signature in the traditional sense, nothing which suggests that the work is striving to announce itself through authorship first and foremost, as though assuming that the client's priority has been to buy into a name and that matters of individual taste and lifestyle must always be subordinate to this. Instead, as we gather from what Chipperfield himself has written on the subject, the enterprise springs from a process of discussion and interpretation, seeking to engage with the occupants' view of their own lives from the broadest of perspectives. The opening sketch thus becomes, as well as a shape made up of enclosed spaces or a simple ground plan, an abstract representation of the kind of existence it is intended to contain.

The Kao House illustrates this perfectly. When we look at an early development sketch, it is not just sheer sturdiness and resilience of line that impress, but the idea of horizontal and vertical planes encountering one another in a fashion that appears both serene and intensely dramatic, rather like those film sequences or photographs we remember of huge chunks of pack ice jostling for position on some polar sea. The effect here is in fact that of a life embodied and imagined, as distinct from one proposed by the space, yet, as elsewhere, Chipperfield's critical, slightly roguish sense of humour seems to come into play. Perhaps this is why I find the work in question one of his most stimulating. For the client is evidently a one-man 'ministry of all the talents', a film producer who is an economics professor, a doctor who directs a medical company, and besides all of these a pianist. He has agreed that the house should reflect the ways in which his different concerns mesh with one another, but instead of insisting on a paradox, as we might expect, created through diversity and homogeneity, Chipperfield, a smile playing across his features, suggests something much more like a children's toybox, whose containing volume will allow all these contrasting enthusiasms to rattle and reverberate safely within it. Only when we look more closely at the interplay between space and substance, vertical and horizontal, do we grasp the serious intention coexisting with what the architect, at least in terms of the lowest storey, has called 'a sort of playground'.

The overall character of the Kao House is as distant as can be imagined from the others in Chipperfield's portfolio. Blank walls here play a symbolic role, whereas in the Aram House they serve to justify the building's presence in an existing residential street governed by local planning restrictions. There is perhaps something a little defensive, or wary at least, about his anonymity vis-à-vis the public space, the face of the house, as it were, being turned towards the garden. Very different to the Lockhart House, a work of positively defiant assertiveness, in which the brief was to combine bedroom, living room, dining room and kitchen with a gallery which, whatever its importance for the owner, should not appear to overwhelm the remainder of the building. The key to the design is surely the external staircase, rising from the ground-level platform outside the gallery to a small landing, and then on to the roof, where a curtain wall conceals the swimming pool. Whatever its architectural uses as a punctuation mark in the gallery's otherwise looming mass or as a link between art and domesticity, the staircase may also be read as forging an essential relationship between the house and its Italian surroundings. Such steep flights of stairs are to be found in villas and palazzi all over Italy – the landing indeed may remind us of those especially precipitous *pietra serena* steps which descend from the corridors of the Galleria degli Uffizi in Florence. We are back once again with Vasari and his staircases as the arms and legs of a body.

One of the most eloquent of all Chipperfield's private house projects is the villa created for clients living outside Berlin, Germany. The zone selected is not necessarily a promising one. For we are in the midst of that kind of suburban affluence, to be found in cities everywhere, which expresses itself in the embourgeoisement of what may formerly have been an agreeably leafy stretch of countryside but one which is now dotted with large villas, eloquent of status and prosperity in the conservatism of their design. The architectural language here is that conventional discourse of 'features' – the balcony, the belvedere, the finial on the pediment, the louvered shutters – which after so many repetitions itself becomes featureless, and the prevailing colours, hinting at a cautious unseriousness, are cream, pastel pink and pale green.

For once Chipperfield makes absolutely no attempt to consult the spirit of place as expressed in these buildings, aware, no doubt, that whatever numinous presence once inhabited the surrounding groves has long since fled. The influence of those elements taking its place would be deadening indeed. Nor do his clients seek to integrate themselves more than is necessary with a notional community, supposing such a thing to flourish amid residences whose very identity draws for its significance on their carefully demarcated separateness from one another. The first thing you notice in approaching the house is the emphatic presence of a high garden wall, as if what you were about to enter were a convent of an enclosed order, or one of those dwellings in an Islamic city where the imagination, not altogether accidentally, is tantalised by ideas of an eternally unreachable domesticity beyond.

The dominant medium here, as indeed for the whole structure, is brick, and brick, let it be said, of a particularly evocative type, decidedly out of keeping with those kinds which elsewhere among the encroaching villas alternate with painted stucco and stonework. Not just the colour, a salmon pink fading almost to white, but the pointing as well makes allusions to that world in which brick was first extensively used as a basic material for domestic as well as public buildings. Looking at these surfaces, one is reminded of the walls of Roman basilicas and baths, though there is an equally strong link with palaces, castles and town houses in the northern Italian cities of Lombardy or Emilia. The unevenness and roughness to the touch of the handmade brick courses heightens an awareness of that physicality mentioned earlier, an architecture for the senses, a house as something directly vulnerable, in the best interpretation of the term, to the nature which encompasses it. Anything more spiritually unlike the villas which stand opposite or alongside cannot possibly be imagined. In such incongruity there is a superbly offhand insolence.

Within the house the Roman air endures as a quality more vaguely explicable in terms of the classical and the antique, but nevertheless pervasive. Maybe the poem inscribed on the *pietra serena* doorstep has something to do with this, or perhaps it is simply the sudden height of the hallway, or the well of shadow above the staircase leading down to the guest apartment below. From the big room opening onto the garden, however, we look out onto the wooden decking which Chipperfield's Japanese inspirations have made a notable feature of the Henley River and Rowing Museum, and which in Japan itself figures in, among other works, the Matsumoto Headquarters. Here such a platform is more obviously a prelude to the sweep of the lawn beyond. And the garden itself is not without its element of surprise, for Italian allusions return with the sequence of stepped terraces, like those of the villa gardens of Tuscany and Lazio, descending towards an indoor swimming pool. As if this sort of reference were not enough, the owners have placed a single terracotta oil jar at the terrace's edge, calculated to wrench us away from the lukewarm, filtered sunlight of northern Europe towards climates whose brilliance has a greater candour and vibrancy.

If the whole place seems much larger than it actually is – can we read the main staircase as a *scala d'onore* and the upper floor as a *piano nobile*? – then this is partly because the clients have deliberately avoided that traditional feature of what architects refer to for convenience as 'the domestic programme', namely living alongside one's guests. Even a guest wing will normally incorporate bedrooms on the same level as those of the family. Here, on the other hand, there is a calculated separation between host and visitor. It is not quite a total banishment, as in the *foresteria* or *palazzina* attached to certain Palladian villas, where the guests are kept at a distance from the main dwelling, but the autonomy granted to them, the notion of an independent realm with its own kitchen, bathroom and garden, means that their reappearance within the main body of the house must always be attended by some element of novelty and surprise. Not that there is any hint of them staggering out of subterranean darkness like the prisoners from Beethoven's *Fidelio*, since each level of the building receives its due share of daylight and these guest rooms are anything but cellar-like in their atmosphere.

The architectural collusion – we can only call it that – with light genuinely comes into its own on the upper floor of the house. Any properly inhabited sequence of domestic spaces must always involve some kind of imbalance between those rooms we assign to entertainment or purely practical purposes and those we colonise and stake out as personal territory, littering them with our possessions, imprinting ourselves in various ways, whether physical or abstract, upon their surfaces, so that they become in some fashion autobiographical, to be read as inalienably ours even if we are temporarily absent from them. This floor then, with its bedroom, bathrooms, closets and a pair of studios very different in character from one another, seems like some well-arranged urban apartment rather than the uppermost level of a semi-rural villa. As furnished with books and paintings, it has something of the grenier, the attic storey about it, and we ought perhaps to be looking out upon clustered rooftops or into a darkness punctuated by the glimmer from neighbouring windows and street lamps wreathed in fog.

Instead these rooms offer what is after all the most strongly idiomatic guarantee of their architect's presence, whether in our awareness that they have not been conceived in some narrowly specific fashion which precludes other kinds of use, or in the individuality conferred upon each by the different use of light. In the long studio overlooking the garden, for example, the medium is directly engaged with, in the Chipperfieldian sense of a building as something not at all finite or bounded by the limits of its site but encountering and participating with the space that surrounds it. Here nevertheless an alternative source of illumination appears, like a gloss or variant reading, in the narrow skylight running over the opposite wall, where the presence of a large bookcase helps to create a sort of gallery within the extant space. In the smaller of the two studios, light defines the room as very much belonging to its owner. Like others in the house, the place becomes an episode in a narrative of personal taste. That spirit of the Mediterranean, the archetypal feeling of 'Kennst du das Land wo die Zitronen blühn', we catch with the presence of the high garden wall, the terraces and the brickwork's flesh-tones, is heightened today by the way in which the sunlight stripes the stone platform of the little balcony with the shadow of its rails. And below, as if to confirm this, the brick-paved courtyard seems to demand lizards and a gnarled fig-tree and a well with a snake living under its masonry, though the language here is of course that of allusion rather than commonplace replica seeking authenticity.

In the garden again, trying to get some sort of distance from a building which operates a peculiar if unmistakable technique of visual seduction, I become absorbed by the house's inherently dramatic qualities in a setting which seems to defy any possibility of theatre. Theoretically the plainness and linearity of the overall form ought to be proclaiming a certain self-effacement, an ascetic rejection of the world, so that the villa, in its classic role as a retreat from the town and the crowd, becomes a kind of hermitage and that curtain wall to the street acts as a warning not to disturb the contemplative process supposedly taking place within. What actually happens is that this notional severity is disturbed by the varied sizes and seemingly deep incision of the windows, as well as by the games the design plays with differing levels on the slope of the site. Hints are continually thrown out, by such features as the tall, narrow passageway which opens from the terraced garden onto the courtyard, or the entrance to the stairs leading down to the guest rooms, that this house is a good deal larger than it wants us to know, and that there must always be parts of it we have not seen, which the owners are, for whatever reason, deliberately keeping secret from us.

In his book *Theoretical Practice* David Chipperfield, writing about the Jazzie B. House project of 1992, speaks of its 'reinforcement of the physical world, the abstraction and engagement of nature as part of the compositional material of architecture'. The exterior, he says, 'completes the process of manipulation which is adopted for the construction of interior space'. That word 'manipulation' is calculated to put us on our guard. Inevitably we associate it with deviousness, with concealed strategies of control, and its various interpretations are generally pejorative.

Yet architecture, with all its attempts at marshalling and containment of human activity, not to speak of its immemorial capacity for harnessing symbolism to the purpose of making a suitable impression on the beholder, is – or often seems to be – a sublimely manipulative art. One thinks in this regard of the very English habit, but one not confined to England alone, of creating follies and eyecatchers (a temple, a ruined castle, a grotto, an obelisk) as the governing elements in a landscape whose arrangement, or in most cases rearrangement, turns it into a text requiring skilful yet not overcomplicated decoding. Perhaps by no mere accident, Chipperfield's description quoted above speaks of the house (absorbing an older building in a north London conservation area) as trying to 'establish its own interior landscape, both internal and external'.

Manipulation, in this way, becomes an interpretative process, one of assessing the fluidity and responsiveness of already existing mass and space. In this case it is not a confrontational activity, a matter of immediate impact on those who see the building for the first time, so much as the kind of performance – one can only call it that – which involves transformation and astonishment. 'Change', John Donne tells us in one of his poems, 'is the nursery of music, joy, life and eternity'. So this Jazzie B. House renews itself in a range of different forms, of contrasting tower-like structures with a walled garden beyond them, resulting in ideas of a complex, a settlement, a community even, rather than a single, all-encompassing capsule of domesticity.

While projects like this remain unrealised, the recently completed apartment in Kensington, London, emphasises this principle of intuitive collaboration and the shaping of domestic space around the client's awareness of individual needs in dramatically uncompromising style. Part of a modern block, looking out on older residences and expanses of garden and trees, this was a neutral, generally characterless space arranged over two levels. The owners decided that the most fundamental aspects of wall surface, flooring, lighting and structure should be allowed their own contributions, more assertively offered, in a final analysis, than those made by incidental decorative features such as pictures (these have indeed been swept away entirely) or furnishings, though in the latter case the architect was asked to design chairs, sofas and other pieces, such as the curved screen behind a bed, which would play a responsive role within the ensemble.

The result is surely the most 'all or nothing' among its architect's essays in this form. Monumentality, grandeur, consequence, while never provoked to overstatement, are all present here in the ongoing vertical rivalry between the lofty walls and the high windows of the living area, from which a curving staircase (a sober adaptation of a similar design in Chipperfield's Joseph shop) and the carefully incised perspectives of the hallway and upper landings seem to tug us free from any danger of being crushed by so much immensity. Elsewhere too, this vast candour and openness is cunningly countered by the sense of the apartment as something layered and honeycombed into smaller rooms, behind screens and folding doors, creating an idea of this place as infinite, self-perpetuating, always as large or compact as its owners wish it to be at any given time. Their imagination, working with the architect's, has seen what it might be, but its perfect physical realisation entails nothing finite or absolutely determined as regards the potential of its different areas and forms.

Does a single clue, a leitmotif, a ruling passion bind Chipperfield's houses together, or is each simply a matter of grasping intuitively the site's capabilities and setting out single-mindedly to embrace them? Obviously there is no concept of standard type or model dwelling involved here, and the ideal ordinances of the Vasarian palace seem remote unless in terms of a sympathy between the building and its reservoir of human sensibility and aspiration. The messianic certainty with which architects have operated in the past, guided by an apparently robust decorum which in turn encourages a prescriptive approach to the styles of living suitable for each building (thereby making architecture into an arid science of definition) is no longer possible or necessarily desirable, however much we occasionally hanker after it. If we are looking at a Chipperfield house as the expression of a theology, a system of belief, then our glance reaches beyond what is actually there. Doubtless I am not alone in finding reassurance in the obstinate diversity of these creations from one another. The Lockhart House, in all its truculent, assertive dismantling of the initial rectangular premise, the Kao House, with its synthesis of intense energy and suspended movement (an apotheosis of the pause, as it were) and the Kensington apartment, its plasticity invoking the sense of a perpetually unachieved horizon – none of these reaches beyond immediacy towards the generic outline provided by some inflexible rule-book of construction and habitation drawn up for private houses. If a pivotal principle emerges, then, as the villa in Germany so powerfully suggests, it is that of domestic architecture as inherently a process of encounter and mutual acknowledgement between houses, their inhabitants and those elements of the natural world which reach out to embrace them.

Asked to describe his impressions of a certain Mediterranean island, an 18th-century French traveller reduced the whole visit to a single epigram. 'Its inhabitants' he said 'have always made more history than they are capable of consuming locally'. Nowadays his words spring irresistibly to mind when we visit Berlin. Maybe it is not the Berliners themselves who have produced most of the history, yet an awareness of the city staggering under a greater burden of past experience than it seems possible for any community to support is potent wherever we turn. Since the Wall came down in 1989 and Berlin reassumed its role as the capital of a united Germany, the process of joining its segments together again has involved the absorbing exercise, for a number of its most important buildings, of retrieval through a process of eliciting new meanings and intentions for them. What were raised as the symbols of youthful energy and self-confidence in the new Prussian Kingdom of Friedrich Wilhelm I and Frederick the Great, or as arrogant images of the bellicose and competitive empire of Kaiser Wilhelm II on the eve of the Great War, are now accorded a different kind of dignity altogether as unquestionable signifiers in the urban profile, enduring well beyond the aspirations which originally empowered them.

The Neues Museum on the western edge of the Museum Island in the River Spree is a case in point. Built on the site of what had once been the pleasure gardens of the old Electoral Schloss, it formed part of a layout which soon came to resemble one of those temple-complexes to be found in the ancient cities of the Orient, and was endowed with a similarly exalted purpose. The ensemble, beginning with Karl Friedrich Schinkel's Altes Museum of 1824 and ending with Alfred Messel and Ludwig Hoffmann's loomingly purposeful Pergamon Museum started in 1906, represented more than a simple Kulturforum of the kind whose late twentieth-century equivalent, housing the Gemäldegalerie and the Kupferstichkabinett, now stands close to Potsdamer Platz and its brashly revitalised arteries. The task of the assembled museums was both to instruct Berlin's citizens and to affirm the authority and international status of German scholarship as manifested in every field from archaeology to the study of classical literature and art history.

Idealism, as typical of the era in general as of the national culture itself, inspired Friedrich August Stüler, Schinkel's pupil, in his creation of the Neues Museum, begun in 1843. Flanking the older master's Altes Museum, it was intended to embody an elaborately detailed synthesis of concepts derived from the close study of antique architecture in the successive civilisations of Egypt, Greece and Rome. The exterior included a colonnade, a domed feature with allusions to the mausoleum of

Halicarnassus and a decorated pediment above two triple rows of windows divided by Corinthian and Ionic columns. Behind the building Stüler devised a further semicircular portico giving onto terraced gardens with flights of steps, dominated by an equestrian statue of King Friedrich Wilhelm IV.

The interior mingled learning, stylistic eclecticism and a dimension of palatial grandeur appropriate to a project initiated by such an ambitious and artistically-inclined monarch. Some of the exhibition halls plainly recalled Pompeii, while others were more closely related to the architecture of early Christian basilicas. At least one large room replicated the effect of an Egyptian temple, the bases of its tapering pillars adorned with hieroglyphs and pharaonic figures. Surely the most crucial of the building's features were the triple windows referred to earlier. These dominated the western side of the great staircase hall, with its loftily-conceived murals representing scenes from history by the painter Wilhelm Kaulbach, and were answered at the eastern end by a pseudo-Erectheum, on a windowed landing, of caryatids beneath a ponderous architrave.

Stüler's design transcends whatever politico-religious message may have been intended by Kaulbach's inclusion of the Lutheran reformation among his historical panels. Magnificently simple indeed is the idea of beckoning the visitor upwards towards a redeeming enlightenment, and it is this luminous metaphor which prevails in what is left of the museum today. A distinguished casualty of World War II, it continued to baffle the civic authorities, in a divided or united city, until David Chipperfield and his Berlin team proposed a dramatic reclamation of what endured from Stüler's original building, in terms of a modern museum displaying the spectacular Egyptology collections of the Prussian state, while successfully validating the survival of this splendid 19th-century carcass as something more than a noble ruin.

Restoration in a conventional sense is not what Chipperfield envisages here, even while all around the Neues Museum, on the island itself and in central Berlin generally, the emphasis is on wholesale reconstruction or else on substitution through completely new building. Though none of these enterprises necessarily constitutes a deliberate attempt to efface the memory of Berlin's bitter experience of National Socialism and Communist domination, the effect is sometimes to suggest an over-hasty, callous, perhaps even embarrassed reordering of the city's past, as if a certain sanitising process were necessary in order to make it acceptable to a rising generation of residents and tourists safely out of touch with the historical events which shaped its destiny in the second half of the twentieth century.

The Neues Museum, maimed and lopped though it may be, resists this process of cosmetic adjustment. Exploring it on a grey morning in February, I am struck at once by the building's strangely personal qualities of sturdiness and autonomy, as it hunkers down, still bomb-scarred as the war left it, beside the viscous blackness of the Spree. Gutted it may be, the windows apparently bleared and sightless, but there is nothing dead about Stüler's museum, even empty of the grand didactic collections for which he planned it.

As I walk through the vaulted undercroft, clamber up scaffolding towards roofless late antique arcades or the remains of covered Pompeiian ceilings, and watch as a photographer takes careful archive shots of the decorated metal roof trusses with their Etruscan lions passant regardant, I am reminded, through no very paradoxical association, of Graham Greene's story 'The Destructors'. In it a group of delinquent children living in south London succeeds in demolishing, beyond hope of any repair, a superb seventeenth-century house attributed to Sir Christopher Wren. While the boys gut the various rooms, with horrifying efficiency, their leader stands back to contemplate them at work. 'In a way' says Greene, 'destruction is a form of creation. A kind of vision had seen what this might become'.

In this case Chipperfield's design for the Neues Museum utilises one of the city's most powerful images of destruction as the basis for a new work. A kind of vision indeed has seen what this might become, in terms of a museum which, while it performs the traditionally expository functions associated with such a place, questions our ideas of buildings like this one as guaranteeing a particular type of cultural continuity. So the Neues Museum, only mildly affected by the need for a practical infrastructure, will remain to a large extent Stüler's battered yet enduringly sumptuous concept, preserving details such as the fragments of the extraordinary blue-and-gold papered ceiling adorned with ancient Egyptian astronomical motifs, but not seeking to reproduce, according to whatever criterion of authenticity, the complete original decorative scheme, as though the intervening experiences of modern history had never taken place.

Enthusiasm lightens the gloom for me when I stand in the great staircase hall, from which the stairs themselves have vanished and where there is nothing but builders' scaffolding, dusty concrete flooring and the high walls scabbed with alternating patches of plasterwork and bare brick. Or almost nothing, since the light – such of it as there is today – peers in, however wanly, through the tall windows. Chipperfield's introduction to the project speaks of the 'dramaturgy' within this space, and so truly this quality appears. The past neither falls away here completely nor accepts the kind of polite rationalisation which seeks to neutralise its impact. Instead the visitor, when the whole achievement is realised, will hear several voices within the museum, clearly identifiable yet not in dispute with one another or vying for undivided attention. The collection itself is to be contained within a series of rooms which harmonise the historic survivals with freshly conceived spaces, while around these will spread the carapace of Stüler's exalted design, perceptible to us as much in its ethical as in its physical dimension.

Preserving the building's autonomy should not mean a wholesale divorce from the other components of the Museum Island complex. On the contrary, Chipperfield's masterplan for the island involves the co-ordination of the five existing museums via the presence of a so-called 'Archaeological Promenade', intended to connect the various buildings so that the visitor to each will be able to ascend from this subterranean route into a sequence of wholly diverse experiences, encouraging bizarre if enthralling notions of troglodytic existence dedicated to wandering between one museum and another without any special temptation to quit such an enriching milieu.

Can this all work? A further prominent feature of the scheme is a glass box standing high on a stepped plinth overlooking the river, and enclosing an entire Pharaonic temple, while a similar adjacent structure will hold what is surely the most famous of all Berlin's Egyptological icons, the image of Queen Nefertiti. Risk-taking, though not a theatrical end in itself where Chipperfield's architecture is concerned, forms an arresting element in his work. One can think of the experiments with light, heat sources and energy in the Olivetti project, for example, or of what the architect himself calls 'the controlled confusion' in the dialectic of the Kao House, on the extravagant sweep of whose seemingly immense exterior planes the windows act as restraining hands. At first glance the addition of these boxes to the Neues Museum, whatever their structural echoes of Stüler's building, might seem to lessen the possibility of coherence between any of the features already in place within the museum itself. In fact their presence enhances the totality of the achievement, and by no special irony returns us to that spirit of an ideal didacticism which inspired Schinkel, his distinguished pupil and their royal patron in the creation of the Museum Island in the first half of the nineteenth century.

For what is shown here, as we can envisage the building once completed, is in some sense an essay in museum biography, a tribute to the building's origins as well as to its resilience in the wider context of Berlin's reinvention of itself as a city. The point of course is that such a biography should remain unfinished and, as such, call into question the nature of our beliefs as to the role of institutions like this one in an evolved society. All structures of this kind traditionally make assumptions on our behalf and seek to draw attention to their own significance. A counter-concept, the idea of a lost or invisible museum, full of non-exhibits, the casualties of war, time and oblivion, or the products of hearsay and urban myth, was wittily posited by Sir Thomas Browne in the seventeenth century as a perverse alternative to the self-consequence of those so-called 'cabinets of curiosities' which provided our earliest modern experience of the whole phenomenon. It could be said that loss and invisibility already form potent elements in the Neues Museum – here we can scarcely ignore what was or what might have been. But Chipperfield's project is unique, so far as I know, in harnessing such qualities to the business of restoring dignity to an already existing work by an earlier architect.

Either as a partial ruin or in its eventual renaissance, the Neues Museum invites several questions as to the role of a museum in the urban *mise-en-scène*, let alone as a symbol of popular, dynastic or scholarly aspirations. Orthodoxy, of the 'truth universally acknowledged' variety, dictates the need, in every great city, for an array of galleries, corridors, staircases and vitrines under one roof, which take shared curiosity for granted and guarantee status and perspective to the surrounding settled community. Berlin incorporates these institutions as an ineluctable fact of its history. But what meaning can a place like Henley-on-Thames, whose distance from the Museum Island is planetary as much as geographical, find for such buildings?

Lying on what is doubtless the most unctuously beautiful stretch of the River Thames, in the heartland of one of southern England's richer, more politically conservative areas, only a brief commuter ride from London, Henley has been famous in the world of international rowing since the beginning of the twentieth century. Competitive boating has now flourished long enough to merit the dignity of a museum, and it seems appropriate that a display of rowing craft and of the whole mystery of what the local writer Kenneth Graham, in his children's classic *The Wind In The Willows*, famously summed up as 'messing about in boats', should combine with an exhibition of the river itself, the Thames from its source in a Gloucestershire field to its swifter-flowing incarnations as London's waterway, hurtling onwards into the North Sea among shingle and mudflats.

Chipperfield was scarcely the most obvious choice for the River and Rowing Museum's designer. Works such as the Lockhart House and the Joseph Shop offered no compromises with their surroundings through any sort of straightforward vernacular mimicry (the former, indeed, created for a client living part of each year in rural Italy was positively confrontational in its stance) and the 1980s, with all of their strident enthusiasm for retro-chic, heritage and the sacred mantra of 'in keeping' as the only acceptable face of contemporary architecture, was not benignly disposed towards this sort of creative imagination. Approval, what is more, when the museum was finally completed after what appear to have been significant delays, may not have arrived in a form Chipperfield was necessarily concerned to acquire. It affords a certain wry amusement, for example, to find the magazine *Perspectives on Architecture*, frequently vocal in its attack on the more aridly disdainful excursions of modernism, conferring a blessing on him for his 'rejoining of several of the lost pathways of Modern architecture'. Elsewhere in the trade press, with a similar absence of irony, the River and Rowing Museum has been viewed as a species of Trojan Horse, smuggled into a bastion of bourgeois philistinism and indifference to contemporary achievements in the fields of building design. Which of these is more accurate, the vision of Chipperfield as self-consciously striving towards what *Perspectives* calls 'an appropriate Modernism for England' or the notion of him as a sly saboteur within the enemy's camp? It seems extraordinary that a work so manifestly without assumptions as this one, so eminently disposed to opening a civilised dialogue with its setting and its public, should turn out to be one of its architect's most controversial achievements, at any rate from the point of view of the inferences drawn from it.

Set back from the river amid willows and water meadows, the building on the contrary appears at first almost coy in its desire not to obtrude too noisily into the fringes of the townscape. What do the shapes here initially recall? Chipperfield himself claims the point of origin as the long marquees raised during the summer regatta to hold boats and to shelter different sorts of hospitality. Apparently there are also nuances derived from local boathouses and the shingled wooden barns of east Oxfordshire and the Chiltern hills.

The pleasure of these forms – those of two pitched-roof structures with oak cladding along their upper stories and across gable-ends rendered more assertive by the flat-topped ridge of the roof, the pair linked to a third hall which takes on a more obvious shed-like appearance – is in their sheer range of suggestion. Up to a point I share the view of them as nothing less than immense upturned boats which some eight formed from a vanished race of giants has hefted from the river. Something in me harks back instead to illustrations of Dayak tribal longhouses in the jungles of Borneo, red-painted barns in the woods of New England or those massive rope-walks of the Corderia in the Venetian Arsenal, nowadays used as exhibition halls for the Biennale.

Eclectic association games of this kind are surely not offensive to the peculiar essence of Chipperfield's design, one of the most extensive and ambitious of all his projects during the past twenty years and one which, in addition to its many other resonances, is inflected with touches of autobiography and what the Scots like to call a 'pawky' sense of humour, dryly oblique in its direction. This latter quality emerges most strongly in what began life as a purely practical detail connected with the likelihood (increasing, as it seems, with the gradual onset in England of a monsoon climate in the wake of global warming) of floodwater from the Thames at certain seasons of the year. In order to avoid this, the halls of the museum needed to be raised off the ground on a concrete plinth supported by low pillars.

The impact of this platform transcends its humdrum usefulness in rescuing the boat halls and other areas from being ravaged by the very element they were intended to celebrate. Henley's planetary distance from Berlin contracts to nothing all of a sudden, and we are back within a Schinkel-Stüler-like frame of reference, in which a museum becomes a temple, taking on aspects of the Parthenon or Agrigento, and by implication making similar demands for a suitable reverence from those who enter its portals. In the case of the Rowing Museum the gesture seems more light-hearted than solemn, celebrating, on the one hand, a sporting enthusiasm traditionally strong in well-watered England and gently mocking, on the other, that intensity which raises such activities to the level of a religion.

Elsewhere, nevertheless, the plinth takes on a more personal meaning for Chipperfield, in relation to certain of his earlier achievements. We recall that much of his important formative experience as an architect during the 1980s was via a range of different projects in Japan, for shops and department stores in Tokyo, for a hotel in Yokohama and a private museum in Chiba Prefecture. A Japanese inspiration contributes to the impact of the Henley building, not just in the reminiscences of the raised palaces and temples of Kyoto which the plinth induces, but in the terraces extending beyond the principal entrance areas, restaurant and shop. Their oak planks, while essentially like those which form the decking of a boat's hull, also return us to the platforms which surround a Japanese temple and seem made for cross-legged meditation by robed and shaven-headed figures. And as if this were not explicit enough as an allusion, consider the windows behind, for all the world like the papered screens typical of the older type of Japanese house.

As elsewhere in his work, Chipperfield has taken the components of certain widely differing styles and proposed fresh identities and conjunctions for them. To me, a visitor to the River and Rowing Museum on a peculiarly ingratiating afternoon in mid-August, when the river is noisy with pleasure craft, the surrounding green of fields and trees is almost hysterically vivid and Henley looks, as we might say, its unashamedly Henleyest, the signature and authenticity of the architect's touch are present most strongly in his idiomatic handling of light.

This individualising mastery of what is one of the guiding fundamental factors of the entire medium has been praised elsewhere, notably by the architectural historian and critic Joseph Rykwert, whose introduction to Chipperfield's book *Theoretical Practice* notes light as 'programmatic to him, all part of the very sympathetic low-tech aspects of his work'. Inside the Henley museum it is impossible not to sense light as wielding a formative influence on us, an almost palpable substance which, in its turn, is somehow exploiting our own palpability, moulding the ways in which we contemplate the exhibits and whereby we move about the various levels of the building.

The dramaturgy here is just as important as it appears in the seemingly diverse context of Berlin's Neues Museum. There light took on the role – one altogether consonant with the aesthetic of German Romanticism in its later phases – of a spiritual guide, like the character of Diotima, of whom Socrates speaks in Plato's *Symposium*, a classical figure with considerable appeal to the cultivated imagination in nineteenth-century Germany. In the English setting light assumes another significance altogether, as something mimetic, which enacts the part of water itself, as much engaged in creating the illusion of a wave, a channel, a current of those lapping patterns set up by the progress of vessels across the surface as defining, through its essential liquidity, the purpose of the museum and giving a vital backdrop to what is displayed here, from the boats suspended in the roof spaces to the sequential exhibition devoted to the river and its history.

It is the sheer diversity of light as material which brings a beauty to this building that transcends the somewhat too well-laundered, ever so slightly suburbanised and neatly manicured ruralism of the Henley setting. Everything shows a concern with returning us to a state of 'outdoorness' from a cultural exercise traditionally carried out in sequestered and protected conditions: those transparent floors, for example, with their varying suggestions of depth, as if we could almost hear the plop of a stone dropped into them, the different washes of daylight from the larger windows around the entrance and above the ramp, from those along the side of the boat hall reached across a glass bridge, or via the filtering through the panels on the lowest floors, and the deftly graded intensity of contrasting luminescence by the first staircase. Unlike museum visiting, rowing is, after all, one of the archetypal human engagements with nature, an act of trust in the most notoriously untrustworthy of the elements. Light, as used in the

Henley building, gives us back something of the experience to which the place is dedicated, or even prompts those who have never rowed a boat to desire it for themselves. So perhaps the notional Englishness of this achievement, its pragmatism, its inherent reasonableness, is not so distant in mood from the Neues Museum. Both works are speculations upon function, quality and type in the creation of a museum, yet each is concerned to provide us with something larger, more reverberate, in terms of our moral response to what surrounds us.

Cemeteries distil a specialised romance, even for those whose chief business in visiting them is grieving and remembrance. More than simple markers concluding a rite of passage into a hypothetical future realm, the graves indicate a residence, a settlement, something territorial, as if what certain poets and novelists ask us to believe were true, and the dead formed their own community, resentful of interference, sociable among each other and vocal amid the decorous silence of gravel paths, cypress trees and flower-beds.

Certain countries are keener than others in cherishing this idea of a gathering of tombs as essentially a cluster of inhabited dwellings, with doors, windows and rooms, to all of which names and even faces are attached. Nowhere cultivates this air of an imperishable human presence more assertively than Italy. Following traditions surely as old as the Etruscans, whose tombs became little houses with frescoed walls and images of the departed wearing their smartest clothes and lying at their ease on elegant couches, an Italian cemetery is a place in which the exchange of one state of being for another is sanctified not just by dignity, decorum and silence but by an appeal to that very worldliness which, according to religious orthodoxy, we should all be eager to leave behind.

A typical note of Italian elegance and fantasy in the funerary *mise-en-scène* makes an inevitable impact on the traveller hailing from a culture where death's visitations are less flamboyantly acknowledged. The great parade of nineteenth-century monuments along the hillside terraces at Staglieno in Genoa, their life-size figures dressed in bustles, top hats and frock coats of the era, is as compelling in its bizarrerie as the more restrained hilltop necropolis of Ancona, where each mausoleum rises like a watchtower over the sea below it, or the solemnly hierarchical little graveyard at Spoleto, where members of the town's so-called 'good families' lie under a mock-Renaissance loggia, looking down, in death as in life, upon those their rank and money enabled them to dominate.

None of these places, however, has tugged more strongly at the impressionable visitor than the island of San Michele, lying out in the lagoon a little to the north of the city of Venice. This is the origin of the *Toteninsel*, the isle of the dead, depicted by the German Symbolist Arnold Bocklin, and the mere prospect of its high brick walls sheltering their clumps of cypresses, viewed from the Fondamenta Nuove through a curtain of rain or mist across the water, is a spur to that sort of generalised morbidity and amorphous romance which cemeteries seem calculated to induce.

Like that of so much other hallowed Venetian ground, the history of San Michele is more muddled than it first appears. Once the island was known as Cavana de Muran, a refuge for boatmen on their way across to Murano, 'the glass republic' to the north. Here in 1469 the monks of Camaldoli commissioned Mauro Codussi to design their church, and the finished achievement, in white Istrian marble, with its deft interplay of curves and planes, is one of the most dramatic Renaissance buildings in the Venetian lagoon. Behind this lies the monastery cloister, itself lined and paved with tombstones, from which an archway leads into the garden beyond, extending the walled cemetery begun in 1861 by Annibale Forcellini.

The paths we trace behind this wall, among the cypress alleys and the rows of numbered graves, thread their way across the conjunction of two islands. When Venice became part of Napoleon's 'Kingdom of Italy' in the first years of the nineteenth century, a new law decreed that on grounds of health the dead must henceforth be buried at a suitable distance beyond the municipal boundary of towns and cities. The little island of San Cristoforo accordingly became the Venetian burial ground, while San Michele was later used for the detention of political prisoners. Only in 1835 were the two joined together to create the area which exists today.

This inherently artificial quality, this blurring of different layers of experience in a fisherman's rest which became a haven for hermit monks, transformed into a prison before achieving its present role, is mirrored in the experience of the dead themselves. Rest on San Michele is no more perpetual than in many another such spot. The bodies, once decomposed, are reassembled in ossuary compartments along the walls, before cremation and the placing of the ashes in urns for reburial. So the tension here is continually sprung between ideas of tranquil permanence and a destined migration through a series of alternate states, in which the acts of memory, homage and respect carried out by the living become ever more important as the physical presence of those they have lost decreases.

Doubtless there is an irony in the fact that while the population of Venice declines and the idea fades of the city itself as a group of vibrant neighbourhoods focusing on local needs rather than those of seasonal tourism, the cemetery of San Michele should become too crowded, losing whatever it might have possessed in the way of proper context for ritual and remembrance. Yet the traditional pessimism in which we like to indulge whenever the name Venice is mentioned, almost as if the place had been designed with the deliberate intention that it should slide into melancholy decay over a thousand years, is hardly validated by the recent spate of restoration and recovery of its ancient fabric. The burnt-out shell of Teatro La Fenice may still be a bone of contention,

309

the proverbial political football kicked among conflicting pressure groups, but elsewhere the face of the city now seems less sullenly resigned to squalor and imminent collapse. Not just the restored palaces and churches, but the canals themselves mirror this determined resilience. For it is with the mud dredged from them that a new island is now to be added to the existing San Michele, its gardens facing southwards onto the stretch of lagoon which gently curves along the Fondamenta Nuove.

Such a project is obviously both practical and symbolic. With their profusion of religious emblems, memorial inscription, photo-portraits of the departed, flowers either natural or artificial, the burial plots reflect a continuing hope of resurrection, a faith in the promise of perpetuity as opposed to total extinction. Releasing the scheme to an international competition rather than confining it to Italy implies a similar kind of expectation, in the idea of Venice as a visual palimpsest, a cosmopolitan text ready, whatever the weight of its historical experience, to receive addition and commentary from contemporary architects in the name of an abiding renewal.

As the winner of the San Michele commission David Chipperfield is hardly a stranger to the Italian architectural scene, and his 1999 entry for a similar competition to design new law courts in the ancient southern university town of Salerno implies certain intriguing affinities with the Venetian project. A comparable sense of the city as something organic, feeding on layers of historical experience while never absorbing them to a point at which they disappear entirely, is even more strongly apparent in Chipperfield's designs for the recovery of Salerno's historic centre grouped around a sequence of monasteries and convents on a hillside above the harbour, a notorious casualty of aerial bombardment in World War II.

Both these schemes do more than simply tip a casual nod in the direction of Salerno as it already exists – the victim, like other towns in the area, not just of past wars and earthquakes, but of complex and deep-rooted traditions of corrupt clientelism brought to bear on urban reconstruction in southern Italy after 1945. The very site of the new law courts seems to challenge the imagination. A scattered industrial zone around the railway station is to be brought into closer integration with the city whose communal value system (on however idealised a level) the courts must serve. Justice should not seem either remote from the reach of the ordinary citizen or a species of luxury item whose purveyors (not unlike the glass-workers of Murano under the old Venetian Republic) are confined to their own isolated, inward-turning world.

Thus Chipperfield and his team announce their initially surprising intention to 'colonise' the industrial area. The word is used advisedly, even considering its heavily-shaded historic overtones, with the idea of taking possession of the site on the city's behalf, so that whatever happens there will be central to a shared existence, though the occupying power will be altogether more benevolent and less exploitative in its purpose than the traditional variety of colonist.

The problem of aspect and image nevertheless remains. Classically a law court is intended, through the metaphorical role of its architecture, to fulfil three purposes. One of these is to overawe the potential culprits or defendants brought there for trial, enforcing notions of the law as a fortress against wrongdoing. By the same token the very substantiality of such buildings is calculated to reassure those in search of adequate redress for suffering. And as a backdrop for the workings of the legal profession, with all its well-known shades of theatricality and its emphasis on procedure as a framework for the practical dispensation of justice, the place needs to offer an appropriate perspective in which lawyers, judges, magistrates or juries can act out their distinct roles.

Whatever the fundamental demands of security in buildings of this kind – and recent experience might suggest that intimidation or actual violence can now be taken for granted as a more than merely theoretical menace – the heart of Chipperfield's design for the Salerno law courts is a direct openness to contact with the city, whether in a physical or an abstract sense. The old concept of such an institution as a citadel, frowning, monolithic and dehumanised, is banished in favour of something whose shape possesses the more sociable aspect of a collegiate or monastic structure, gathered around a sequence of interconnecting quadrangles with their accompanying colonnades and gardens.

Light – through long association a feature abhorred by the law (so often portrayed in novels and poems as a fog, a thick cloud or a realm of impenetrable shadow) – therefore becomes a vital component. Via the presence of such open areas, these new law courts assume, or at least imply, a moral function which some might cynically imagine was totally alien to the legal state of mind. The whole theme of disclosure, central to the concept of justice, is highlighted by the very nature of these buildings, while the opening up of perspectives, both within the quadrangles and from the public spaces surrounding the courts, suggests an openness to popular scrutiny which challenges ideas of the law as inherently disdainful of those it is intended to serve.

The humane inspirations of the project ultimately coalesce in the profile of the courts when viewed as an ensemble. What such buildings have tended to express in the past is the grimly serene countenance of legality, its features saturninely composed, its terminology both pure yet inaccessible to the layman and its details resistant to any hint of change. Chipperfield's alternative is a complex of different shapes and heights, more like a university, as noted earlier, than a government institution. The relationships here seem deliberately aimed at exploding the view of statutes and penalties as elements in a merely impersonal system triumphant through its remoteness. Instead it is hardly too far-fetched to say that we can hear as well as see this juxtaposition, rather like some still life from the hand of Chardin or Zurbarán, in which the things grouped within the perimeter of the canvas exchange a sterile individuality for a mutually evolved discourse which in its turn creates an air of inevitability in the roles designed for them by the artist.

It is the courtyards which forge a link between the ensemble and Salerno itself, as well as relating the whole scheme to certain more deeply resonating features of life in the Italian Mezzogiorno. Their function is as much practical as emblematic, hinting as they do at a sort of sociability easily adapted from the world of daytime meetings in the piazza or the immemorial evening drift of the *passeggiata*. To hang out and rendezvous in the law courts, of all places, may at first appear preposterous, but is not this only another means of defusing the utilitarian grimness associated with the practical execution of justice?

In fact, by placing such enclosed spaces at the centre of his design, Chipperfield has caught hold of one of the basic shapes in which Italians from the Alps to Sicily have always chosen to live. In northern regions such as Lombardy and Emilia the courtyard, within its defensive square of domestic buildings and workshops, is a classic feature of the countryside, known as the *cascina* and incorporating barns, cowsheds and sometimes even a chapel. Accommodating more than one family, these *cascine*, in the days of medieval feudalism, were essentially little fortresses, their gates locked at night, but the central yard space was the area for meeting and communal labour, an alternative to the frequent loneliness of work in the fields beyond.

In southern Italy these spaces are much more closely related to a particularly exotic cultural layer, of which certain forms, colours, faces and sounds will occasionally remind us. For in the historic core of the towns and larger villages of Campania, Puglia or Calabria, the classic form is Islamic, that of a *medina* made up of cellular clusters of houses entered through arched alleys leading out of narrow streets onto which these dwellings appear to turn their backs. Muslim Africa is only a day's boat journey away, and the Arabs were settlers as well as raiders in Italy's heel and toe. Echoes of this style, its huddled, impacted quality influenced as much by a need for coolness and shade in a hot climate as by economic or space-saving considerations, can be traced everywhere from Bari and Taranto to the tunnel-like *bassi* of Naples.

All such places maintain a curious balance between inward sociability and wariness. The most ancient of them are generally perched on those hillsides where perhaps the original Greek settlers of the town, as early as the tenth or ninth centuries BC, planted their first dwellings. Typical in this respect, Salerno's historic centre clings around a number of former monasteries and conventual buildings whose mass and bulk enhance that air of palpable physicality which southern Italian cities always convey more readily than their northern counterparts. Any project for revitalising this quarter of the town must call into question the part such structures are destined to play in a world where monks, nuns and friars of the various religious orders, their original occupants, no longer enjoy a pivotal role in society. The fact that at least one of these convents was eventually converted for use as a women's prison hardly dictates another institutional purpose, though given such space and substance, the imagination turns easily towards ideas of a school, a museum or municipal offices. Many an old monastery, on the other hand, not just in Italy but throughout the whole of Catholic Europe, has been transformed into a hotel or divided into apartments whose handsomeness induces a certain *frisson* when we think of the sparsely-furnished cells to which the monks themselves would have retired for fasting, prayer and contemplation.

Chipperfield's project for Salerno's historic centre takes no such functions for granted. The guiding principle derives instead from that physicality mentioned earlier, from the rhythms set up in the twisting of a lane or the sudden cascade of a flight of steps, from the tensions sprung between the angles and planes of roofs, terraces, balconies and buttressed walls, the sheer unsystematized growth of the old city as a human dimension of the landscape. To impose a limited ordinance on a place of this kind, whose essence is its apparent planlessness, must seem both arrogant and implausible. Here as elsewhere Chipperfield rejects the idea – which architecture has not altogether unwittingly borrowed, or perhaps inherited, from evangelical Protestantism – of a predestined purpose within any given building, a purpose it is heresy or sacrilege thereafter to forsake in favour of some altogether different use.

What the present scheme advocates is none other than Alexander Pope's classic injunction to Lord Burlington, 'Consult the genius of the place in all'. Rather than dictating a function or offering a drastic rationalisation of the whole area into some sort of flavourless civic amenity, Chipperfield's plan, taking the *genius loci* as its inspiration, is not unlike one of those critical editions of a familiar text whose apparatus of notes and variant readings help the reader to elaborate ideas and evolve connections between its various elements, as well as prompting a range of distinct interpretations. Thus, as with the law courts in the modern city at the foot of the hill, the three convent buildings (or complexes as in fact they are) are more closely integrated with the houses and streets surrounding them, losing in the process their air of slightly forlorn – we might almost say pointless – monumentality. Stripped of later accretions and given a context to trees, gardens and terraces, they form part of a broader scheme involving a sequence of public spaces paved with the local basalt and reached by ramps and stairways, creating essential moments of stasis amid transience and fluidity.

These ideas are devoted to revitalising a moribund quarter of a city to which history and nature have dealt several harsh blows. Their general drift is typical of Chipperfield's desire to evolve architectural solutions from what already exists, rather than a determination to carry the architecture to the place in question as a ready-formulated truth, overriding all possible dispute. Yet the project has not been accepted by Salerno's municipal authorities and may, alas, join that group of works in the portfolio of every architect from Palladio to the present, a file whose label of convenience is 'the Great Unbuilt'.

From a living city in the throes of binding itself more closely together it is, however paradoxically, no very distant a step to a city of the dead undergoing an equally significant process of reinvention and reintegration. Here again the equilibrium between enclosure and openness provides a dominant theme. For in the Venetian cemetery of San Michele the problem is one of a certain dreariness in the prospect of the graveyard as it currently exists beyond the tantalising brick curtain walls, which seem from a distance to rise sheer out of the waters of the lagoon. Exuberance and entertainment may not be exactly what we feel entitled to expect from such a spot, but an overall air of resignation in the present layout of the numbered burial plots, between alleys of indiscriminately planted cypress trees and straggling rose beds, merely adds to whatever shades of personal sadness most visitors are likely to be experiencing.

Chipperfield's design for the extension (part of it, as we have seen, created from the very same mud on which Venice itself is based) assumes a form much closer in spirit to one of the smaller island settlements of the lagoon. The effect is inherently that of a village, whatever the more sombre purposes allotted to several of its structures. A chapel and a crematorium look onto a little harbour, and beyond these lie courtyards given over to different uses, some enclosing graveyards, others holding family tombs and planted with gardens. On an adjacent islet stands another ensemble of funerary buildings, this time acting as a prelude to a sequence of gardens stretching southwards to allow an uninterrupted prospect of Venice – otherwise (at present) more or less invisible from San Michele as we have come to know it.

That emphasis on a closer relationship between a city and its civilising forces which emerges so strongly in the Salerno project is prompted in this case by the different allusions the architect makes to some of the most inalienably Venetian elements of urban living. Arriving on San Michele for the first time, some of us may feel that as matters stand at present the visual impact of the cemetery ensemble is curiously delusive. The brilliance of Mauro Codussi's church lacks that species of crowded context through which much less spectacular works by the same Renaissance master (one thinks of San Giovanni Grisostomo or Santa Maria Formosa) gain their significance. Passing through the cloister and out onto the stone terrace in front of the grander family monuments, we survey the burial place beyond with an odd awareness of how un-Venetian, non-specific and lacking in reference points everything here suddenly seems.

What the new island contrives, not just by turning its face with such a blatant openness towards the eastern end of the Fondamenta Nuove, is a renewal of those architectural constants of Venetian life, the *campo*, the *calle* and the *canal*. The lanes which divide the courtyards – themselves of unequal height and area – recall the deeply-incised *calle* of central Venice, generally running in dead-straight line to meet each other with a dramatic abruptness, or else to emerge upon a *campo*, the classic open space with its well-head (*la vera da pozzo*), its cats and pigeons and children kicking a football. None of these paved expanses can be called a 'square' in the traditional civic sense understood from other European cities. The name *campo* implies the original presence of a field or an orchard during Venice's earliest centuries. Such places, always irregular in the disposition of their surrounding palaces and churches, act as nurturing pauses in the complex urban argument, rather as the city's bell towers seem to function as its diacritical marks.

Chipperfield's *campi* at San Michele differ in size and serve to accentuate the reserved dignity of the funerary buildings standing back from them on all sides. The glance towards Venice which the whole complex encapsulates is further signalled by the presence of that ultimate emblem of the city's otherness, a canal running between two islands and crossed by small bridges. For the first time since it received its established form, via the designs of Annibale Forcellini in 1861 (like Chipperfield, a competition winner) San Michele prepares to achieve a direct integration with that element creating the plane from which the startling Venetian perspective rises to meet the viewer. Water becomes the point of origin and departure. The canal and harbour reflect the city's insistence, sometimes arrogant or desperate, on controlling and rationalising what John Ruskin in the *The Stones of Venice* poetically calls 'the wild sea-moor'. Yet it is the garden levels beyond them which, sloping to meet the waves of the lagoon, acknowledge its ultimate supremacy over wooden piles and Istrian marble.

Earlier I wrote of Chipperfield's potent awareness of what a given place communicates. Both the San Michele design and the two Salerno projects, one in progress, the other, let us hope, 'wished until it were', are as strong an example as any of such a consciousness, forming a major imperative in his architectural process. In several different ways his eye is that of a critic, in the constructive rather than the pejorative sense of the term. An existing text is broken down into its components, from which new and powerful metaphors are developed, collaborating with our all too often unused faculties of reference and association. Where better than in Italy, with its almost implausible wealth of human occupational layering, for such architecture to commend the value of past urban experience in shaping new forms of public space?

There are times when architects can appear perfectly monstrous in their self-absorption. But should we blame them for this? As dealers in the massive, the expansive, the solid, the voluminous, as exponents of an art which by its very nature negates concealment and aspires to the ideal condition of the cynosure, gazed at and admired by all, they can be forgiven for their moments of selfishness and occasional flourishes of pomposity. Not for nothing has architecture evolved its own realm of grandiloquent fantasy. Piranesi's *Carceri dell'Invenzione*, their titanic vaulting enclosing perspectives of a desperate infinity, or Sir John Soane's views of his own work in the ruinous condition to which 'the after-times' must inevitably reduce it, are different proclamations of that peculiar species of hubris through which architects (or in Piranesi's case, dreamers of architecture) invest their achievement with an imperishable glamour. 'Even in our ashes live their wonted fires', as the poet Thomas Gray puts it. Even a ruin – perhaps especially a ruin – acknowledges those sensations of perpetuity, of survival against all odds, which the building's creator assumes in our experience of it. For whatever reason Greek mythology (unlike the Jewish scriptures, with their cautionary tale of the Tower of Babel) does not include the story of an architect punished for defiance of the gods. Arachne is turned into a spider for challenging Pallas Athene with her skill as a tapestry weaver, the cunning musician Marsyas is flayed alive by his infuriated rival Apollo, but the makers of temples and towers remain unpunished in their arrogant presumptions of the everlasting and the power of reaching towards the heavens.

Added to which, there is the desire to impose, to present the given building as a statement, a tract, a polemic, a thesis, disdainful of anything in the way of origins or context, and as such more deserving of our attention than whatever else may occupy the available prospect. The 'notice me' factor in architecture is perhaps its most exasperating characteristic, if only because our natural instinct is to do precisely the opposite, in a bid to remind the architect of his mortal status in relation to the rest of humanity. Swagger, done properly with a certain panache, we are inclined to allow, but the self-consequence with which certain buildings force themselves upon us, taking their supremacy for granted, evokes a pardonable wish to turn the back, to refuse to be impressed, recalling Voltaire's story of the Doge of Genoa who, when taken to Versailles with the expectation that he would be suitably overawed by the palace and the gardens, remarked that the most astonishing feature of the whole place was his own presence there, not withstanding the achievements of Mansart, Levau and Le Nôtre.

To some extent our era itself has colluded in developing this phenomenon of the overweening architect. In the closing years of the twentieth century and the earliest phase of the new millennium, nothing quite rivals fashion design in the quintessential chic it confers on its practitioners, but architecture surely comes a close second. The various kinds of consciousness raising, whether by the media or by pressure groups and special interests or by patrons of the individual projects themselves, which have given building design a new kind of urgency, simultaneously bestow on its creators a significance, not to say a smartness, by which they can scarcely avoid feeling flattered. Once this was merely a respectable profession. Now it comes wreathed in an aura of positively global elegance.

Yet whatever his presumptions or imaginings, the architect works within a social system, even if he manages to avoid working with it. Operation may not imply co-operation, but certain lines are already drawn, certain demands already formulated, and a framework exists which compels the acceptance of a number of realities seemingly calculated to crush or at least to mishandle the creative impulse. Architecture has long perceived a need to dignify such spheres of activity as politics, religion, academic study and cultural rituals – theatre going, museum visits, attendance at concerts and opera – but what of our more commonplace business, especially that which, above all, sustains the dominant rhythm of urban life? Does architecture want to know – or would it much rather not know – about shopping?

Designs for shops, or buildings which incorporate shops, are not a novelty of capitalism in its more sophisticated forms from the nineteenth century onwards. The medieval London Bridge featured what are now called 'retail outlets' in its design, the Elizabethan Royal Exchange, built in 1570, was intended as a shopping complex, and in the Tuscan town of San Miniato an entire block of Renaissance houses incorporates traders' booths in its lowest storey. The tendency in the twentieth century, however, has been increasingly utilitarian. In European and American cities before the Great War, a deliberate attempt was made, especially by the proliferating department stores, to lure a shopper into a building which should combine a palace with a hotel, so that the experience of shopping should involve something more memorable than a purely commercial transaction. This sense of dignifying the ordinary, of turning it into an exceptional moment, on the perfectly pardonable assumption that the lives of most of us who shop are not inherently varied or interesting, has largely vanished from the calculations of both the retailer and the architect. The shop, more especially in its most familiar incarnation as a component of the modern mall, has become a void, an area of space in the least encouraging sense either term will bear, to be crammed with merchandise but not in itself a contributor to what for so many is a significant recreational exercise.

This reluctance to provide the adequate dimension is curious, given how much attention is currently paid to shopping in its more abstract aspects. Theoreticians may not have devised the appropriate philosophy or semiotics, a Tao of Shopping may not yet exist, but increasingly we satisfy ourselves with an awareness that the process must involve something more complex and specialised than a series of disparate activities centred around payment for purchases and reasons for choosing or rejecting them. Whether viewed as an act of self-projection or self-indulgence, as a therapy offering multiple consolations or as a simple surrender to the blandishments of capitalism, the exercise invites some sort of setting, a perspective which ventures beyond the idea of it as a simple business of goods exchanged for money.

David Chipperfield's work has included a range of different projects designed to display architecture's potential for engaging seriously and unselfconsciously with such an apparent commonplace of civilised existence. The shops themselves are almost all connected with luxury items in some form or another, or with objects which only the most sophisticated line of reasoning might argue were fundamental to our survival. We may say that for this or that item of clothing 'we would kill' or that we could not live without it, but the very act of acquiring these things celebrates a freedom from absolute necessity and the pleasure of indulging alternative impulses involving taste, selectivity, proclamation of status or even sheer competitiveness. To commission an architect of Chipperfield's stature and experience in the creation of a suitable mounting for these clothes, let alone for those who choose to wear them, authenticates the designers' conviction in the value of their achievement and brings an unwonted dignity to the seemingly ephemeral business of buying a smart frock.

Some might detect the springing of a tension here, between the apparent impermanence of fashion, with its perpetually critical eye trained on the new, the recondite or the bizarre, and a deliberate solidity, saturnine and unbudgeable in view of whatever is placed upon them or against them, in Chipperfield's forms and surfaces in these shop projects. How, we might ask, can objects as perishable as belts, shoes, dresses and coats survive the reproachful permanence of these stone floors and plinths or those massive white rectangular columns? Others would as easily argue for fashion's most recently evolved bid, vindicated by everything from the textile departments of museums to the serious academic scrutiny of costume as a social indicator, for the role of quintessential barometer of the zeitgeist, the ultimate pointer towards wishes and aspirations too profound for verbal articulation. Chipperfield's handling of the project, viewed in this light, brings an appropriate weight and resonance to an increasingly complex discourse.

The Issey Miyake shop in Sloane Street, London, effectively mirrors this ambiguity in our possible approaches, perhaps more radiantly so since it was the very earliest essay in the genre by the architect and his office. The design includes several features which Chipperfield has since developed in similar projects. For one thing, we notice that an absolute clarity of enunciation, in such elements as the lighting, the floors and the low plinths and ledges along the walls, is intended to honour the clothes themselves with the kind of display which solicits rather more than a crude eagerness for possession on the part of the consumer. We are here not just to buy what Miyake has made, but to admire his perceptions in terms of fabric and form. In an ordinary fashion outlet a garment has no beauty or meaning allowed it except on the body of the wearer. Here a different sort of participation is invited. The clothes seem almost like objects of veneration and awe, hung up like *ex-votos* or those items of apparel one sometimes finds in cathedrals preserved above the tombs of medieval knights. While it is not a sin on this occasion to touch or remove them from their rails and hangers, it is also not reprehensible to enjoy these things for what they are, in a context which renders them suitably epoch-making.

Essential to Chipperfield's approach seems to be the removal of those varieties of clutter and distraction in detail which the average shop contains, the advantage in this case being that the product for sale is exclusively that of the named design house. Display is a matter of carefully isolated presentation, which means, incidentally, that the eye has the leisure to delight in what surrounds the clothes as well as the individual pieces themselves. I am reminded of the music critic who wisely remarked of Handel's concertos that it was not just the sequence of the notes we relished, but the quality of the spaces in between them.

So far Chipperfield's portfolio has not included a theatre, but his shops seem to me his most abundantly theatrical buildings. Those who supervise architects in the creation of different sorts of auditorium and performance areas place much emphasis on sight-lines, those extended vistas whereby the audience is enabled to view as much of the stage as possible without necessarily having its illusion of the scenic picture troubled by inopportune glimpses into the wings or the orchestra pit. Sight-lines in a Chipperfield store are compulsive, the motivators and engines of the design. In the Kenzo shop, for example, think of what the glance enfolds as we look towards the steps ascending to the highest level, with a balcony to our left and a set of free-standing shelves balancing the whole effect. The setting invites parade, gesture, projection of various kinds – for this is, after all, a fashion store, in whose creations we shall become something rather more than we know ourselves genuinely to be, or else uncover fresh identities in rising to the challenge made by the garment on display.

The Joseph shop in Sloane Avenue, London, catches fashion's continual fling in the direction of the dramatic more decisively because the clothes themselves are the very reverse of flamboyant overstatement. Vistas are positively epic, within what is not in fact an entirely new building but the deft conversion of a 1960s office block which has successfully transformed its overall shape and character. The place now seems made for surprise appearances and grand transmogrifications, while not lacking in essentially theatrical touches of concealment here and there, in its screens, its wing-like pillars and its patches of shadow. Most abundantly histrionic of all, though without the least hint of camp or shallow staginess, is the sudden intervention of a spiral staircase whose swirling elegance grows the more entrancing through its interplay of irregular shapes, a deep curve in one baluster, the suggestion, on the other, of a casually ruffled piece of paper, the reversing flight supported on what looks like the billow of an unfurled sail, the whole thing not a little rococo in its implication that beauty does not always need solemnity to validate it.

There is one shop indeed among Chipperfield's most recent works, where this touch of what I am tempted to call amused sincerity comes fascinatingly into play in moderating the nature of the design. I suspect, what is more, that the unexpectedness of the setting had as much to do with this as the peculiarly potent idiom, a dialect rather than an accent, governing the look of the clothes in this particular store. The older end of Bond Street, after all, has until recently been associated with jewellers and dealers in old masters rather than with fashion houses, so that the shop fronts have tended to preserve a Victorian or Edwardian appearance, making a conscious appeal to ideas of well-established respectability and the kind of smartness which feels no need to advertise itself.

The arrival of Dolce & Gabbana in the midst of this relative sobriety signals the advent of a different sort of smartness altogether, rather as if some gorgeously-accoutred carnival party had burst in upon the solemn meeting of a religious chapter and refused thereafter to be dislodged. The label is well known as one of the most impertinently original in modern design, powerfully marked in its overall style by the fusion of its creators' northern Italian and Sicilian origins, an inspired reconciliation, as it must seem, of the traditionally irreconcilable. We might call Dolce & Gabbana the most ethnically Mediterranean in idiom among the great Milanese fashion houses, and it is hard not to feel, as we are ushered into the shop, that the temperature has suddenly risen by several degrees, as if the climate had been imported to provide a sympathetic environment for the clothes.

Not inopportunely, the sun is shining today in any case, which heightens the *meridionale* effect of Chipperfield's exterior prelude to the design, a sturdy sequence of concrete columns between the windows, a sequence which seems to play somewhat with the gradient of the street itself in making the pavement appear steeper than it actually is. The shape of these vitrines possesses a certain monumentality which, though never pompous, invites us to view the work on display as something serious and enduring, an achievement transcending the inbuilt limitations of the fashion design medium.

Inside, the very floors and steps we walk on are Italian, of that rich grey basaltina which we have seen used for palace staircases and the paving of chapels. There is always more than a hint or two of Catholic devotion in Dolce & Gabbana's peculiar rhetoric, and the idly associative glance falling upon the stone ledges surrounding the showrooms on both floors makes an inevitable link with the altar on which a dress or a shirt has been laid as an offering. The principle I noted earlier in the Issey Miyake shop is just as vital here, that the clothes should be objects of wonder as well as desire. The type of stone chosen plays an important role in shaping a distinctive identity for the shop. Its volcanic sombreness creates instant associations with Sicily (where Domenico Dolce was born) and the shadow of an eternally unpredictable Mount Etna. From a more practical aspect, this same quality of subdued smouldering – 'even in our ashes live their wonted fires' seems still more appropriately remembered in such a context – offers an almost organic setting for the handsomeness of everything exhibited here, as if these coats, handbags, boots and sweaters had sprung naturally from a dark surrounding fertility of pumice and lava.

That Dolce & Gabbana, Bond Street, was intended to display significant differences from other stores of its kind is made clear from Chipperfield's preliminary sketches, evolved during discussion with the two designers themselves, a veritable self-contained album rather than a disparate collection of drawings and ideas. The points of departure are, on the one hand, the essential individuality of these clothes as artefacts and, on the other, their intrinsic delicacy of conception and execution. Thus out go the traditional long racks and rails, a gesture of deliberate rejection calculated to challenge the thoughtless idleness of the modern shopper and invite a more directly responsible engagement between the purchaser and the creation. Instead, the emphasis is on presence and presentation, on the shop as a species of forum, piazza or arena – those classic open spaces of the Mediterranean world at various stages of its history – in which our awareness of a surrounding amplitude will heighten the abundance of beauty and fantasy inherent in Dolce and Gabbana's work. Clothes are gathered in small – we could even say conversational – groups on simple wooden stands, or offered to the view in lacquer trays. Whether on hangers or on free-standing mannequins (of the kind dressmakers used to call 'Bloody Maries') these garments seem to acquire a greater volume and contour than their equivalents in the rival emporia of Bond Street and its satellites. Doubtless this explains why, browsing the shop on an ordinary weekday, I gain an odd but entirely congenial impression of there being more people within it than simply the customers and the assistants.

This sense of movement and vitality is best expressed by that scarcely translatable Italian word *popolare*, which itself relates to Dolce & Gabbana's concept of an exclusivity without snobbery. Yet for such animation, nothing is allowed to disturb the serenity of Chipperfield's planes of colour, the incandescent southern whiteness of the walls, the glass screens filtering light through black chiffon, the cinder-grey basalt flooring, plinths and stairs. There is none of the customary illusion of cupboard and shelf space built into the wall. Everything seems autonomous, mobile within the overarching permanence of the architect's design, which, while making no preconditions for the client, is strong enough to sustain a whole variety of fresh groupings and arrangements among the components assembled within it. In addition its elemental simplicity is untroubled by the characteristic touches of 'set-dressing' and Italianate theatricality through which Dolce and Gabbana establish their inalienable possession of the domain. There are swanky rococo thrones in the main body of the shop, while the fitting rooms, with the aid of immense curtains of blood-coloured velvet, have been turned into the boxes of an opera house.

I use words like 'domain' and 'inalienable', but surely the whole aim of this achievement, mixing glamour with irony and purposefully blurring the distinctions between where we are and where we ought to be, is to transcend the more banal considerations of typology, categorising and restricted function. What strikes us here is the versatility, or better still, the susceptibility of these spaces, presenting themselves in the most unembarrassed fashion as open to a range of uses and interpretations, not necessarily related to each other and in certain cases widely removed from the destiny proposed for them by the original commission. A certain well-tempered Renaissance grandeur in the staircase to the basement level, for example, made from one of those types of stone which Vasari, in his *Lives*, praises for 'withstanding the assaults of time', is not more than a mere shop deserves because Chipperfield and his clients have not conceived this project purely in terms of the usual commercial cycle of product, sale and profit. Ambiguity of association conjures up a variety of roles for this place – a studio, a laboratory, a chapel, a performance venue – and by this means we return to elemental questions as to the purposes of architecture and the architect's privilege of dignifying even the most earthbound aspects of human existence.

In this context of the Dolce & Gabbana shop and its implicit triumph over dogmas of form and function, I am reminded – not inappropriately, given where the two designers' discourse is coming from – of one of my favourite Italian buildings. Its location is unremarkable, in the small town of Monte San Savino, above the Val di Chiana in southern Tuscany, a spot noted in the history of art solely as the birthplace of the Renaissance sculptor Andrea Contucci, who became known as Sansovino. It was he who designed the Loggia dei Mercanti in the town's principal Corso. A simple arcade with storage space above, it was intended as a shelter for the local corn merchants and dealers in cocoons for the region's silk industry. The traders have long since gone, but the Loggia remains, a work of unassuming elegance whose proportions proclaim the presence, or more significantly the possibility, of beauty and harmony as defining values in a society which theoretically ought to seem entirely uninterested in them. For what moves us as much as the formal purity of this Renaissance colonnade is the fact that the merchants themselves should have seen it as desirable and appropriate to their activities in the first place.

> 'Because a man has shop to mind
> In time and place, since flesh must live,
> Need spirit lack all life behind,
> All stray thoughts, fancies fugitive,
> All loves except what trade can give?

These lines of Robert Browning, from a poem called 'Shop', dealing with, among other important themes, the conflict between capitalism and the imagination, have their resonance under the Loggia dei Mercanti and in the Bond Street emporium of Dolce & Gabbana. Chipperfield's 'stray thoughts, fancies fugitive', guided by an unerring sense of the strong line, of where it leads and what it makes, have prompted him to ask the ultimate question as to whether a space like this one might actually be habitable? While not setting himself up as a moralist, he appears continually to enforce the moral dimension surrounding an architect's work, whether in sharpening our apprehensions of beauty even in human activity's most commonplace spheres, or through ennobling this same activity by allowing it sufficient room in which to achieve, or at least aspire to, a sufficient dignity and grace. This, therefore, is an architecture which proposes rather than ordains: our acceptance of it measures our humanity.

David Chipperfield

Biography

1953   Born in London, UK
1978   Diploma in Architecture, Architectural Association, UK
1978–84 Worked for Douglas Stephen, Richard Rogers, and Norman Foster
1985   Established David Chipperfield Architects
          Founder member of 9H Gallery, London, UK
1992–97 Trustee of the Architecture Foundation, London, UK

Teaching

1979–82 Design tutor, North London Polytechnic, UK
1981   Design tutor, Cardiff School of Architecture, UK
1982   Design tutor, South Bank Polytechnic, UK
1984–85 Design tutor, Birmingham Polytechnic, UK
1985–86 Design tutor, University College London, UK
1987–88 Visiting Professor, Harvard University, Cambridge, Massachusetts, USA
1988–90 Design tutor, Royal College of Art, London, UK
1992   Visiting Professor, University of Graz, Austria
          Visiting Professor, University of Naples, Italy
1993–94 Visiting Professor, Ecole Polytechnique, Lausanne, Switzerland
1995–2001 Professor of Architecture, Staatliche Akademie der Bildenden Künste,
          Stuttgart, Germany
1997–   Visiting Professor, London Institute, UK
2001   Mies van der Rohe Chair, Barcelona School of Architecture, Spain

Awards and Prizes

1981   Schinkel Prize, special mention
1990   British Design and Art Direction Award
1991   Andrea Palladio Award for the Toyota Auto Kyoto building, Kyoto, Japan
          Andrea Palladio Award, second prize
          British Design and Art Direction Award
          Financial Times Award, special mention
          Pantone Colour Award
1998   AIA Award (UK) for Kaistraße studios, Düsseldorf, Germany
          RIBA Regional Award for the River and Rowing Museum, Henley-on-Thames, UK
1999   Civic Trust Award for the River and Rowing Museum, Henley-on-Thames, UK
          Mies van der Rohe Award-Shortlist for the River and Rowing Museum,
            Henley-on-Thames, UK
          RIBA Category Award – Architecture in Arts and Leisure Award for the River and
            Rowing Museum, Henley-on-Thames, UK
          Royal Fine Art Commission Trust/British Sky Broadcasting Building of the Year
            Award – Best Building Award (England) for the River and Rowing Museum,
            Henley-on-Thames, UK
          Stirling Prize Shortlist for the River and Rowing Museum, Henley-on-Thames, UK
          The Tessenow Gold Medal Award
2002   Stirling Prize Shortlist for the Ernsting Service Center, Coesfeld-Lette, Germany

Projects

Current Projects 2002

Alessi tea and coffee service, Italy
Almere Blok 2, Almere, The Netherlands
Ansaldo City of Cultures, Milan, Italy
Apartment Buildings, Shanghai, China
Barcelona City of Justice, Barcelona, Spain
BBC Scotland, Glasgow, UK
BFI Film Centre, London, UK
Des Moines Public Library, Des Moines, Iowa, USA
Diagonal, Barcelona, Spain
Figge Arts Center, Davenport, Iowa, USA
Gormley Studio, London, UK
Hamburg brewery and hotel, Hamburg, Germany
House in Frankfurt, Germany
House in Miami, Florida, USA
House in New York, New York, USA
House in Portofino, Italy
Kojun Building, Tokyo, Japan
Lenée-Dreieck apartment building, Berlin, Germany
Maasport, Venlo, The Netherlands
Literature Museum, Marbach am Neckar, Germany
Neues Museum, Berlin, Germany
New Entrance Building, Berlin, Germany
Oosterdokseiland Hotel, Amsterdam, The Netherlands
Palace of Justice, Salerno, Italy
Polo Culturale, Verona, Italy
San Michele Cemetery, Venice, Italy
Social housing, Madrid, Spain
Teruel urban development, Teruel, Spain

Projects 1983–2002

The project list indicates the year that the project was completed or in the case of unrealized projects the year in which the main body of work was completed.

1983
Davis House [interior], London, UK

1985
Cleveland Square Apartment, London, UK
Issey Miyake, Sloane Street, London, UK [in collaboration with Ken Armstrong]
Mews studio, London, UK [in collaboration with Ken Armstrong]

1986
Courtauld showroom, London, UK
Equipment, Rue d'Argout Étienne Marcel, Paris, France
Hedley Apartment, London, UK
Issey Miyake, Permanente: Sapporo, Kyoto, Osaka, Sendai, Ginza and Shibuya-Tokyo, Tokorozawa, Nihon-Bashi, Japan
Monkton House restoration, Sussex, UK
Seibu department store, Suibuya, Toyko, Japan
Sound studios, London, UK

1987
Agar Grove studios, London, UK
Arnolfini Gallery, Bristol, UK
Architectural Press exhibition stand, Interbuild, Birmingham, UK
Bingo Bango Bongo discotheque, Roppongi, Japan
Brownlow Mews, London, UK
Gotoh Museum, Chiba, Japan
Monkton House, Sussex, UK
Hanna Olin office, Philadelphia, Pennsylvania, USA

1988
Palais de Congress [with Yves Lyon], Nantes, France
Wilson & Gough Gallery, London, UK

1989
Draper House and Pavilion, London, UK
Fabian Carlsson Gallery, Bond Street, London, UK
Toyota Auto Kyoto, Kyoto, Japan

1990
Aram House, London, UK
Equipment Shirt; Lyon, Toulouse, and Lille, France
Gormley House – addition and renovation, London, UK
Kenzo, Brook Street, London, UK
Light industrial units, Southern Row, London, UK

1991
Betty Jackson shop, London, UK
Equipment Shirt, Blvd. St. Germain, Paris, France
Equipment Shirt, Brook Street, London, UK
Equipment Shirt concessions in department stores in Japan, London, Paris
Knight House, Richmond, UK
Sara Sturgeon shop, London, UK
Screenprinting studio, London, UK
Virgin Records reception, Harrow Road, London, UK
Joseph warehouse, London, UK

1992
Equipment Shirt, Sloane Street, London, UK
Joseph, Rue du Cherche, Paris, France
Matsumoto Corporation Headquarters, Okayama, Japan
Restoin Apartment, Paris, France

1993
Chatters showroom, London, UK
Lockhart Saatchi House, Umbria, Italy
Equipment, Istanbul, Turkey
Jazzie B House, London, UK
Kao House, Boston, Massachusetts, USA
Natural History Museum, central hall, London, UK
Natural History Museum, plant gallery, London, UK

1994
Apartment in London, UK
Grassi Museum, Leipzig, Germany
Joseph, Sloane Street, London, UK
Joseph concessions; Liberty and Simpsons, London, UK
Olivetti Hypo-Bank theoretical project, Italy
Tate Modern, London, UK

1995
Chatters Residence, London, UK
Equipment, Hong Kong
First Church of Christ Scientist, Richmond, UK
Joe's Café, London, UK
Joseph, Old Bond Street, UK
Wagamama restaurant, London, UK

1996
Bristol Centre for Performing Arts, Bristol, UK
Dundee City Arts Centre, Dundee, UK
Equipment, New York, New York, USA
Equipment, Tokyo, Japan
Faggionato Fine Art Gallery, London, UK
L'Express, Sloane Street, London, UK
Lühn Apartment, London, UK
Munich Tourist Office, Munich, Germany
Phaidon Stand, Frankfurt book fair, Germany
Phoa & Williams apartments, London, UK
Private house, Berlin, Germany

1997
Adolf Würth Art Gallery, Schwäbisch Hall, Germany
Aalemannkanal Housing, Berlin, Germany
Circus Restaurant, London, UK
Cornerhouse Art Centre, Manchester, UK
Diocesan Museum, Cologne, Germany
Joseph, Sloane Avenue, London, UK
Kaistraße Studios, Düsseldorf, Germany
Lockhart Saatchi House, Martha's Vineyard, Massachusetts, USA
River and Rowing Museum, Henley-on-Thames, UK

1999
Apartment in Kensington, London, UK
Centre of World Cultures, Göteborg, Sweden
Dolce & Gabbana, Milan, Italy
Dolce & Gabbana, Old Bond Street, London, UK
Dolce & Gabbana, Osaka, Japan
Dolce & Gabbana, Porto Cervo, Sardinia, Italy
Dolce & Gabbana, Menswear, Milan, Italy
Laban Centre, London, UK
Royal Collections Museum, Madrid, Spain
Vitra Showroom, London, UK

2000
Apartment on Park Lane, London, UK
Dolce & Gabbana, Los Angeles, California, USA
Dolce & Gabbana, Sloane Street, London, UK
Dolce & Gabbana, Zurich, Switzerland
Knight House, Richmond, UK
Lever House, office building refurbishment, New York, New York, USA
National Gallery of Art, Rome, Italy

2001
Bliss Spa, London, UK
Bryant Park Hotel, New York, New York, USA
Church of the Pentecost, Milan, Italy
Dolce & Gabbana, Moscow, Russia
Ernsting Service Center, Coesfeld-Lette, Germany
Hugh Lane Municipal Gallery, Dublin
Landeszentralbank, Gera, Germany
Museum of Modern Art, Bolzano, Italy
Pasquale Bruni showroom, Milan, Italy
Reece Mews, London, UK
Shore Club Hotel, Miami, USA
Spreedreieck, Berlin, Germany
Vigo Congress Hall, Vigo, Spain

2002
Dolce & Gabbana, New York, USA
Dolce & Gabbana, Paris, France
House in Galicia, Corrubedo, Spain
Moscow Shopping Village, Moscow, Russia

Furniture and Products

1992
Cassina IXC. Ltd., Air Frame furniture, Japan
Okamura furniture, Japan

1994
Interlübke, furniture, Germany

1996
Slegten & Toegemann, ceramics, Belgium

1998
B&B Italia, Mirror Chair, Italy
Cassina IXC. Ltd., Air Frame Mid range furniture, Japan

1999
Fontana Arte, Abaco light, Italy
Hitch Mylius, upholstered furniture, UK

2000
Czech & Speake, brassware, UK

2001
Conceptual Domestic Bathroom, ceramics and brassware, Ideal Standard, Italy

2002
Alessi tea and coffee service, silverware, Italy
Brassware and ceramics, Ideal Standard, UK
Cassina IXC. Ltd., Air Frame desks and office system, Japan
Valli & Valli, door furniture, Italy

1981
Schinkel Prize [in collaboration with   2nd prize
  Roger Huntley], Berlin, Germany

1982
Botanical Museum, Kew, London, UK

1988
British ambassador's residence, Moscow, Russia

1990
Docklands restaurant, London, UK

1991
Channel 4 studios, London, UK   Shortlisted
Museum of Scotland, Edinburgh, UK

1992
DAM: Ideas for Frankfurt Osthafen,
  Frankfurt, Germany
Nordbahnhof, Vienna, Austria   Shortlisted
Red Cross Station, Graz, Austria   1st prize
Spedale di Santa Maria della Scala
  [in partnership with Richard Rogers], Sienna, Italy

1993
Central Library, Berlin, Germany
Neues Museum, Berlin, Germany   2nd prize

1994
Maselakekanal housing masterplan, Berlin   1st prize
Tate Modern, London, UK   Shortlisted

1995
Leipzigerplatz, Berlin, Germany   3rd prize
Lisbon Fair Building, Expo 98, Portugal   Shortlisted

1996
Bristol Centre for Performing Arts, Bristol, UK
Cathay Pacific lounge, Hong Kong
Dundee City Arts Centre, Dundee, UK
Lindengalerie an der Komischen Oper,   1st prize
  Berlin, Germany

1997
Adolf Würth Art Gallery, Schwäbisch Hall, Germany
Diocesan Museum, Cologne, Germany   4th prize
Hackney Empire, London, UK
Neues Museum, Berlin, Germany   1st prize
Salle Philharmonique, Luxembourg

1998
Ernsting Service Center, Coesfeld-Lette, Germany   1st prize
Extension of San Michele Cemetery, Venice, Italy   1st prize
Mid Wales Centre for the Arts, Welshpool, UK   1st prize
Redevelopment of the Old Town, Salerno, Italy   Special
                                                   mention
White Cube Gallery, London, UK   Shortlisted

1999
Centre of World Cultures, Göteborg, Sweden   2nd prize
Hamburg Deichtor office building, Hamburg,   Shortlisted
  Germany
Laban Centre, London, UK   Shortlisted
Lamborghini showroom, Munich, Germany
Palace Hotel, Lugano, Switzerland   Shortlisted
Palace of Justice, Salerno, Italy   1st prize
Reina Sofia Museum extension, Madrid, Spain   Shortlisted
Royal Collections Museum, Madrid, Spain   Shortlisted

2000
Ansaldo City of Cultures, Milan, Italy   1st prize
Figge Arts Center, Davenport, Iowa, USA   1st prize
Fritz Kaiser Business Centre, Liechtenstein   1st prize
German Embassy, Tokyo, Japan   Shortlisted
Haus Witt, Hamburg, Germany   3rd prize
Japanese Palais, Dresden, Germany   Shortlisted
Lenée-Dreieck apartment building, Berlin,   2nd prize
  Germany
Museum and Auditorium, Lugano, Switzerland   Shortlisted
National Gallery of Modern Art, Rome, Italy   Shortlisted
Ponte Parodi, Genoa, Italy   Shortlisted
Royal College of Art extension, London, UK   Shortlisted
Salisbury Magna Carta, Salisbury, UK   Shortlisted

2001
BBC Scotland, Glasgow, UK   1st prize
BFI Film Centre, London, UK   1st prize
Church of the Pentecost, Milan, Italy   2nd prize
Des Moines Public Library, Des Moines,   1st prize
  Iowa, USA
Dreef Complex, Haarlem, The Netherlands
Museum of Art and Technology, New York,
  New York USA
Museum of Modern Art, Bolzano, Italy   2nd prize
Polo Culturale, Verona, Italy   1st prize
Richemont International, Geneva, Switzerland   2nd prize
Teruel urban development, Teruel, Spain   1st prize
Vigo Congress Hall, Vigo, Spain   2nd prize
Villanova, Barcelona, Spain   Shortlisted

2002
Barcelona City of Justice, Barcelona, Spain   1st prize
Hamburg brewery and hotel, Hamburg, Germany   1st prize
Kojun Building, Tokyo, Japan   1st prize
Literature Museum, Marbach am Neckar, Germany   1st prize
Natural History Museum, Los Angeles,   Shortlisted
  California, USA
Sammlung Brandhorst Museum, Munich, Germany
Trieste Waterfront, Trieste, Italy

1983
'Ten Young Architects', RIBA, London, UK

1985
'40 Under 40', Royal Institute of British Architects, London, UK

1986
'Recent Work', Gund Gallery, Harvard University, Cambridge, Massachusetts, USA

1987
'Four London Architects', 9H Gallery, London, UK

1988
'Correspondances', Institut Français d'Architecture in collaboration with 9H Gallery and British Council, Paris, France
'Gotoh Museum', Fabian Carlsson Gallery, London, UK

1989
'Latter Day Modernism', Camden Arts Centre, London, UK
'The British Week', Scala Gallery, Copenhagen, Denmark

1990
'David Chipperfield Architecture 1985–1990', Naples, Italy
'Metropole '90', Pavillon de l'Arsenal, Paris, France

1991
'David Chipperfield Architecture 1985–1991', Rome, Lisbon, Antwerp

1992
'Light and Architecture', Ingolstadt, Germany
'Projects in Japan – David Chipperfield', Ljubljana, Slovenia

1993
'Das Schloß' in collaboration with Peter St. John and Adam Caruso, Berlin, Germany
'David Chipperfield Architecture 1985–1992', Bolzano, Klagenfurt, Zurich

1994
'Three Houses', Galerie für Architektur, Hamburg, Germany

1995
'Houses, Offices and Museums', Aedes Gallery, Berlin, Germany

1997
'David Chipperfield', Jaroslav Fragner Gallery, Prague, Czech Republic
'Grassimesse', Museum für Kunsthandwerk, Leipzig, Germany
'Living Design Exhibition', British Council, London, UK
'New Works/Future Visions: An exhibition of British Architecture', São Paulo, Brazil

1998
'Architects as Designers', Kunstgewerbemuseum, Berlin, Germany
'Cities of the Future', traveling exhibition [Far East] for The British Council
'Contemporary Houses for Hamburg', Galerie Renate Kammer, Hamburg, Germany
'Futuropolis', The British Council, Worldwide

1999
'Architecture and Design of Second Modernism', Zentrum für Kunst und Medientechnologie, Karlsruhe, Germany
'Architecture for a New Century', The River and Rowing Museum, Henley-on-Thames, UK
Exhibition for the 6th Mies van der Rohe Award for European Architecture, Barcelona, Spain
Heinrich Tessenow Exhibition, Dresden and Hamburg, Germany
'Home', Glasgow, UK
'Little Buildings, exhibition at Purves & Purves showroom, London, UK
'Museums for a New Millennium: Concepts, Projects, Buildings', Art Centre Basel, Switzerland
'New British Architecture and Product Design', British Consulate, New York, New York, USA
'New Urban Environments', The Royal Academy, traveling exhibition
'Recent Projects', Galerie Renate Kammer, Hamburg, Germany
'The New Architecture', Venice, Italy

2000
'da! Architektur in Berlin 2000', exhibition by the Berliner Architektenkammer, Berlin, Germany
'Der Masterplan Museuminsel, ein Europäisches Projekt', Neues Museum, Berlin, Germany
'Stadt der Architektur. Architektur der Stadt. Berlin 1900–2000', Neues Museum, Berlin, Germany
'Summer Exhibition 2000', Royal Academy of Arts, London, UK

2001
'Building Inside the City', Suitcase Architecture, Berlin, Germany
'David Chipperfield', Cube Gallery, Manchester, UK
'Visions for a New Film Centre: Three Competition Schemes for the British Film Institute', Architecture Foundation, London, UK

2002
'David Chipperfield: Progetti in Italia', Palermo, Italy
Venice Biennale, Venice, Italy

Bold text denotes current staff

Brigitte Abele-Becker
Ricardo Aboim Inglez
Ram Ahronov
Erik Ajemian
Gabrielle Allam
Maha Alusi
Sandor Ambrus
Francesco Apuzzo [Berlin]
Motohisa Arai
Tomomi Araki
Sofia Arraiza Ruiz de Galarreta
Alberto Arraut
Nse Veronica Asuquo
Philipp Auer
Tamami Baba
Renata Bailey
Duncan Bainbridge
Conxita Balcells
Christoph Bartscherer [Berlin]
Alexander Bauer
Wolfgang Baumeister [Berlin]
Johannes Baumstark
Cesar Bautista
Nigel Beedles
Renato Benedetti
Jennifer Beningfield
Helen Beresford
Jitse van den Berg [Berlin]
Dagmar Bernady [Berlin]
Doreen Bernath
Veronique Berthon
Martina Betzold [Berlin]
Clemens Beyer [Berlin]
Cristiano Billia
Giuseppe Boezi
Franz Borho
Nathalie Bredella
Louise Brooker
Judith Brown
Daniela Brun [Berlin]
Andrew Bryce
Roberta Buccheri
Katja Buchholz [Berlin]
Clemens Bühring [Berlin]
Kord Büning-Pfaue
Janna Bunje [Berlin]
Mirjam von Busch [Berlin]
Tristan Butterfield
Cinzia Calandra
Amanda Callaghan
Patrick Campbell
Kevin Carmody
Darren Carroll
Jorge Carvalho
Natalie Cheng
David Chipperfield
Christian Clemares
Jan Coghlan
Simon Colebrook
Sarah Conrado
Mario Cottone
Melanie Crick
Peter Crompton
Paul Crosby
Michael Cullinan
Eamen Cushnahan
Valerie Dodge
Rachel Doherty
Luca Donadoni
Nipa Doshi
Maryla Duleba [Berlin]
Adrian Dunham [Berlin]
Ashley Dunn
Martin Ebert
Harald Eggers [Berlin]
Claudia Eggert

Martin Eglin
Mansour El-Khawad
Rebecca Elliot
Reenie Elliot
Petra Elm
Leyla Ergun
Christoph Felger [Berlin]
Dirk Feltz-Suessenbach
Massimo Fenati
Jens Finkensiep
David Finlay
Annette Flohrschütz [Berlin]
Jamie Fobert
An Fonteyne
Robin Foster
Olwen Fowler [Berlin]
Michael Freytag [Berlin]
Anke Fritzsch [Berlin]
Spencer Fung
Pablo Gallego Picard
Christian Galvao
Christopher Gaylord
Anna Momo Gediehn [Berlin]
Dieter von Gemmingen
Max Gentz [Berlin]
Bettina Georg [Berlin]
Carsten Gerhards [Berlin]
Alec Gillies
Jochen Glemser
Ulrich Goertz [Berlin]
Amos Goldreich
Jason Good
Michael Greville
Catherine Griffin
Suzanne Grills
Andrew Groarke
Regina Gruber
Dirk Gschwind [Berlin]
Manuel Gujber
Katja Gursch [Berlin]
Amelie Haake [Berlin]
Russ Hamilton
Ulrich Hannen [Berlin]
Andrew Hapgood
Chris Hardie
Andrea Hartmann [Berlin]
Takeshi Hayatsu
Joanna Healey
Jens Hecht [Berlin]
Isabelle Heide
Mette Heide
Klaus Heldwein [Berlin]
Christian Helfrich [Berlin]
Mercedes Henderson
Anne Hengst [Berlin]
Christoph Hesse
Barnaby Hewitt
Ian Hill
Christine Hohage
Christopher Howker
Anthony Hoyte
Josef Huber
Sue Hust
Ferruccio Izzo
Jean-Paul Jaccaud
Serena Jaff
Richard Jeffery
Victoria Jessen-Pike
Melissa Johnston
Hannah Jonas [Berlin]
Laura Joyce
Lynn Joyce
Stephania Kallos
Ina Kaminski
Judit Kampian
Emelie Karlsson
Isabel Karig [Berlin]
Ryoji Karube

Michael Kaune [Berlin]
Naoko Kawamura [Tokyo]
Thomas Keller
Eileen Kenny
Daniel Keppel [Berlin]
Rosemary Kerrison
Julie Keys
Essicka Kimberly
Darryl King
Wolf Kipper
Hikaru Kitai [Berlin]
Martin Kley
Stephan Klopp [Berlin]
Maren Köhler [Berlin]
Hartmut Kortner [Berlin]
Talar Kouyoumdjian
Akira Koyama
Nicola Kraemer
Nicolas Kretschmann [Berlin]
Merethe Hjorth Kristensen
Michael Kruse
Avril Ladbrook
Amy Lam
Madeleine Lambert
Gustav Langenskiöld
Harvey Langston-Jones
Cecilia Lau
Susan Le Good
Katrin Lembke [Berlin]
Martina Leucht [Berlin]
Reto Liechti
Genevieve Lilley
Antonio Lipthay
Andrew Llowarch
Holger Lohrmann
Daniel López-Pérez
Patrick McInerney
Rebecca McKay
Steve McKay
Ian McKnight
Ian McMillan [Berlin]
Alessandra Maiolino
Antonio Marín-Oñate
Karoline Markus
Carlos Martínez de Albornoz
Claudia Marx
Laurent Masmonteil
Marcus Mathias [Berlin]
Emanuele Mattutini
Julia Mauser [Berlin]
Werner Mayer-Biela [Berlin]
Robert Maxwell
Sabrina Melera-Morettini
Claire Meller
Christiane Melzer [Berlin]
Courtney Miller
Patricia Miyamoto
Guy Morgan-Harris
Haruo Morishima
Dieter Morscheck [Berlin]
Samatha Morse
Louise Muir
Sandra Mullaly
Harald Müller [Berlin]
Tina Sophie Müller
Cristina Murari
Takayuki Nakajima
Jeneva Nash
Ultan Nelson
Aubrey Newman
Angela Ng
Rentaro Nishimura
Kristina Nisson
Branka Njegic
Rik Nys
Nina Nysten
Lisa Obertautsch [Berlin]
Cecilia Obiol Cordón

Kaori Ohsugi
Pablo Olalquiaga Bescos
John Onken
Christian Pabst
Louise Parmenter
Julia Paterson-Todd
Johannes tho Pesch
Ignacio Peydro
Andrew Phillips [New York]
Gregory Phillips
Christof Piaskowski [Berlin]
Sashwin Pillai
Tracy Pinniger
Sergio Pirrone
Andrea Plaetzer-Guzmán [Berlin]
Janelle Plummer
Simon Pole
Caterina Polidoro
Naomi Porter
Billy Prendergast
Tatiana von Preussen [Berlin]
Gundula Proksch
John Puttick
Gene Pyo
Susanne Rabey
Mark Randel [Berlin]
David Regester
Martin Reichert [Berlin]
Andrea Reinacher
Donna Riley
John Robins
Óscar Rodríguez
Michele Rossi
Franziska Rusch [Berlin]
David Saik [Berlin]
Elke Saleina [Berlin]
Peter Sattrup
Christiane Sauer [Berlin]
Silvia Scarpat [Milan]
Tanya Scendeffy
Eva Schad [Berlin]
Stefan Scharf [Berlin]
Boris Schebesch [Berlin]
Annika Scherwen
Sven Schichor [Berlin]
Antonia Schlegel [Berlin]
Claudia Schmidt
Melanie Schubert
Heidrun Schuhmann
Silvana Schulze [Berlin]
Douglas Schwab
Alexander Schwarz [Berlin]
Lorna Scutt
Jonathan Sergison
Maurice Shapero
Hae Won Shin [Berlin]
Olivia Silverwood-Cope
Jordi Sinfreu Alay
Franziska Singer [Berlin]
Jennifer Singer
Vivienne Sizer
Zoka Skorup
Amalia Skoufoglou
Ewa Skrzypczak [Berlin]
Jonathan Slaughter
Graham Smith
Heeri Song
Alessandro Sorcini
Doreen Souradny [Berlin]
John Southall
Cordula Stach
Joachim Staudt
Tim Stefan
Florian Steinbächer [Berlin]
Evelyn Stern
Kurt Stern
Christian Stiller [Berlin]
Tobias Stiller [Berlin]

Claudia Stück
Mechthild Stuhlmacher
Henning Stummel
Jill Sudbury
Yuki Sumner
Tanya Szendeffy
Anat Talmor
Hannah Tame [Berlin]
Vincent Taupitz [Berlin]
Eddie Taylor
Cassius Taylor-Smith
Sara Tempesta
Phillip Thomanek
Axel Timm [Berlin]
Simon Timms
Sarah Titman
Jane Tobin
Katherina Troost [Berlin]
Hau Ming Tse
Aglaia Tsohas
Jonathan Tuckey
Elizabeth Tukker
Bernard Tulkens
Abigail Turin
Patrick Überbacher
Oliver Ulmer
Ma Prem Varta
Laura Vega Arroyo
Alan Vihant
Milka Vjestica
Philippe Volpe
Toshiki Wakisaka
Rosalind Walters
Kim Wang
Wilfried Wang
Thomas Weaver
Evan Webber
Jan Wesseling [Berlin]
Peter Westermann
Michele White
Thomas Wiedmann [Berlin]
Laura Wilkinson [Berlin]
Jonathan Wong
Sarah Wong
Mickey Woo
Susannah Woodgate
Nicole Woodman
Adrian Wright
Reiko Yamazaki
Oshri Yaniv
Toni Yli-Suvanto
Mirei Yoshida
David Yum
Ada Yvars Bravo
Giuseppe Zampieri
Er Ming Zhang
Ute Zscharnt [Berlin]
Mark Zogrotzski

Adolf Würth Art Gallery

Location:	Schwäbisch Hall, Germany
Competition Date:	1997
Client:	Sammlung Würth
Gross Floor Area:	3,000 m²
Team:	Franz Borho, Nathalie Bredella, Martin Kley, Alexander Schwarz, Henning Stummel
Structural Engineer:	Jane Wernick Associates: Jane Wernick
Models:	A-Models
Photographs:	Richard Davies
Bibliography:	'David Chipperfield 1991–1997', *El croquis*, no. 87, 1998, pp. 170–175

Air Frame Furniture [p. 34]

Manufacturer:	Cassina IXC. Ltd., Japan
Date:	From 1992
Team:	Jamie Fobert, Victoria Jessen-Pike, Rik Nys
Photographs:	Nacása & Partners
Bibliography:	'Metal Works', *Design*, October 1992, no. 526, pp. 19–21

Almere Blok 2

Location:	Almere, The Netherlands
Completion Date:	Due 2005
Client:	Almere Hart C.V.
Gross Floor Area:	16,000 m²
Contract Value:	£ 9,940,000
Team:	Martin Ebert, Martin Eglin, Chris Hardie, Ryoji Karube, Cordula Stach, Reiko Yamazaki
Contact Architect:	B&M den Haag: Rob Hilz
Structural Engineer:	Pieters Bouwtechniek: Jan Neele
Services Engineer:	Huygen Elwako: Stefan Hudepohl
Photographs:	David Chipperfield Architects

Ansaldo City of Cultures [p. 40]

Location:	Milan, Italy
Competition Date:	2000
Completion Date:	Due 2007
Client:	Comune di Milano
Production Directors:	Anna Fontanella, Giovanni Varesi
Gross Floor Area:	45,500 m²
Contract Value:	£ 45,000,000
Team:	*Competition in association with P+ARCH:* Renata Bailey, Patrick Campbell, Amos Goldreich, Takeshi Hayatsu, Ferruccio Izzo, Wolf Kipper, Amy Yee Ping Lam, Gustav Langenkiöld, Alessandra Maiolino, Tina Sophie Müller, Jonathan Slaughter, Henning Stummel, Anat Talmor, Hau Ming Tse, Oliver Ulmer, Nicole Woodman, Toni Yli-Suvanto, Giuseppe Zampieri
	P+ARCH: Francesco Fresa, Germán Fuenmayor, Gino Garbellini, Monica Tricario
	Preliminare: Ram Ahronov, Judith Brown, Kevin Carmody, Mario Cottone, Luca Donadoni, Amos Goldreich, Jason Good, Ferruccio Izzo, Serena Jaff, Alessandra Maiolino, Carlos Martinez de Albornoz, Sabrina Melera-Morettini, Sergio Pirrone, Silvia Scarpat, Sara Tempesta, Toni Yli-Suvanto, Giuseppe Zampieri
	Definitivo: Tomomi Araki, Luca Donadoni, Manuel Gujber, Akira Koyama, Emanuele Mattutini, Rentaro Nishimura, Sashwin Pillai, John Puttick, Silvia Scarpat, Melanie Schubert, Sara Tempesta, Patrick Überbacher, Oliver Ulmer, Laura Vega, Giuseppe Zampieri
	Esecutivo: Roberta Buccheri, Christian Clamares, Luca Donadoni, Akira Koyama, Claudia Lucchini, Emanuele Mattutini, Luca Parmeggiani, John Puttick, Oscar Rodriguez, Silvia Scarpat, Melanie Schubert, Sara Tempesta, Patrick Überbacher, Oliver Ulmer, Giuseppe Zampieri
Contact Architect:	F&P Architetti: Emanuele Bottigella, Barbara Camocini, Leopoldo Freyrie, Giovanni Gabardini, Francesco Leoni, Marco Pestalozza, Gianluca Saibene, Andrea Sormani
Structural Engineer:	Sajni e Zambetti s.r.l.: Alfio Sajni, Angelo Zambetti
Services Engineer:	Ove Arup & Partners: Ned Crowe, Emmanuelle Danisi, Emily Emerson, Tim Hanson, Martin Hockey, Ian Knowles, Richard Kuehn, Florence Lam, Andrew Sedgwick
	Manens Intertecnica: Dino Boni, Giorgio Marchioretti, Ugo Piubello, Gaetano Viero
Quantity Surveyor:	Tim Gatehouse Associates: Malcolm Atwill, Tim Gatehouse
	F&P Cantieri: Antonella Flores, Angela Todisco
Models:	A-Models
	David Chipperfield Architects
	Matthew Marchbank
	Vista models
Photographs:	Richard Davies
	Tom Miller
Bibliography:	'Milano 2001', *Casabella* supplement, June 2001, pp. 5–99
	'Chipperfield wins competition for museum', *Architectural Record*, February 2001, p. 47
	'Building Inside the City', *Selected Views* (Berlin: Suitcase Architecture, 2001), pp. 6–10
	'The City of Culture: International Design Competition', *Abitare*, special issue, no. 396, June 2000
	'Milan to Build Vast Cultural Complex in Industrial Buildings by 2004: The British Chipperfield Group wins for its tactful and practical plan', *The Art Newspaper*, June 2000, p. 11
	'Building Blocks, *Observer Magazine*, 11/6/00, pp. 20–24
	'La città delle culture', *Modo*, no. 204, May/June 2000, pp. 9–11
	'Città nelle Città', *Costruire*, May 2000, pp. 60–62
	'Concorso Internazionale per la Città delle Culture', *Abitare*, no. 394, April 2000, pp. 187–191
	'Città delle Culture', *Bauwelt*, 20/4/00, p. 5
	'Ansaldo: Ciudad de Culturas', *Pasajes de Arquitectura y Crítica*, no. 17, p. 5
	'New Contracts', *World Architecture*, no. 85, p. 34

Apartment in Kensington [p. 48]

Location:	London, UK
Completion Date:	1999
Client:	Carole and Neville Conrad
Gross Floor Area:	500 m²
Team:	An Fonteyne, Patrick McInerney, Billy Prendergast, Hau Ming Tse, Abigail Turin
Structural Engineer:	Dewhurst Macfarlane and Partners: Stephen Haskins
Services Engineer:	BDSP: Adrian James, John Perry
Quantity Surveyor:	Tim Gatehouse Associates: Malcolm Atwill, Tim Gatehouse
General Contractor:	Chisolm and Winch: Tony Winch
Photographs:	Hélène Binet

Barcelona City of Justice

Location:	Barcelona, Spain
Competition Date:	2002
Completion Date:	Due 2007
Client:	GISA
Gross Floor Area:	330,000 m²
Contract Value:	£130,000,000
Team:	*Competition in association with b720 Arquitectura:* Motohisa Arai, Tomomi Araki, Alberto Arraut, Alessandra Maiolino, Alexander Bauer, Johannes Baumstark, Doreen Bernath, Roberta Buccheri, Christian Clemares, Luca Donadoni, David Finlay, Jochen Glemser, Chris Hardie, Isabelle Heide, Serena Jaff, Michael Krusse, Reto Liechti, Takayuki Nakajima, Rentaro Nishimura, Ignacio Peydro, Sashwin Pillai, John Puttick, Jordi Sinfreu Alay, Jennifer Singer, Cordula Stach, Hau Ming Tse, Patrick Überbacher, Giuseppe Zampieri
Associate Architect:	b720 Arquitectura: Ana Bassat, Eduard Miralles, Magdelena Ostornol, Adriana Plasencia, Fermín Vázquez
Landscape Architect:	Manuel Colominas
Structural Engineer:	Jane Wernick Associates: Jane Wernick Obiol, Moya i Associats: Agusti Obiol
Services Engineer:	Ove Arup & Partners: Andrew Sedgwick Grupo JG: Joan Gallostra
Quantity Surveyor:	Tim Gatehouse Associates: Tim Gatehouse
Models:	b720 Arquitectura David Chipperfield Architects Matthew Marchbank Vista Models
Photographs:	Richard Davies
Bibliography:	'Barcelona City of Justice', *Architecture Today*, no. 128, May 2002, pp. 12–24

BBC Scotland [p. 56]

Location:	Glasgow, UK
Competition Date:	2001
Completion Date:	Due 2005
Client:	BBC Property
Gross Floor Area:	30,000 m²
Contract Value:	£47,000,000
Team:	*Competition:* Johannes Baumstark, Kevin Carmody, Mario Cottone, Paul Crosby, Andy Groarke, Manuel Gujber, Victoria Jessen-Pike, Kaori Ohsugi, Billy Prendergast, Hau Ming Tse, Oliver Ulmer, Jonathan Wong, Toni Yli-Suvanto, Giuseppe Zampieri *Stage B:* Paul Crosby, Martin Ebert, Andy Groarke, Victoria Jessen-Pike, Hau Ming Tse, Giuseppe Zampieri *Stage C:* Gabrielle Allam, Paul Crosby, Martin Ebert, David Finlay, Robin Foster, Andy Groarke, Victoria Jessen-Pike, Hau Ming Tse
Structural Engineer:	Jane Wernick Associates: Jane Wernick Faber Maunsell: Scobie Alivs, David Irving
Services Engineer:	Ove Arup & Partners: Graham Beadle, Gil Van Buuren, Nigel Clift, Darren Connolly, Fred Robinson, Alan Rowell, Andrew Sedgwick, Paul Sloman, Martin Surridge, Ian Thompson
Quantity Surveyor:	Gardiner & Theobald: John Meechan, Sandy Park, Roy Weller
Models:	David Chipperfield Architects Matthew Marchbank Vista Models
Photographs:	Richard Davies
Bibliography:	'Chipperfield back in the UK', *Building Design*, 25/5/01, p.1

BFI Film Centre [p. 62]

Location:	London, UK
Competition Date:	2001
Completion Date:	Due 2007
Client:	British Film Institute
Gross Floor Area:	20,000 m²
Contract Value:	£50,000,000
Team:	Louise Brooker, Victoria Jessen-Pike, Amy Lam, Carlos Martínez de Albornoz, Ignacio Peydro, Billy Prendergast
Quantity Surveyor:	Turner and Townsend: Martin Sudweeks
Models:	David Chipperfield Architects
Photographs:	Richard Davies
Bibliography:	'Let's do the show right here', *The Observer*, 30/12/01, p. 10 'Chipperfield lands star role in BFI's new South Bank centre', *Architects' Journal*, 23/8/01, p. 6

Bristol Centre for Performing Arts

Location:	Bristol, UK
Competition Date:	1996
Client:	Bristol Centre for the Performing Arts
Gross Floor Area:	21,000 m²
Team:	Philipp Auer, Renato Benedetti, Jan Coghlan, Alec Gillies, Victoria Jessen-Pike, Harvey Langston-Jones
Structural Engineer:	Ove Arup & Partners: Peter Ross, Toby Savage, Jane Wernick
Services Engineer:	Ove Arup & Partners: Tom Barker, Andrew Sedgwick
Quantity Surveyor:	Tim Gatehouse Associates: Tim Gatehouse
Models:	David Chipperfield Architects
Photographs:	Richard Davies
Bibliography:	'David Chipperfield Architects Centre for Performing Arts Bristol', *Architecture Design*, May/June 1999, no. 139, pp. 24–25 'What a Performance', *RIBA Journal*, May 1996, pp. 18–19 'David Chipperfield. Recent work', *2G International Architecture Review*, no. 1, 1997, pp. 106–111

Brownlow Mews

Location:	London, UK
Completion Date:	1987
Client:	Carroll, Dempsey & Thirkell
Gross Floor Area:	280 m²
Contract Value:	£100,000
Team:	John Southall
Structural Engineer:	Price and Myers: Nick Hanika
Services Engineer:	M.F. Rogers & Co.
Quantity Surveyor:	Michael F. Edwards & Associates: Mike O' Hanlen
General Contractor:	Pritchett Contractors: M.J. Bull, A. Newman
Photographs:	Richard Bryant
Bibliography:	'Brownlow Mews Conversion', *A+U*, October 1997, no. 205, pp. 103–106 'Studios Conversion', *Architects' Journal*, 15/7/87, pp. 24–29

Centre of World Cultures, Göteborg   [p. 68]

Location:	Göteborg, Sweden
Competition Date:	1999
Client:	Centre Of World Cultures
Gross Floor Area:	14,048 m²
Team:	Erik Ajemian, Tristan Butterfield, Mansour El-Khawad, Petra Elm, Takeshi Hayatsu, Mette Heide, Amy Lam, Daniel Lopez-Perez, Jonathan Slaughter, Hau Ming Tse, Oliver Ulmer, Jonathan Wong, Ada Yvars Bravo, Giuseppe Zampieri
Structural Engineer:	Jane Wernick Associates: Jane Wernick
Services Engineer:	Ove Arup & Partners: Andrew Sedgwick
Models:	A-Models
	David Chipperfield Architects
	Matthew Marchbank
Photographs:	Richard Davies
Bibliography:	'Vaggar och Terrassea', *Concept*, no. 6, August 1999, pp. 24–33

Church of the Pentecost

Location:	Milan, Italy
Competition Date:	2001
Client:	Diocese of Milan
Gross Floor Area:	1,600 m²
Team:	Kevin Carmody, Andy Groarke, Manuel Gujber, Takeshi Hayatsu, Carlos Martínez de Albornoz, Kaori Ohsugi, Bernard Tulkens, Giuseppe Zampieri
Structural Engineer:	Jane Wernick Associates: Jane Wernick
Services Engineer:	Ove Arup & Partners: Andrew Sedgwick
Quantity Surveyor:	Tim Gatehouse Associates: Tim Gatehouse
Models:	Matthew Marchbank
Photographs:	Richard Davies
Bibliography:	'Una chiesa per Milano', *Casabella* supplement, September 2001, pp. 3–35

Circus Restaurant

Location:	London, UK
Completion Date:	1997
Client:	Christopher Bodker
Gross Floor Area:	400 m²
Contract Value:	£800,000
Team:	Nathalie Bredella, Jean-Paul Jaccaud, Richard Jeffrey, Genevieve Lilley
Structural Engineer:	Dewhurst Macfarlane: Chris Akins, James O'Callaghan
Services Engineer:	Atelier Ten: Patrick Bellew, Clive Buckle, Scott Munro, Mark Smith
Quantity Surveyor:	M. Porter & Associates: Terry Magennis
General Contractor:	Pat Carter
Photographs:	Richard Bryant
Bibliography:	'Circus Restaurant – Leisure Time', *Abitare*, February 1999, pp. 72–75
	'David Chipperfield 1991–1997', *El croquis*, no. 87, 1998, pp. 86–91

Des Moines Public Library

Location:	Des Moines, Iowa, USA
Competition Date:	2001
Completion Date:	Due 2004
Client:	Public Library of Des Moines
Gross Floor Area:	110,000 m²
Contract Value:	£14,000,000
Team:	Doreen Bernath, Martin Ebert, Michael Kruse, Kaori Ohsugi
Associate Architect:	Herbert Lewis Kruse Blunck Architecture: Cal Lewis, Brian Lindgren, Paul Mankins
Landscape Architect:	Zimmer, Gunsul, Frasca Partnership: Brian McCarter, Don Miller
Structural Engineer:	Jane Wernick Associates: Jane Wernick
Services Engineer:	Ove Arup & Partners: Martin Hockney, Andrew Sedgwick, Nigel Tonks
General Contractor:	The Weitz Company, Des Moines: Robert Anderson
Photographs:	David Chipperfield Architects
Bibliography:	'Des Moines Library', *Architectural Record*, vol. 190, no. 6, June 2002, p. 36

Diagonal

Location:	Barcelona, Spain
Project Date:	2001
Completion Date:	Due 2004
Client:	Layetana/Llave de Oro
Gross Floor Area:	57,468 m² / 34,088 m² / 23,380 m²
Team:	Alberto Arraut, Mario Cottone, Luca Donadoni, Manuel Gujber, Serena Jaff, Emmanuele Mattutini, Takayuki Nakajima, Rentaro Nishimura, Kaori Ohsugi, Melanie Schubert, Sara Tempesta, Hau Ming Tse, Patrick Überbacher, Giuseppe Zampieri
Associate Architect:	b720 Arquitectura: Marc Abiol, Ana Bassat, Katrin Baumgarten, Itziar Imaz, Eduard Miralles, Magdalena Ostornol, Adriana Plasencia, Doris Sewczyk, Fermín Vázquez
Structural Engineer:	Obiol, Moya i Associats: Robert Brufau
Models:	b720 Arquitectura
	David Chipperfield Architects
	Matthew Marchbank
	Vista Models
Photographs:	Richard Davies

Diocesan Museum

Location:	Cologne, Germany
Competition Date:	1997
Client:	Diocese of Cologne
Gross Floor Area:	2,500 m²
Team:	Philipp Auer, Alexander Schwarz, Henning Stummel
Models:	A-Models
	David Chipperfield Architects
Photographs:	Richard Davies
Bibliography:	'Wettbewerb fur den Neubau des Kolner Diozesanmuseums', *Bauwelt*, 18/7/97, pp. 1518–1519
	'David Chipperfield 1991–1997', *El croquis*, no. 87, 1998, pp. 166–169

Dolce & Gabbana [p. 76]

Location:	Milan, Italy
Completion Date:	1999
Client:	Dolce & Gabbana
Gross Floor Area:	775 m²
Contract Value:	£900,000
Team:	Franz Borho, Andy Groarke, Takeshi Hayatsu, Stephania Kallos, Genevieve Lilley, Ian McKnight, Mark Randel
Contact Architect:	P+ARCH: Francesco Fresa, German Fuennnmayor, Gino Garbelli, Monica Tricario
Structural Engineer:	Studio Associato: Francesco Ferrari da Grado
Services Engineer:	Progetto EDI: Franco Gasparini, Mauro Triulzi
General Contractor:	Sice Previt: Arturo Caprio
Photographs:	Dennis Gilbert
Bibliography:	'All shopped out', *Architectural Design*, 2000 December, no. 148, pp. 48–51
	'Tienda Dolce & Gabbana en Milán', *Diseno Interior*, no. 109, pp. 136–141

Location:	Old Bond Street, London, UK
Completion Date:	1999
Gross Floor Area:	800 m²
Contract Value:	£1,400,000
Team:	Patrick Campbell, Andy Groarke, Takeshi Hayatsu, Patricia Miyamoto
Structural Engineer:	Michael Hadi Associates: Michael Hadi
Services Engineer:	BDSP: Carsten Ernst, Adrian James, Anjum Osman, John Perry
Quantity Surveyor:	Scott Chandler Robinson: Richard Robinson, Mike Scott
General Contractor:	EC Sames: Michael Boyle, Richard Kendall, Steve Murphy, John Quinn
Photographs:	Dennis Gilbert
Bibliography:	'Dolce & Gabbana London', *Architectural Record*, January 2001, pp. 116–118
	'Clothes are not enough: Dolce & Gabbana, Old Bond Street', *Blueprint*, no. 167, December 1999, pp. 39–41

Location:	Sloane Street, London, UK
Completion Date:	2000
Gross Floor Area:	400 m²
Contract Value:	£950,000
Team:	Mansour El-Khawad, Andy Groarke, Patricia Miyamoto, Jonathan Wong
Structural Engineer:	Michael Hadi Associates: Michael Hadi, Malachy McNamara
Services Engineer:	Environmental Engineering Partnership: Nigel Bowater, David Simcox
Quantity Surveyor:	Scott Chandler Robinson: Richard Robinson, Mike Scott
General Contractor:	EC Sames: Michael Boyle, Richard Kendall, Steve Murphy, John Quinn
Photographs:	Dennis Gilbert

Location:	Los Angeles, California, USA
Completion Date:	2000
Gross Floor Area:	523 m²
Contract Value:	£2,000,000
Team:	Andy Groarke, Amy Lam, Patricia Miyamoto
Contact Architect:	Gruen Associates: Pritish Gupta, Karl Swope, Ashok Vanmali
Structural Engineer:	WHL Consulting Engineers: Lauren Carpenter
General Contractor:	Hurst & Siebert: Scott Hurst
Photographs:	Dennis Gilbert
Bibliography:	'Chipperfield at the Rodeo', *World Architecture*, no. 94, April 2001, p. 26
	'Dolce & Gabbana's new look is set in stone', *Building*, vol. 266, no. 8166, 26/1/01, p. 16

Location:	New York, New York, USA
Completion Date:	2002
Gross Floor Area:	1,250 m²
Contract Value:	£2,000,000
Team:	Kevin Carmody, Andy Groarke, Melissa Johnston
Contact Architect:	Lou Batsch Architecture: Lou Batsch, Silvia Benelli
Structural Engineer:	Robert Silman Associates: Emily MacDonald, Nat Oppenheimer
Services Engineer:	AVCON Design Group: Tony Condurso, Ella Malkin
General Contractor:	Richter + Ratner Contracting Corp.: Mark Humphreys, Marialisa Walton
Photographs:	Dennis Gilbert

Dundee City Arts Centre

Location:	Dundee, UK
Competition Date:	1996
Client:	Dundee City Arts Centre
Gross Floor Area:	6,000 m²
Team:	Philipp Auer, Jan Coghlan, Pablo Gallego Picard, Harvey Langston-Jones, Patrick McInerney, Giuseppe Zampieri
Structural Engineer:	Ove Arup & Partners: Jane Wernick
Quantity Surveyor:	Tim Gatehouse Associates: Tim Gatehouse
Models:	David Chipperfield Architects
Photographs:	David Chipperfield Architects
Bibliography:	'David Chipperfield. Recent work', *2G International Architecture Review*, no. 1, 1997, pp. 100–105
	'David Chipperfield 1991–1997', *El croquis*, no. 87, 1998, pp. 156–161

Ernsting Service Center [p. 86]

Location:	Coesfeld-Lette, Germany
Completion Date:	2001
Client:	Kurt Ernsting
Gross Floor Area:	14,000 m²
Contract Value:	£15,000,000
Team:	Erik Ajemian, Jennifer Beningfield, Martin Ebert, Mansour El-Khawad, Jochen Glemser, Johannes tho Pesch, Heidrun Schuhmann, Henning Stummel, Peter Westermann
Contact Architect:	Schilling Architekten: Johannes Schilling, Jochem Vieren
Landscape Architect:	Wirtz International: Peter Wirtz
Structural Engineer:	Arup GmbH: Joachim Güsgen
	Jane Wernick Associates: Steve Haskins, Jane Wernick
Services Engineer:	Planungsgemeinschaft Haustechnik PGH: Hilmar Göhre, Albert Hoffmann, Thomas Scislowski
General Contractor:	E. Heitkamp GmbH: Heinz-Peter Dämgen, Uwe Galka, Marcus von Rüden
Models:	A-Models
	David Chipperfield Architects
Photographs:	Christian Richters
	Edmund Sumner
Bibliography:	'Ernsting's Family', *Bauwelt*, 16/8/02, pp. 12–17

Equipment Store, Brook Street

Location:	London, UK
Completion Date:	1991
Client:	Equipment UK (Joseph Ltd)
Gross Floor Area:	50 m²
Contract Value:	£200,000
Team:	Renato Benedetti
Structural Engineer:	Whitby, Bird & Partners
General Contractor:	T.E.C. Ltd.: Lawrence Noakes
Photographs:	Alberto Piovano
Bibliography:	Deyan Sudjic, *Equipment Stores: Architect David Chipperfield* (London: Wordsearch, 1992)

Figge Arts Center [p. 94]

Location: Davenport, Iowa, USA
Competition Date: 2000
Completion Date: Due 2004
Client: Davenport Museum of Art
Gross Floor Area: 10,000 m²
Contract Value: £19,700,000
Team: Johannes Baumstark, Franz Borho, Jochen Glemser, Reto Liechti,
                       Jennifer Singer, Hau Ming Tse
Contact Architect: Herbert Lewis Kruse Blunck Architecture: Doug Frey, Cal Lewis,
                       Jill Swanson
Structural Engineer: Jane Wernick Associates: Jane Wernick
Services Engineer: Ove Arup & Partners: Andrew Sedgwick
General Contractor: Russell Construction Company: James Russell
                       Pepper Construction: Mike Stensland
Models: A-Models
                       David Chipperfield Architects
Photographs: Richard Davies
Bibliography: 'London Firm Comes to Town', *The Leader*, 11/8/01, A1
                       'Art House', *Wallpaper**, no. 33, November 2000, p. 60
                       'Building Blocks [and Blobs]', *Observer Magazine*, 11/6/00, pp. 20–22
                       'Chipperfield has Designs on New Museum', *The Dispatch & The Rock
                       Island Argus*, 26/10/99, H5
                       'A Visit with David', *The Quad-City Times*, 24/10/99, 2A
                       'Architect Holds Crystal Image of New Museum', *The Dispatch &
                       The Rock Island Argus*, 4/10/99, A5
                       'Museum Project Moves Ahead', *The Quad-City Times*, 8/8/99, M1

First Church of Christ Scientist

Location: Richmond, UK
Completion Date: 1995
Client: First Church of Christ Scientist
Gross Floor Area: 450 m²
Contract Value: £282,000
Team: Renato Benedetti, Jonathan Sergison, Simon Timms
Structural Engineer: Whitby, Bird & Partners
General Contractor: Burgess Owen Property Services
Photographs: Margherita Spiluttini
Bibliography: 'Faith in the Community', *Architects' Journal*, 14/3/96, pp. 36–42
                       'Christian Science Church', *Church Building*, no. 41, 1996, pp. 34–35
                       'David Chipperfield. Recent work', *2G International Architecture Review*,
                       no. 1, 1997, pp. 26–33

Gormley Studio [p. 102]

Location: London, UK
Completion Date: 2003
Client: Anthony Gormley
Gross Floor Area: 1,000 m²
Team: Kevin Carmody, Paul Crosby, Andy Groarke, Victoria Jessen-Pike,
                       Kaori Ohsugi
Structural Engineer: Jane Wernick Associates: Jane Wernick, Tim George
Services Engineer: Environmental Engineering Partnership: Nigel Bowater, David Simcox
Quantity Surveyor: Capita Property Services: Brendan Henessey, Joe Lehane
General Contractor: Leonard Field
Models: David Chipperfield Architects
Photographs: David Chipperfield Architects
                       Richard Davies

Gotoh Museum [p. 106]

Location: Chiba, Japan
Completion Date: 1991
Client: Morio Gotoh
Gross Floor Area: 420 m²
Contract Value: £950,000
Team: Andrew Bryce, Jamie Fobert, Spencer Fung, Michael Greville,
                       Naoko Kawamura, Haruo Morishima, Alan Vihant
Contact Architect: Kamitani Spatial Planning: Yoshihiko Kamitani
Structural Engineer: Tanaka Teruaki Architects: Teruaki Tanaka
Services Engineer: Yasuda Setsubi Design: Shigeru Yasuda
General Contractor: Kasahara Koumuten: Shouzou Kasahara
Photographs: Hiroyuki Hirai
Bibliography: 'Chiba, Gotoh Museum', *Lotus*, no. 76, 1993, pp. 54–59
                       'Gotoh Museum', *Japan Architect Annual*, no. 2, Spring 1991–1992,
                       pp. 38–41
                       'Gotoh Museum', *Hi Fashion*, no. 200, December 1990, pp. 192–193
                       'Into the artistic and cultural '90s', *Fusion Planning*, no. 33, November
                       1990, p. 49
                       'David Chipperfield', *Nikkei Architecture*, December 1990, pp. 128–135
                       'Opening up the Japanese Honeypot,' *Building Magazine*, 19/01/90,
                       pp. 49–57
                       'Gotoh Museum', *Japan Architect*, no. 9, 1990, pp. 304–309
                       'Palladio Prize', *Picabia*, no. 6, 1990, p. 31
                       'Il Museuo Privato Gotoh a Tokyo', *Casabella*, no. 559, August 1989,
                       pp. 42–43
                       'Gotoh Museum', *AMC*, no. 23, December 1988, pp. 36–43
                       'Out of the '80s,' *Building Design*, November 1987, p. 32

Grassi Museum

Location: Leipzig, Germany
Project Date: 1994
Client: Stadt Leipzig Hochbauamt
Gross Floor Area: 35,000 m²
Team: Wolfgang Baumeister, Steven Brown, Mirjam von Busch,
                       Pablo Gallego Picard, Dirk Gschwind, Björn Hausmann,
                       Jean-Paul Jaccaud, Harvey Langston-Jones, Genevieve Lilley,
                       Christiane Sauer, Eva Schad, Stefan Scharf, Kai Schreiber, Eddie Taylor,
                       Hau Ming Tse
Contact Architect: Stefan Hemmann
Restoration Consultant: Julian Harrap Architects: Julian Harrap
Structural Engineer: Arup GmbH: David Lewis, Sarah Taylor
Services Engineer: Arup GmbH: David Lister, Michael Schmidt
Quantity Surveyor: Tim Gatehouse Associates: Tim Gatehouse
Bibliography: 'David Chipperfield. Recent work', *2G International Architecture Review*,
                       no. 1, 1997, pp. 70–75
                       'David Chipperfield 1991–1997', *El croquis*, no. 87, 1998, pp. 152–155

House in Galicia [p. 114]

Location: Corrubedo, Spain
Completion Date: 2002
Client: Evelyn Stern
Gross Floor Area: 210 m²
Contract Value: £200,000
Team: Louise Brooker, Luca Donadoni, Pablo Gallego Picard,
                       Victoria Jessen-Pike, Daniel López-Pérez, Carlos Martínez de Albornoz,
                       Tina Sophie Müller, Anat Talmor, Oliver Ulmer, Giuseppe Zampieri
Contact Architect: Carlos Fontenla, Carlos Seoane
Structural Engineer: Javier Estévez Cimadevila
General Contractor: Serinfra: Reinaldo Nuñez, Domingo Vidal
Models: David Chipperfield Architects
                       Matthew Marchbank
                       The Network: Richard Armiger
Photographs: Hélène Binet
Bibliography: 'Lust auf Urlaub pur', *DBZ*, December 1998, p. 30
                       'David Chipperfield: Contro la retorica del nuovo – 3 progetti',
                       Casabella, no. 638, October 1996, pp. 34–43
                       'David Chipperfield. Recent work', *2G International Architecture Review*,
                       no. 1, 1997, pp. 82–87
                       'David Chipperfield 1991–1997', *El croquis*, no. 87, 1998, pp. 148–151

House in New York

Location:	New York, New York, USA
Completion Date:	Due 2002
Client:	Nathaniel Rothschild
Gross Floor Area:	500 m²
Team:	Kevin Carmody, Andy Groarke, Victoria Jessen-Pike, Kaori Ohsugi, Andrew Phillips
Contact Architect:	Richard Lewis Architects: Jason Gold, Richard Lewis
Landscape Architect:	Miranda Brooks Landscape Design: Miranda Brooks
Structural Engineer:	Dewhurst Macfarlane and Partners: Russel Davies
General Contractor:	Townhouse Construction: Dennis Leftwick
Models:	David Chipperfield Architects
Photographs:	David Chipperfield Architects

Issey Miyake, Sloane Street

Location:	London, UK
Completion Date:	1985
Client:	Issey Miyake Limited
Gross Floor Area:	100 m²
Contract Value:	£72,000
Team:	Kenneth Armstrong
Structural Engineer:	Whitby, Bird & Partners
Services Engineer:	Dale & Goldfinger: R. Singer
General Contractor:	Shin & Setford: Richard Setford
Photographs:	Peter Cook
Bibliography:	'David Chipperfield: laden fur Issey Miyake', *Bauwelt*, 20/2/87, p. 230

Jazzie B House

Location:	London, UK
Project Date:	1993
Client:	Jazzie B
Gross Floor Area:	800 m²
Team:	Renato Benedetti, Harvey Langston-Jones, Genevieve Lilley
Structural Engineer:	Whitby, Bird & Partners
Quantity Surveyor:	Tim Gatehouse Associates: Tim Gatehouse
Photographs:	David Chipperfield Architects
Bibliography:	'David Chipperfield 1991–1997', *El croquis*, no. 87, 1998, pp. 122–125

Joseph, Sloane Avenue [p. 126]

Location:	Sloane Avenue, London, UK
Completion Date:	1997
Client:	Joseph Ltd.
Gross Floor Area:	600 m²
Contract Value:	£980,000
Team:	An Fonteyne, Patrick McInerney
Structural Engineer:	Dewhurst Macfarlane & Partners: Steven Haskins
Services Engineer:	BDSP: Adrian James, John Perry
Quantity Surveyor:	Tim Gatehouse Associates: Tim Gatehouse
General Contractor:	Heery International Limited: Keith Obourne
Models:	David Chipperfield Architects
Photographs:	Richard Bryant
Bibliography:	'Menswear Shop in London', *Detail*, no. 40, March 2000, pp. 222–224
	'Joseph', *Architecture in Greece*, no. 33, pp. 158–159
	'Mo'joe', *The Independent on Sunday Magazine*, 20/9/97, pp. 34–36
	'Bare-faced boom', *Blueprint*, no. 142, September 1997, p. 14
	'David Chipperfield 1991–1997', *El croquis*, no. 87, 1998, pp. 92–97

Kaistraße Studios [p. 132]

Location:	Düsseldorf, Germany
Completion Date:	1997
Client:	Helge Achenbach
Gross Floor Area:	3,300 m²
Contract Value:	£2,500,000
Team:	Jan Coghlan, Nicola Kraemer, Genevieve Lilley, Henning Stummel
Contact Architect:	Ingenhoven, Overdiek und Partner: Max Schultheis
Structural Engineer:	Arup GmbH: Andrew Butt, Eva Hinkers, David Lewis
Services Engineer:	DS Plan: Christian Fischer
General Contractor:	Strabag Bau AG: Horst Brandt
Models:	David Chipperfield Architects
	Matthew Marchbank
Photographs:	David Chipperfield Architects
	Christian Richters
Bibliography:	'Stirling Shortlist', *Building Design*, 6/11/98, p. 2
	'El Trío del Rin', *Arquitectura Viva*, May 1998, pp. 92–95
	Architecture 1998 (London: Ellipsis, 1998), pp. 36–39
	'Signature tuned', *Building Design*, 27/3/98, pp. 14–19
	Tijdschrift voor Architectuur (Munich: Ernst & Sohn, 1997), pp. 108–122
	Katrin Johnsen, *Medienmeile Hafen Düsseldorf* (Wuppertal: Müller + Busmann, 1997), pp. 58–61
	'David Chipperfield: Contro la retorica del nuovo – 3 progetti', *Casabella*, no. 638, October 1996, pp. 34–43
	'Karg und Klar', *VFA Profil*, January 1996, p. 30
	'David Chipperfield. Recent work', *2G International Architecture Review*, no. 1, 1997, pp. 76–81
	'David Chipperfield 1991–1997', *El croquis*, no. 87, 1998, pp. 106–113

Kao House

Location:	Boston, Massachusetts, USA
Project Date:	1993
Client:	John Kao
Gross Floor Area:	750 m²
Team:	Genevieve Lilley
Models:	The Network: Richard Armiger
Photographs:	Andrew Putler
Bibliography:	'David Chipperfield 1991–1997', *El croquis*, no. 87, 1998, pp. 130–133

Knight House	[p. 140]
Location:	Richmond, UK
Completion Date:	Stage One: 1989
Client:	Nick and Charlotte Knight
Gross Floor Area:	200 m²
Team:	Michael Cullinan, Jamie Forbert, Michael Greville, Cecilia Lau, Zoka Scorup
Structural Engineer:	Price & Myers: Nick Hannika
Quantity Surveyor:	Roger Rawlinson Associates: Roger Rawlinson
General Contractor:	B Maguire Building Services: Roger Morgan
Models:	David Chipperfield Architects
Photographs:	Martin Charles
	Alberto Piovanni
Bibliography:	'Space: The Final Frontier', *Tatler*, April 1997, pp. 156–161
	'Elogio alla luce', *Casa Vogue*, May 1994, pp. 50–57
	'Fiestre come astrazione', *Ville Giardini*, April 1994
	'Un sensibile minimalismo', *Interni*, no. 431, June 1993, pp. 82–87
	'Radikaler Umbau', *Architektur und Wohnen*, January 1993, pp. 46–49
	'In Control of the Modern', *World Architecture*, no. 16, 1992, pp. 66–69
	'Pur, Weiss und Wehnlich', *Häuser*, November 1991, pp. 148–151
	'Maison à Richmond', *Architecture d'Aujourd'hui*, April 1991, pp.124–126
	Premio Internazionale di Architettura (Milan: Electa, 1991), pp. 28–33
	'Haus Knight', *Bauwelt*, 12/9/90, pp.1934–1939
	'La Boite', *Techniques & Architecture*, June 1990, pp. 56–57
	'Casa Knight, Londra', *Domus*, no. 716, May 1990, pp. 56–63
	'White Knight', *Architectural Review*, April 1990, pp. 77–82
	Nikkei Architecture, 1990, pp. 128–135
	Biennal de Barcelona, October 1989, pp. 30–31

Completion Date:	Stage Two: 2001
Gross Floor Area:	170 m²
Team:	Paul Crosby, Russ Hamilton, Harvey Langston-Jones, Ian McKnight, Claire Meller, Henning Stummel, Anat Talmor, Ada Yvars Bravo
Landscape Architect:	Miranda Brooks, Alan Hart
Structural Engineer:	Michael Hadi Associates: Michael Hadi
Services Engineer:	BDSP Partnership: Alan Farnfield, Anjum Osman
Quantity Surveyor:	Tim Gatehouse Associates: Tim Gatehouse
General Contractor:	Chisholm and Winch: Simon Castle, Ali Rostami, Tony Winch
Models:	David Chipperfield Architects
	Matthew Marchbank
Photographs:	Hélène Binet
	Richard Davies
	Dennis Gilbert
Bibliography:	'Knight Vision', *The Sunday Telegraph Magazine*, 13/1/02, pp. 35–37
	'Subversion in the Suburbs', *Domus*, no. 843, December 2001, pp. 44–53
	'Knight's Tale', *Harpers Bazaar*, July 2001, p.142

Laban Centre	
Location:	London, UK
Competition Date:	1999
Client:	Laban Dance Centre
Gross Floor Area:	8,500 m²
Team:	An Fonteyne, Patrick McInerney, Mark Randel, Abigail Turin
Models:	Matthew Marchbank
Photographs:	Richard Davies

Landeszentralbank	[p. 150]
Location:	Gera, Germany
Completion Date:	2001
Client:	Landeszentralbank in den Freistaaten Sachsen und Thüringen
Gross Floor Area:	5,471 m²
Contract Value:	£17,000,000
Team:	Philip Auer, Petra Elm, Mansour El Kawad, Robin Foster, Isabelle Heide, Tina Müller, Gundula Proksch, Alexander Schwarz, Florian Steinbächer, Henning Stummel
Contact Architect:	Architekturbüro Krüger + Krüger: Klaus Krüger, Stefan Krüger
General Contractor:	IFB Horst Grün Gmbh: Ralph Kettenis
Landscape Architect:	Büro Thomanek & Duquesnoy: Karl Thomanek, Irene Winterstein, Annette Konrad, Jörg Michel, Hieltrud Dusquen
Structural Engineer:	Ingenieurbüro Joachim Trogisch: Hilmi Candogan, Joachim Trohisch
Services Engineer:	Ingenieurbüro Quirin: Hans Quirin, Astrid Quirin-Nied
Project Management:	BAL AG: Norbert Krenz, Johannes Bittcher
Artist:	Michael Craig-Martin
Models:	David Chipperfield Architects
	Mathew Marchbank
Photographs:	Richard Davies
	Stefan Müller

Literature Museum	[p. 158]
Location:	Marbach am Neckar, Germany
Competition Date:	2002
Completion Date:	Due 2005
Gross Floor Area:	3,500 m²
Contract Value:	£5,000,000
Client:	Deutsche Schillergesellschaft
Team:	Martina Betzold, Mirjam von Busch, Andrea Hartmann, Christian Helfrich, Franziska Rusch, Alexander Schwarz, Tobias Stiller, Vincent Taupitz
Structural Engineer:	Ingenieurgruppe Bauen: Gerhard Eisele
Quantity Surveyor:	Nanna Fütterer
Models:	Architektur-Modelle-Berlin: Gunter Schwob
Photographs:	David Chipperfield Architects
	Richard Davies
Bibliography:	Wettbewerbe Aktuell, *Sonderdruck*, March 2002, p. 97

Lockhart Saatchi House, Martha's Vineyard	
Location:	Martha's Vineyard, Massachusetts, USA
Project Date:	1997
Client:	Doris Lockhart Saatchi
Gross Floor Area:	200 m²
Team:	Victoria Jessen-Pike, Genevieve Lilley, Giuseppe Zampieri
Structural Engineer:	Kent Healy
General Contractor:	Doyle Construction: Joe Chapman, Neal Gallahan
Models:	A-Models: Christian Spencer-Davies
	David Chipperfield Architects
Photographs:	Richard Davies
Bibliography:	'House in Martha's Vineyard', *A+U*, 1998, no. 338, pp. 54–55

Lockhart Saatchi House, Umbria	
Location:	Umbria, Italy
Project Date:	1993
Client:	Doris Lockhart Saatchi
Gross Floor Area:	900 m²
Team:	Jan Coghlan, Genevieve Lilley, Rik Nys
Models:	The Network: Richard Armiger
Photographs:	Andrew Putler
Bibliography:	'David Chipperfield 1991–1997', *El croquis*, no. 87, 1998, pp. 126–129

Matsumoto Corporation Headquarters

Location:	Okayama, Japan
Completion Date:	1992
Client:	Matsumoto Corporation
Gross Floor Area:	4,172 m²
Contract Value:	£6,600,000
Team:	Renato Benedetti, Jan Coghlan, Jamie Fobert, Naoko Kawamura, Haruo Morishima, Rik Nys, Jonathan Sergison
Contact Architect:	Matsumoto Corporation: Hiroshi Asano
Structural Engineer:	Matsumoto Corporation: Heihachiro Kishida
Services Engineer:	Matsumoto Corporation: Akimasa Hatamoto
General Contractor:	Matsumoto Corporation: Toshiaki Uemura
Photographs:	Hiroyuki Hirai
Bibliography:	'Force tranquille: le siège de l'enterprise Matsumoto', *Architecture Interieure Cree*, October 1992, pp. 122–127
	'David Chipperfield 1991–1997', *El croquis*, no. 87, 1998, pp. 38–55

Moscow Shopping Village

Location:	Moscow, Russia
Project Date:	2002
Client:	Mercury Distribution
Gross Floor Area:	64,100 m²
Team:	Wolfgang Baumeister, Martina Betzold, Dirk Gschwind, Klaus Heldwein, Boris Schebesch
Models:	Architektur-Modelle-Berlin: Günter Schwob
Photographs:	David Chipperfield Architects

Museum of Modern Art [p. 168]

Location:	Bolzano, Italy
Competition Date:	2001
Client:	Autonomous Province Bolzano – South Tyrol
Gross Floor Area:	8,000 m²
Contract Value:	£10,000,000
Team:	Johannes Baumstark, Franz Borho, Martin Ebert, Mansour El-Khawad, Jochen Glemser, Christoph Hesse, Gustav Langenskiöld, Tina Sophie Müller, Johannes tho Pesch, Hau Ming Tse, Giuseppe Zampieri
Structural Engineer:	Jane Wernick Associates: Jane Wernick
Services Engineer:	Ove Arup & Partners: Andrew Sedgwick
Quantity Surveyor:	Tim Gatehouse Associates: Tim Gatehouse
Models:	David Chipperfield Architects
	Vista Models
Photographs:	Richard Davies
Bibliography:	'2. Preis', *Wettbewerbe Aktuell*, June 2001, pp. 46–47
	'Museum für Modern Kunst', *Bauwelt*, 27/4/01, p. 8

National Gallery of Modern Art

Location:	Rome, Italy
Competition Date:	2000
Client:	Soprintendenza Speciale Arte Contemporanea
Gross Floor Area:	7380 m²
Team:	Ricardo Aboim Inglez, Renata Bailey, Franz Borho, Luca Donadoni, Amos Goldreich, Jason Good, Thomas Keller, Gustav Langenskiöld, Sabrina Melera-Morettini, Anat Talmor, Hau Ming Tse, Oliver Ulmer, Nicole Woodman, Toni Yli-Suvanto, Giuseppe Zampieri
Associate Architect:	Alberto Izzo and Partners: Ferruccio Izzo
Structural Engineer:	Jane Wernick Associates: Jane Wernick
Services Engineer:	Ove Arup & Partners: Andrew Sedgwick
Quantity Surveyor:	Tim Gatehouse Associates: Tim Gatehouse
Models:	A-Models
	David Chipperfield Architects
Photographs:	Richard Davies

Natural History Museum

Location:	Los Angeles, California, USA
Competition Date:	2002
Client:	Natural History Museum, Los Angeles
Gross Floor Area:	50,000 m²
Team:	Motohisa Arai, Johannes Baumeister, Christiano Billia, Jens Finkensiep, Jochen Glemser, Regina Gruber, Chris Hardie, Reto Liechti, Takayuki Nakajima, Rentaro Nishimura, Caterina Polidoro, John Puttick, Giuseppe Zampieri
Structural Engineer:	Jane Wernick Associates: Jane Wernick
Services Engineer:	Ove Arup & Partners: Andrew Sedgwick
Quantity Surveyor:	Tim Gatehouse Associates: Tim Gatehouse
Models:	David Chipperfield Architects
	Matthew Marchbank
Photographs:	David Chipperfield Architects

Neues Museum [p. 172]

Location:	Berlin, Germany
Competition Date:	1997
Completion Date:	Due 2009
Client:	Stiftung Preußischer Kulturbesitz represented by Bundesamt für Bauwesen und Raumordnung
Gross Floor Area:	20,500 m²
Contract Value:	£97,000,000
Team:	*Competition:* Philipp Auer, Franz Borho, Nathalie Bredella, An Fonteyne, Robin Foster, Mario Hohmann, Martin Kley, Harvey Langston-Jones, Patrick McInerney, Ian McKnight, Claudia Marx, Guy Morgan-Harris, Rik Nys, Mark Randel, Eva Schad, Alexander Schwarz, Haewon Shin, Graham Smith, Henning Stummel, Giuseppe Zampieri, Mark Zogrotzski
	Preliminary design: Isabel Karig, Harald Müller, Mark Randel, David Saik, Eva Schad, Alexander Schwarz, Florian Steinbächer
	Final design: Janna Bunje, Adrian Dunham, Harald Eggers, Annette Flohrschütz, Michael Freytag, Anke Fritzsch, Isabelle Heide, Isabel Karig, Christiane Melzer, Harald Müller, Mark Randel, Martin Reichert, Franziska Rusch, Eva Schad, Alexander Schwarz, Christian Stiller
	Working drawings: Daniela Brun, Katja Buchholz, Annette Flohrschütz, Michael Freytag, Anke Fritzsch, Ulrich Goertz, Anne Hengst, Michael Kaune, Marcus Mathias, Werner Mayer-Biela, Harald Müller, Martin Reichert, Franziska Rusch, Elke Saleina, Eva Schad, Alexander Schwarz, Doreen Souradny
Landscape Architect:	Levin Monsigny: Martina Levin, Luc Monsigny
Structural Engineer:	Ingenieurgruppe Bauen: Gerhard Eisele
Services Engineer:	Jaeger, Mornhinweg + Partner: Xavier Calvo, Ernst Göppel Kunst und Museumsschutz: Jörg-Dieter Haack, Lutz Henske, Thorsten Schöne
History Consultant:	Julian Harrap Architects: Julian Harrap, Caroline Wilson
Restoration Consultant:	Pro Denkmal: Uwe Bennke, Janna Bunje, Wolfgang Frey, Heiner Sommer
Quantity Surveyor:	Nanna Fütterer
Site Supervision:	Lubic & Woehrlin Architekten: Alexander Lubic, Stefan Woehrlin
Models:	A-Models
	Rüdiger Hammerschmidt
	James McKinnan
	Gareth Paterson
Photographs:	Jörg von Bruchhausen
	David Chipperfield Architects
	Hans Joosten
	Planungsgruppe Museuminsel
	Roman März
	Stefan Müller
Bibliography:	*Die Baumeister des Neuen Berlin* (Berlin: Nicolaische Verlagsbuchhandlung GmbH, 2001), pp. 198–201
	'Langsam tickender Zeitmesser', *Bauwelt*, 3/11/00, pp. 20–25
	'Stadt der Architektur – Architektur der Stadt', *Bauwelt*, 14/7/00, p. 2
	'Museums Galore', *The Economist*, 19/2/00, pp. 82–85
	Masterplan Museumsinsel Berlin – Ein Europäisches Projekt (Berlin: G+H Verlag, 2000), pp. 76–80
	Wege zum Masterplan (Berlin: G+H Verlag, 2000), pp. 28–31
	'Berlin Island Job', *Building Design*, 18/6/99, p. 6
	Vittorio Magnago Lampugnani (ed.), *Museums for a new Millennium* (London: Prestel, 1999), pp. 174–179
	'Museuminsel', *Casabella*, no. 657, June 1998, pp. 46–51
	'Haus Proud', *Guardian Weekend*, 11/4/98, p. 53
	'Gedeckte Bruken für den Raschen Kunstkonsum', *Art – Das Kunstmagazin*, January 1998, p.103
	'Chipperfield Attempts to Heal the Prussian Patient', *World Architecture*, no. 63, 1998, p. 98
	Berlin – Visionen Werden Realitat (Berlin: JOVIS, 1998), p. 41
	Bau und Raum Jahrbuch 1998 (Osterfildern-Ruit: Hatje Cartz Verlag, 1998), pp. 132–141
	'Restoring a Torso', AV Monograph – Museums of Art, 1998, pp. 94–103
	'Entscheidung Neues Museum in Berlin', *Bauwelt*, 5/12/97, p. 2565
	'Chipperfield beats Gehry in Berlin bid for Museum', *Building Design*, 14/11/97, p. 3
	'Museuminsel', *Architecture d'Aujourd'hui*, February 1995, p. 81
	'Museumsinsel', *Domus Dossier*, no. 3, 1995, pp. 14–27
	'Idee per il centro di Berlino', *Casabella*, no. 615, September 1994, pp. 30–43
	'David Chipperfield. Recent work', *2G International Architecture Review*, no. 1, 1997, pp. 88–93
	'David Chipperfield 1991–1997', *El croquis*, no. 87, 1998, pp. 176–185

New Entrance Building [p. 188]

Location:	Berlin, Germany
Completion Date:	Due 2009
Client:	Stiftung Preußischer Kulturbesitz
Gross Floor Area:	10,500 m²
Contract Value:	£35,000,000
Team:	*Scheme Design:* Franz Borho, Adrian Dunham, Mansour El-Khawad, Carsten Gerhards, Mette Heide, Gustav Langenskiöld, Christof Piaskowski, Mark Randel, Hau Ming Tse, Oliver Ulmer, Tony Yli-Suvanto
	Preliminary Design: Wolfgang Baumeister, Mirjam von Busch, Christoph Felger, Dirk Gschwind
	Final Design: Wolfgang Baumeister, Mirjam von Busch, Christoph Felger, Dirk Gschwind, Mark Randel, Alexander Schwarz
Landscape Architect:	Levin Monsigny: Martina Levin, Luc Monsigny
Structural Engineer:	Ingenieurgruppe Bauen: Frank Arnold, Alexander Rausch
Services Engineer:	Jaeger, Mornhinweg + Partner: Xavier Calvo, Ernst Göppel Kunst und Museumsschutz: Wolfgang Fuchs, Wolfgang Liebert, Dirk Pankau, Lutz Henske
Quantity Surveyor:	Nanna Fütterer
Models:	Rüdiger Hammerschmidt
	Architektur-Modelle-Berlin: Gunter Schwob
Photographs:	David Chipperfield Architects
	Richard Davies
Images:	3D Works: Markus Groeteke

Olivetti Hypo-Bank

Location:	No site – theoretical project
Project Date:	1994
Team:	Jamie Fobert, Madeleine Lambert
Services Engineer:	Ove Arup & Partners: Jane Wernick
Models:	The Network: Richard Armiger
Photographs:	Andrew Putler
Bibliography:	'Olivetti Projectos, O Banco', *Architecti*, Winter 1996, pp. 72–79
	'Three designs for Banks by Three European Architects', *Domus*, no. 764, October 1994, pp. 20–23
	'David Chipperfield. Recent work', *2G International Architecture Review*, no. 1, 1997, pp. 62–67
	'David Chipperfield 1991–1997', *El croquis*, no. 87, 1998, pp. 134–1137

Oosterdokseiland Amsterdam Hotel

Location:	Amsterdam, The Netherlands
Completion Date:	Due 2005
Client:	MAB
Gross Floor Area:	26,500 m²
Contract Value:	£20,000,000
Team:	Gabrielle Allam, Regina Gruber, Isabelle Heide, Victoria Jessen-Pike, Laurent Masmonteil, Billy Prendergast
Contact Architect:	B+M: Rob Hilz
Landscape Architect:	Agence Ter: Henri Brava
Structural Engineer:	Arcadis: Dieneke Grimmelius
Services Engineer:	Deerns: Xavier Crolla
Quantity Surveyor:	MAB
Models:	David Chipperfield Architects
Photographs:	David Chipperfield Architects
	'David Chipperfield. Recent work', *2G International Architecture Review*, no. 1, 1997, pp. 62–67
	'David Chipperfield 1991–1997', *El croquis*, no. 87, 1998, pp. 134–1137

Palace of Justice [p. 198]

Location: Salerno, Italy
Competition Date: 1999
Completion Date: Due 2004
Client: Comune di Salerno
Gross Floor Area: 71,400 m²
Contract Value: £35,000,000
Team: *Competition:* Erik Ajemian, Patrick Campbell, David Chipperfield, Martin Ebert, Mansour El-Khawad, Petra Elm, Amos Goldreich, Jason Good, Rachel Hart, Mette Heide, Ferruccio Izzo, Harvey Langston-Jones, Daniel López-Peréz, Alessandra Maiolino, Claire Meller, Tina Sophie Müller, Louise Parmenter, Jonathan Slaughter, Henning Stummel, Hau Ming Tse, Oliver Ulmer, Jonathon Wong, Nicole Woodman, Mirei Yoshida, Ada Yvars Bravo, Giuseppe Zampieri
  Preliminare: Renata Bailey, David Chipperfield, Amos Goldreich, Jason Good, Ferruccio Izzo, Daniel López-Peréz, Alessandra Maiolino, Sabrina Melera-Morettini, Luca Piscitelli, Jonathan Slaughter, Hau Ming Tse, Oliver Ulmer, Toni Yli-Suvanto, Giuseppe Zampieri
  Definitivo: Ram Ahronov, Judith Brown, Patrick Campbell, David Chipperfield, Mario Cottone, Luca Donadoni, Amos Goldreich, Jason Good, Alessandra Maiolino, Sabrina Melera-Morettini, Claire Meller, Kord Buening-Pfaue, Sara Tempesta, Oliver Ulmer, Amy Yee Ping Lam, Toni Yli-Suvanto, Giuseppe Zampieri
  Esecutivo: Ram Ahronov, Sofia Arraiza Ruiz de Galarreta, Judith Brown, David Chipperfield, Mario Cottone, Jason Good, Manuel Gujber, Alessandra Maiolino, Sara Tempesta, Oliver Ulmer, Toni Yli-Suvanto, Giuseppe Zampieri
Associate Architect: Alberto Izzo & Partners: Maurizio D'Andrea, Carlo Funel, Fabio Gorga, Ferruccio Izzo, Rosario Manzo, Giuseppe Monzo, Barbara Pulli
Contact Architect: Alberto Izzo and Partners: Maurizio d'Andrea, Ferruccio Izzo
Landscape Architect: Wirtz International: Johan Leenaerts, Peter Wirtz
Structural Engineer: Jane Wernick Associates: Stephen Haskins, Jane Wernick
  Pasquale Giancane: Domenico Giancane, Pasquale Giancane
Services Engineer: Ove Arup & Partners: Martin Hockey, Florence Lam, Andrew Sedgwick
  Aniello Castaldo: Aniello Castaldo, Maria Castaldo, Paolo Cicala
Safety Engineer: Ennio Campagnuolo
Quantity Surveyor: Tim Gatehouse Associates: Malcolm Atwill, Tim Gatehouse
Artists: Joseph Kosuth
  Ben Jakober & Yannick Vu
  Franco Scognamiglio
Models: A-Models
  David Chipperfield Architects
  Matthew Marchbank
  Millennium Models
Photographs: Richard Davies
Bibliography: 'The Ideas Merchants of Venice', *Building Design*, 23/6/00, p. 17
  'Building Blocks [and Blobs]', *Observer Magazine*, 11/6/00, pp. 20–24
  'Salerno: Un'altra Italia', *Giornale dell' Archiettura*, no. 22, October 1999, pp. 1, 12

Pasquale Bruni Showroom [p. 210]

Location: Milan, Italy
Completion Date: 2001
Client: Pasquale Bruni SPA
Gross Floor Area: 160 m²
Contract Value: £750,000
Team: Victoria Jessen-Pike, Billy Prendergast
Contact Architect: Mario Filocca Architect: Mario Filocca
Structural Engineer: Dewhurst Macfarlane: Philip Wilson
Services Engineer: Amman Progetti: Luigi Cova
General Contractor: Mario Filocca
Models: David Chipperfield Architects
Photographs: Ornela Sancassani
Bibliography: 'Set in stone', *Frame* 27, July/August 2002, pp. 66–71
  'Showroom Pasquale Bruni,' *Abitare*, April 2002, pp. 220–223

Private House [p. 214]

Location: Berlin, Germany
Completion Date: 1996
Gross Floor Area: 1,450 m²
Team: Philipp Auer, Brigitte Becker, Stevan Brown, Jamie Fobert, Mark Randel, Eva Schad, Mia Sclegel, Mechthild Stuhlmacher, Henning Stummel
Contact Architect: M.J. Zielinski
Landscape Architect: Katrin Lesser Sayrac
Structural Engineer: Rene Becker, Gotthard Gonsior
Services Engineer: Büro Fitz: Hans Jürgen Fitz
General Contractor: Firma Bargenda Bau: Eberhard Bargenda
Artist: Ed Ruscha
Models: The Network: Richard Armiger
Photographs: David Chipperfield Architects
  Richard Davies
  Stefan Müller
Bibliography: Michael Jenner and Meinhard von Gerkan (eds.), *New British Architecture in Germany* (London: Prestel, 2000), pp. 86–89
  Paco Arsenio Cerver, Casas Sorprendentes (Barcelona: Loft Publications, 1999), pp. 36–41
  'Private House in Germany', *A+U*, no. 338, November 1998, p. 38–55
  'Private House in Germany', *Domus*, no. 795, August 1997, pp. 49–55
  'David Chipperfield. Recent work', *2G*, no. 1, 1997, pp. 54–61
  'David Chipperfield 1991–1997', *El croquis*, no. 87, 1998, pp. 74–81

River and Rowing Museum [p. 226]

Location: Henley-on-Thames, UK
Completion Date: 1997
Client: The River and Rowing Museum Foundation
Gross Floor Area: 2,300 m²
Contract Value: £5,000,000
Team: Renato Benedetti, Peter Crompton, Rebecca Elliot, Spencer Fung, Alec Gillies, Victoria Jessen-Pike, Harvey Langston-Jones, Genevieve Lilley, Andrew Llowarch, Rik Nys, John Onken, Peter Andreas Sattrup, Silvana Schulze, Maurice Shapiro, Mechthild Stuhlmacher, Simon Timms
Landscape Architect: Whitelaw Turkington: Paul Barrett, Lindsay Whitelaw
Structural Engineer: Whitby, Bird & Partners: Mark Phillip, Ian Scott
Services Engineer: Furness Green Partners: John Eames, Stephen Green
Quantity Surveyor: Davis Langdon Everest: Stephen Bugg, Alan Davis, Nigel New
General Contractor: Norwest Holst Construction Limited: Phil Bean, Robert Drury, Clive Percival, Mike Robeson, Terry Wood
Models: The Network: Richard Armiger
Photographs: Richard Bryant
  Richard Davies
  Dennis Gilbert
  Ben Johnson
  Margherita Spiluttini
Bibliography: 'Ritorno al Legno', *Costruire*, May 2000, p. 146
  'Modernizing Timber Design', *Canadian Architect*, November 1999, p. 14
  'Museum in Henley-on-Thames', *Detail*, July/August 1999, pp. 827–833
  Royal Fine Art Commission Award, *Building Design*, 11/6/99, p. 3
  'Royal Fine Art Commission Award', *Architects' Journal*, 10/6/99
  6th Mies van der Rohe Award For European Architecture (Barcelona: Fundació Mies van der Rohe, 1999), pp. 38–41
  'River & Rowing Museum,' *Lotus 102*, 1999, p. 99–103
  First Thoughts (London: Wordsearch, 1999), p. 29
  'Welcome to the class of 1998', *Building Design*, 2/10/98, p. 12
  'Toitures à Pentes', *AMC*, no. 89, May 1998, pp. 70–73
  Architecture 1998 (London: Ellipsis, 1998), pp. 36–39
  Philip Jodidio (ed.), *Contemporary European Architects, vol. 6* (London: Taschen, 1998), pp. 82–89
  'Verankert, aber nicht Verwurselt', *Bauwelt*, 12/9/97, pp.1918–1923
  'Museo del Fiume e del Remo', *Abitare*, no. 365, September 1997, pp.140–146
  'Tradition and Innovation – Timber as Rainscreen Cladding', *Arq*, Summer 1997, pp. 54–63
  'Pulling Together', *Architectural Review*, January 1997, pp. 31–35
  'Going with the Flow', *Perspectives on Architecture*, January 1997, pp. 50–53
  New Work, Future Visions (London: RIBA Architecture Centre, 1997), p. 27
  'Henley's Trojan Horse', *Blueprint*, September 1996, no. 131, pp. 50–52
  'Theoretical Practice', *UME*, no. 1, pp. 26–35
  'David Chipperfield. Recent work', *2G International Architecture Review*, no. 1, 1997, pp. 40–53
  'David Chipperfield 1991–1997', *El croquis*, no. 87, 1998, pp. 53–63

Royal Collections Museum   [p. 240]

Location:	Madrid, Spain
Competition Date:	1999
Client:	Registro del Patrimonio Nacional
Gross Floor Area:	30,000 m²
Team:	Patrick Campbell, Luca Donadoni, Jason Good, Takeshi Hayatsu, Mette Heide, Gustav Langenskiöld, Daniel López-Pérez, Alessandra Maiolino, Jonathan Slaughter, Hau Ming Tse, Jonathan Tuckey, Oliver Ulmer, Oshri Yaniv, Ada Yvars Bravo, Guiseppe Zampieri
Structural Engineer:	Jane Wernick Associates: Jane Wernick
Services Engineer:	Ove Arup & Partners: Andrew Sedgwick
Quantity Surveyor:	Tim Gatehouse Associates: Tim Gatehouse
Models:	A-Models
	David Chipperfield Architects
	Matthew Marchbank
Photographs:	Richard Davies

Salerno Old Town

Location:	Salerno, Italy
Competition Date:	1998
Client:	Comune di Salerno
Gross Floor Area:	26,000 m²
Team:	Patrick Campbell, Luca Cuzzolin, Natalie De Leval, An Fonteyne, Tim Greensmith, Andy Groarke, Takeshi Hayatsu, Barnaby Hewitt, Anthony Hoyte, Harvey Langston-Jones, Daniel López-Pérez, Andrew Phillips, Hau Ming Tse, Ada Yvars Bravo, Giuseppe Zampieri
Associate Architect:	Alberto Izzo and Partners: Ferruccio Izzo
Structural Engineer:	Jane Wernick Associates: Jane Wernick
Quantity Surveyor:	Tim Gatehouse Associates: Tim Gatehouse
Models:	David Chipperfield Architects
	Mathew Marchbank
Photographs:	Richard Davies
	Tom Miller
Bibliography:	'Salerno: Un'altra Italia', *Giornale dell' Archiettura*, no. 22, October 1999, pp. 1, 12
	'Progetti per il centro antico di Salerno', *Casabella*, no. 667, May 1999, pp. 22–31

San Michele Cemetery   [p. 250]

Location:	Venice, Italy
Competition Date:	1998
Completion Date:	*Stage One:* Due 2006
	Stage Two: Due 2013
Client:	Commune di Venezia
Gross Floor Area:	*Stage One:* 16,000 m²
	Stage Two: 500,000 m²
Contract Value:	*Stage One:* £ 14,000,000
	Stage Two: £ 28,000,000
Team:	*Competition:* Giuseppe Boezi, Franz Borho, Mansour El-Khawad, An Fonteyne, Takeshi Hayatsu, Joseph Huber, Harvey Langston-Jones, Genevieve Lilley, Holger Lohrmann, Daniel López-Pérez, Steven McKay, Ian McKnight, Nina Nysten, Gundula Prosc, Donna Riley, Peter Andreas Sattrup, Silvana Schulze, Alexander Schwarz, Abigail Turin, Giuseppe Zampieri
	Preliminare: Erik Ajemian, Ada Yvars Bravo, Petra Elm, Mette Heide, Daniel López-Pérez, Alessandra Maiolino, Hau Ming Tse, Oliver Ulmer, Giuseppe Zampieri
	Definitivo: Mario Cottone, Luca Donadoni, Serena Jaff, Carlos Martínez de Albornoz, Sabrina Melera-Morettini, Sara Tempesta, Toni Yli-Suvanto, Jonathan Wong, Giuseppe Zampieri
	Esecutivo: Tomomi Araki, Judith Brown, Mario Cottone, Serena Jaff, Sabrina Melera-Morettini, Giuseppe Zampieri
Production Director:	Franco Gazzarri
Landscape Architect:	Wirtz International: Peter Wirtz
Structural Engineer:	Jane Wernick Associates: James Packer, Jane Wernick
	Forcellini Breda Scarpa: Gianni Breda, Francesco Marson, Romeo Scarpa
Services Engineer:	Ove Arup & Partners: Heather Carter, Andrew Sedgwick
	Studio Associato Vio: Alessandra Vio, Diego Danieli
Quantity Surveyor:	Tim Gatehouse Associates: Malcolm Atwill, Andrea Faggiou, Tim Gatehouse
Geologist:	Cesare Rizzetto
Geotechnical Consultant:	Studio Geotechnic Italiano: Paolo Ascari, Claudio Mascardi
Models:	David Chipperfield Architects
	Mathew Marchbank
	Millennium Models
	The Network: Richard Armiger
	Richard Threadgill Associates
Photographs:	Alessandra Chemollo
	Richard Davies
Bibliography:	'The Venetian Way of Death', *Blueprint*, no. 187, September 2001, pp. 51–54
	'Death in Venice', *Blueprint*, no. 170, March 2000, p. 13
	'Death in Venice', *Independent on Sunday*, 27/2/00, pp. 28–29
	'Chippo's Venice 'Lives'', *Architects' Journal*, 10/2/00, p. 4
	'Competition for the Extension of the San Michele Cemetery in Isola', *Domus*, no. 817, 7/8/99, pp. 42–45
	'Floating Ideas', *Blueprint*, no. 160, April 1999, p. 18
	'Tomb it may Concern', *FX*, November 1998, pp. 42–48
	'Tod in Venedig', *Baumeister*, September 1998, p. 10
	'Preis David Chipperfield London', *Bauwelt*, 7/8/98, pp.1676–1677
	'Tomb with a View', *The Guardian G2*, 6/7/98, pp.10–11
	'Chipperfield takes on death in Venice', *Architects' Journal*, 6/8/98, p. 10
	'Caronte en Venecia', *Arquitectura Viva*, May 1998, pp. 78–79

Slegten & Toegemann Ceramics   [p. 260]

Manufacturer:	Slegten & Toegemann, Belgium
Date:	1996
Team:	Victoria Jessen-Pike, Rik Nys
Photographs:	Christian Aschman

Social Housing   [p. 264]

Location:	Madrid, Spain
Completion Date:	Due 2004
Client:	Empresa Municipal de la Vivienda
Gross Floor Area:	11,698 m²
Contract Value:	£ 4,205,588
Team:	Kevin Carmody, Andy Groarke, Takeshi Hayatsu, Kaori Ohsugi, Bernard Tulkens, Jonathan Wong, Mark Zogrotzski
Contact Architect:	Matías Manuel Santolaya Heredero, José María Fernández-Isla
Models:	Matthew Marchbank
Photographs:	David Chipperfield Architects
	Richard Davies

Spreedreieck   [p. 270]

Location:	Berlin, Germany
Project Date:	2001
Client:	Müller-Spreer & Co. Spreedreieck KG
Gross Floor Area:	65,000 m²
Team:	Martin Ebert, Jochen Glemser, Christoph Hesse, Mark Randel, Franziska Rusch, Toni Yli-Suvanto
Structural Engineer:	Dewhurst MacFarlane: Tim MacFarlane, Marc Simmons, Ian Stephenson
Models:	Architekur-Modelle-Berlin: Gunter Schwob
Photographs:	David Chipperfield Architects
	Richard Davies
Bibliography:	'Das magische Dreieck', *Skyline*, March 2001, pp. 11–23
	'Mies von Morgen', *H.O.M.E.*, July/August 2002, pp. 78–83

Tate Modern

Location:	London, UK
Competition Date:	1994
Client:	Tate Gallery
Gross Floor Area:	30,868 m²
Team:	Renato Benedetti, Jan Coghlan, Eamon Cushnahan, Jamie Fobert, Pablo Gallego Picard, Sarah Hare, Madeleine Lambert, Susan Le Good, Genevieve Lilley, Jonathan Sergison, Stevan Shorter, Zoka Skorup, Simon Timms, Susannah Woodgate
Structural Engineer:	Ove Arup & Partners
Historical Consultant:	Julian Harrap Architects: Julian Harrap
Quantity Surveyor:	Tim Gatehouse Associates: Tim Gatehouse
Models:	The Network: Richard Armiger
Photographs:	Andrew Putler
Bibliography:	'Tate Frames Architecture', *ANY* 13, pp. 28–33
	'Competition for new Tate Gallery', *Progressive Architecture*, April 1995, pp. 16–17
	'Tate Gallery of Modern Art: selecting an architect', *Blueprint supplement*, March 1995
	'How the Swiss swung Bankside', *Architects' Journal*, 26/1/95, pp. 8–9
	'David Chipperfield. Recent work', *2G International Architecture Review*, no. 1, 1997, pp. 94–99
	'David Chipperfield 1991–1997', *El croquis*, no. 87, 1998, pp. 138–143

Teruel Urban Development

Location:	Teruel, Spain
Completion Date:	2003
Client:	Diputación General de Aragón
Gross Floor Area:	7215 m²
Contract Value:	£ 3,900,000
Team:	*Competition in association with b720 Arquitectura:* David Chipperfield
Associate Architect:	b720 Arquitectura: Cristina Algas, Ana Bassat, Emma Dunner, Urtzi Grau, Itziar Imaz, Javier López, Eduard Miralles, Agustín Miranda, Madalena Ostornol, Adriana Plasencia, Doris Sewczyk, Fermín Vázquez, Cristian Zanoni

Toyota Auto Kyoto   [p. 276]

Location:	Kyoto, Japan
Completion Date:	1990
Client:	Toyota Auto Kyoto Corporation
Gross Floor Area:	1,413 m²
Contract Value:	£ 5,000,000
Team:	Jorge Carvalho, Jan Coghlan, Jamie Fobert, Spencer Fung, Michael
Greville,	Naoko Kawamura, Cecilia Lau, Haruo Morishima, Ko Nakatani, Toshiki Wakisaka, Sarah Wong
Contact Architect:	Makoto Nozawa + GETT: Toshiaki Kamo, Makoto Nozawa
Landscape Architect:	Naoko Terasaki
Structural Engineer:	Whitby, Bird & Partners: Mark Phillip, Ian Scott
	Hanawa Structural Engineers: Noriaki Hanawa
Services Engineer:	Nakajima Setsubi Co., Ltd.: Nakajima Setsubi
General Contractor:	Fujita Komuten: Noboru Mizuguchi
Models:	The Network: Richard Armiger
Photographs:	David Chipperfield Architects
	Hiroyuki Hirai
	Alberto Piovano
	Andrew Putler
Bibliography:	'Palladio Prize', *Presenza Techica*, December 1993, pp. 27–29
	'Honourable Lineage', *Building Design*, 8/10/93, pp.12–13
	'Rising Suns Exhibition Guide', *RIBA Journal*, June 1993, p. 42
	'Designzentrum in Kyoto', *Baumeister*, May 1993, pp. 32–38
	'When Less is More', *Estates Gazette*, 3/4/93, pp. 90–91
	Telescope, The Wild, Wild City – TAK, Workshop for Architecture and Urbanism No. 7 (Tokyo: 1992), p. 37
	'In Control of the Modern', *World Architecture*, no. 16, 1992, p. 66
	'Chipperfield in Kyoto', *Blueprint*, no. 82, November 1991, pp. 40–44
	'Tre architetture di David Chipperfield', *Casabella*, no. 584, November 1991, pp. 4–22
	'TAK design centre, Kyoto', *Domus*, no. 732, November 1991, pp. 38–47
	'Aspects of Abstraction', *SD*, September 1991, pp. 96–120
	'Projectos recentes: David Chipperfield, *Arquitectura na Cidade*, April 1991, pp. 8–9
	'David Chipperfield', *Nikkei Architecture*, 1991, 9–16, p. 103
	'David Chipperfield. Recent work', *2G International Architecture Review*, no. 1, 1997, pp. 18–25
	'David Chipperfield 1991–1997', *El croquis*, no. 87, 1998, pp. 24–37

Vigo Congress Hall

Location:	Vigo, Spain
Competition Date:	2001
Client:	Xunta de Galicia
Gross Floor Area:	65,000 m²
Team:	Sophia Arraiza, Johannes Baumstark, Franz Borho, Natalie Cheng, Mario Cottone, Mansour El-Khawad, Ruiz de Galaretta, Jochen Glemser, Urtzi Grau, Christoph Hesse, Johannes tho Pesch, Sergio Pirrone, Hau Ming Tse
Contact Architect:	b720 Arquitectura: Ana Basat, Adriana Plasencia, Fermín Vázquez
Structural Engineer:	Obiol, Moya i Associats
Services Engineer:	Grupo JG i Associats
Models:	David Chipperfield Architects
Photographs:	Richard Davies

Vilanova

Location:	Vilanova i la Geltrú, Barcelona
Competition Date:	2001
Client:	Garraf Mediterrània
Gross Floor Area:	141,700 m²
Team:	Alberto Arraut, Mario Cottone, Luca Donadoni, Manuel Gujber, Serena Jaff, Alessandra Maiolino, Emmanuele Mattutini, Takayuki Nakajima, John Puttick, Melanie Schubert, Sara Tempesta, Patrick Überbacher, Giuseppe Zampieri
Contact Architect:	b720 Arquitectura: Ana Basat, Javier López, Eduard Miralles, Adriana Plasencia, Fermín Vázquez
Models:	Matthew Marchbank
Photographs:	David Chipperfield Architects

Colophon

General editor: Francisco Rei
Editing: Thomas Weaver
Texts: David Chipperfield, Kenneth Frampton, Jonathan Keates, Rik Nys, Thomas Weaver
Design: Atelier Works
Preparation: Yuki Sumner and Cassius Taylor-Smith
Coordination: Montse Holgado
Copy editing: Rafael Galisteo and Sue Brownbridge
Production Manager: Rafael Aranda
Color Separation: Format Digital
Printing: Filabo
Binding: Bardenas

Acknowledgements

Publishing a book on your own work is not an easy exercise at the best of times. To try to bring together work that is completed, with work that is in progress, with that which is abandoned is perhaps a questionable task. In the last few years the scale of the work, the diversity of tasks and the places it is located have expanded geometrically. It is a testament to my colleagues and collaborators that this progress has happened at all while maintaining a sense of coherence. Producing a publication during this period has put one more strain on our powers of organization and I would like to thank all those involved for their patience and commitment through this process. I hope that the resulting book gives some reward and justifies the generous words of Jonathan Keates and Ken Frampton. Finally and most importantly, I thank Evelyn for her support, encouragement and for continuously reminding me of life's priorities.